THE SWINE REPUBLIC

STRUGGLES WITH THE TRUTH ABOUT AGRICULTURE AND WATER QUALITY

CHRIS JONES

ICE CUBE PRESS, LLC
NORTH LIBERTY, IOWA, USA

The Swine Republic:
Struggles with the Truth about Agriculture and Water Quality

Copyright © 2023 Chris Jones

ISBN 9781948509404

Library of Congress Control Number: 2023931994

Ice Cube Press, LLC (Est. 1991)
1180 Hauer Drive, North Liberty, Iowa 52317
www.icecubepress.com steve@icecubepress.com

The paper used in this publication meets the minimum requirements of the American National Standard for Information Sciences—Permanence of Paper for Printed Library Materials, ANSI Z39.48-1992.

Made with recycled paper.

Manufactured in Canada

For my girls

CONTENTS

FOREWORD: THE ROAD TO RACCOON RIVER
—by Tom Philpott

George Orwell, born in 1903, grew up in the bosom of the British Empire at its height. His father worked in the civil service in a poppy-growing region of north-eastern India, overseeing the production of poppy for sale to China as opium[1]—a cog in the Royal narcotics cartel. For his first job out of school, Orwell himself spent much of the 1920s working as a colonial cop in Burma, first providing security for a British petroleum refinery, later serving as a prison guard. Orwell did not let his status as an imperial insider blunt his observational abilities—or his mastery of prose. "In a job like that you see the dirty work of Empire at close quarters," he wrote in a 1936 essay. "The wretched prisoners huddling in the stinking cages of the lock-ups, the grey, cowed faces of the long-term convicts, the scarred buttocks of the men who had been Bogged with bamboos—all these oppressed me with an intolerable sense of guilt."[2]

I think about Orwell a lot when I read the work of Chris Jones—and not just because Chris admires the celebrated writer and cites him often in his work. Chris, too, grew up in the heart of an empire: the domain of the corn, soybeans, and hogs that dominate the former prairies, grasslands, and savannas of the US Midwest. And Jones toiled for his region's sovereign, putting his doctoral degree in analytical chemistry into the service of the Iowa Soybean Association, which employed him as an environmental scientist from 2011 to

---

1 https://www.bbc.com/news/magazine-28739420
2 From "Shooting an Elephant"

2015. The ISA's sponsors include many of the globe-spanning corporations that harvest fat profits from the corn-soybean-hog complex: from seed-pesticide giants Bayer and Syngenta, to grain-trading and meat behemoth Cargill, to that farm-equipment monolith John Deere.[3] Like Orwell, Jones proved incapable of trodding the blinkered path of the loyal colonial functionary. Orwell fled the British Raj and set upon a career as an anti-imperialist journalist. Jones, for his part, bolted the ISA, took a position at the University of Iowa, and soon launched a blog featuring lucid, rigorously documented dispatches on the toxic and deteriorating state of Iowa's water—and crisp refutations of the shameless cant spewed by the corn-soybean-hog complex to justify and hide its mounting depredations.

I'm a journalist myself, and I first encountered Chris' blog in 2019 while in the throes of writing my book *Perilous Bounty*, which documented the downward ecological spiral underway in the two US regions most in the clutches of industrial agriculture: California's Central Valley and the Midwest heartland, centered on Iowa. Too often, my work consisted of carefully reading dense scientific papers and teasing out the damning conclusions hidden beneath their tedious, timid, hard-to-parse prose: documents brimming with vital, often publicly funded research, written as if in fear of offending the very private interests behind the demonstrated damage. Chris' blog hit me like a revelation: Here was a scientist writing in blunt English, calmly laying out the wreckage wrought by his state's dominant industry, with no need for elaborate translation.

His most eye-popping post of that era, "Iowa's Real Population," published in the spring of 2019, established Jones as an essential voice emanating from the ruins of the North American prairielands. In it, he pithily demonstrated the gargantuan scale of livestock pro-

---

3 https://www.iasoybeans.com/about/our-partners

duction in Iowa, and how the state's teeming herds of concentrated hogs, cattle, and egg-laying hens generated far more fecal waste than the land could absorb without fouling streams, rivers, lakes, and tap water. Noting that "a feeder pig is about the same size as a human being, but it excretes 3 times as much nitrogen (N), 5 times as much phosphorus (P), and 3.5 times as much solid matter (TS-total solids)," Jones introduced the grisly concept of Iowa's "fecal equivalent population"—that is, how many humans it would take to churn out as much sewage as the state's livestock. In a state with an actual human headcount of about 3 million, Iowa's 24 million hogs produce as much waste as 83.7 million people, he calculated. Add to that fetid gusher the rear-end output of the state's cattle, chickens, and turkeys, Jones revealed, and Iowa's landscape annually receives a serving of waste equivalent to "that produced by about 134 million people, which would place Iowa as the 10th most populous country in the world, right below Russia and right above Mexico." In the post's most subversive move, Jones teamed with a colleague to generate a map depicting the fecal equivalent populations of Iowa's beleaguered watersheds in terms of the human populations of various famous cities. In it, for example, we learn that the concentrated animals and relatively tiny human population in a discrete chunk of northwest Iowa deliver much waste as everyone who lives in Mexico City; an adjoining watershed to the southeast matches with Tokyo, which itself abuts watersheds that receive fecal outputs equal to those of the two-legged denizens of Chicago, Paris, and Philadelphia. It should be noted that in much of the world, including all the cities named here, human sewage is treated for bacterial pathogens and filtered of nutrients before returning to the wild. Iowa's livestock waste, by contrast, hits the land *au naturel*.

Jones didn't lead us on this scatological plunge into the depths of Iowa's manure cesspits merely to gross us out. Nor was he engaging in a purely academic display of fecal calculus. "There are only a precious-few weeks in a year when this Mt. Everest of waste can be applied to corn and soybean fields," he writes. And raw hogshit is as heavy and expensive to transport as it is repellent to smell. As a result, farmers tend to apply it near their confinements, in amounts well in excess of the land's ability to metabolize it as crop fertilizer. And thus shitloads, so to speak, of nitrogen and phosphorus leach into the state's water resources, poisoning municipal tap water—or causing the need for heroic, expensive efforts to filter it out—and triggering foul algal blooms in Iowa's lakes as well as waterways as far downstream as the Gulf of Mexico (a particular affront to Jones, who writes often of his love for fishing).

In these pages, which gather the greatest hits of Jones' blog, you'll find vivid, ever-timely accounts of how nearly two centuries of US settler-colonial agriculture have transformed one of the globe's most fecund landscapes into a veritable aquatic sacrifice zone—and how the process of destruction accelerated in the post-World War II era with the addition of heavy machinery and synthetic agrochemicals and the withering away of crop diversity. *The Swine Republic* amounts to a damning case against the agricultural interests that have essentially colonized the state's land as well as its political institutions—required reading for anyone hoping to turn today's depleted corn belt into a robust, thriving region capable of delivering a healthy food supply in an era of increasing climate chaos. And that group includes young would-be farmers, who face ever-escalating land prices propped up by various federal crop subsidies as well as lax regulation that allows incumbent barons to pollute virtually unchecked. Unless things change, and fast, Jones warns, Iowa will remain a "place where only the elite can farm and own land"—and one with evermore polluted water.

I know from talking to Chris that breaking the code of obscurity, unto outright propaganda, observed by many agricultural scientists in Iowa's public institutions wasn't an easy choice to make. Again, I think of Orwell. On an overnight train in Burma in the 1920s, young Orwell found himself sitting beside a colleague in the colonial service, he later recounted. "It was too hot to sleep and we spent the night in talking." He continued:

> Half an hour's cautious questioning decided each of us that the other was "safe"; and then for hours, while the train jolted slowly through the pitch-black night, sitting up in our bunks with bottles of beer handy, we damned the British Empire.... It did us both good. But we had been speaking forbidden things, and in the haggard morning light when the train crawled into Mandalay, we parted as guiltily as any adulterous couple.

Orwell published those words in *The Road to Wigan Pier*, released in 1937. His island home country continued to bring misery to—and siphon wealth from—great swaths of the globe, but Orwell was done speaking in hushed tones about its crimes. Jones, for his part, has his eyes, nose, and scientific chops trained on the agricultural empire that reigns over the United States' most important farming region, and he's done with polite silence, too. Tune in before it's too late.

Tom Philpott is a senior research associate at the Center for a Livable Future (Johns Hopkins University). He is the former food and agriculture correspondent for *Mother Jones* (2011-2022) and food editor and columnist at *Grist* (2006-2011). His 2020 book *Perilous Bounty* was named an "editor's pick" by *The New York Times Book Review* and shortlisted for a New York Public Library Helen Bernstein Award for Excellence in Journalism.

WHY THIS BOOK

People in my line of work attend a lot of meetings. A ballpark guess is fewer than 5% of those meetings generate anything consequential; this book is a result of one of those. I came away from that one particular meeting five years ago with the certainty that the Ag establishment here in Iowa had no real interest in cleaning up the state's water and was mostly operating in bad faith when it came to the issue. On that day, I decided I had to do some things differently if I was going to be able to reconcile my publicly funded job with my conscience.

My scientific training and the jobs I've held since—Ph.D. in analytical chemistry, manager of a testing laboratory, environmental scientist for the Iowa Soybean Association, lab supervisor at the Des Moines Water Works and now a research engineer at the University of Iowa—have required me to generate written material. Because of that, I've always felt I was an adequate writer. But my writing was never something I could know for certain was good, good in this sense meaning people will read it because they want to and see quality in the composition. But after the fateful meeting, I felt that writing about my observations of the political and scientific landscape that is Iowa agriculture and the environment, specifically as they relate to the state's wretched water quality, would help me make some sense of what I was doing with my life and my career. I hope the book that now lies in your hands will help people make some sense of the foul green and brown water that has been characteristic of Iowa's streams and lakes for nearly all my sixty-two years.

The content and the style of these essays have been viewed as controversial by many. That fact alone crystallizes much of what you need to know about the problem by telling you we lack the courage as a state to confront our environmental problems honestly and in good faith. At times I am almost ashamed to admit that this book exists largely because so many can't bring themselves to say that grass is green, and the sky is blue. At least not in public, anyway.

The bulk of this book is made up of a series of essays that I wrote and posted on my blog at cjones.iihr.uiowa.edu. I haven't updated these; instead I have added headnotes at the beginning of each one that include comments and new information. Mostly they are presented in chronological order. I also wrote a few new essays; these are at the end of the book, starting with "Bushels or Bobolinks." Writing about the same damn thing all the time can get boring, believe it or not, so these newer pieces explore different (for me) subject matter and approach to writing.

My first real attempt to write seriously for general audiences on the topic of Iowa water quality, an essay titled "This Is What Happened," was posted in February of 2019 and an expanded version of that is the basis for the introductory chapter here, "Upstream." The concluding chapter, "Downstream," is a summary of my thoughts on what is needed to improve the water of our state.

Everybody who writes about agriculture and environment has been inspired in some way by the great Aldo Leopold, and I'm not an exception. When I hear people say I'm too caustic or sardonic, I always know they haven't read Aldo, especially his *River of the Mother of God*. For me, the thing that makes Aldo great is that his words, some written nearly a century ago, seem like they could have been written yesterday. I think Aldo Leopold is really a George Orwell-type figure; he's that great in my opinion.

The other main inspiration for me has been Howard Zinn. More than any other person, Zinn has informed my ideas on what needs to change if our water is going to change for the better. If Zinn's *A People's History of the United States* is Leopold's *Sand County Almanac,* then Zinn's *Declarations of Independence* is Leopold's *River of the Mother of God.* The latter works are lesser-known, but greater, in my opinion. This book wouldn't exist without those two guys.

Before you turn the page to get on with the book, I need you to read one more acknowledgment, and that person would be Larry Weber at the University of Iowa. If he had ever told me even once to stop writing, that the material was too this or too that or that the merit and the quality of the work didn't overcome the controversy that came with writing it, I would have stopped.

He never told me to stop.

UPSTREAM

While indigenous people have populated Iowa for millennia, those of European descent have had their eye on what is now the Hawkeye State only 350 years. Marquette and Joliet were the first of the latter to see Iowa, when the bluffs of today's Pikes Peak State Park appeared before them as their canoes were dispatched by the Wisconsin River into the Mississippi. The better part of two centuries would pass, however, before white settlement, and white agriculture, would begin in earnest. The 1833 Bad Axe Massacre across the Mississippi from New Albin, Iowa, ended the Chief Black Hawk-led Sauk and Fox hold on the region, and a subsequent treaty allowed white immigrants to pour in. Settlers came first to southern Iowa, but by 1850, colonization had spread to the northern half of the new state.

Farmers from rocky New England and Appalachia immediately recognized the soil Nirvana lying beneath Iowa's rolling hills and plains. The Jethro Wood cast-iron plows of the day, however, were no match for the sticky prairie soils. Enter Illinois blacksmith John Deere, who in 1837 fashioned the steel plow that would overturn the great prairie expanse, and later with its drainage tile accomplice, doom hundreds of thousands of wetlands that dotted the landscape from Des Moines to central Alberta.

Settlers of European descent found that an un-engineered Iowa was soggy in a lot of places, a lot of the time, and everywhere some of the time. And as the saying goes, corn doesn't like wet feet. This king of grasses was already established as the preeminent American crop, and the early Iowa farmers grabbed the drier lands first so they could plant and grow *Zea mays*. The wetter areas weren't that way because they were rainier; they were wetter because they were flatter. Wringing the water out would mean bringing the corn in. But draining thousands of square miles required capital and widespread coordination, both beyond the capacity of the early Iowa farmer. Many had arrived with little more than the shirt on their back. So, much of Iowa's soggy and wetland areas in the northern half of the state were acquired by east coast and English land speculators.[1] These barons financed the pipe-laying and ditch-digging in the second half of the nineteenth century that lowered the water table four feet. They then sold off individual tracts of land "improved" for people and corn and annual weeds, but little else. The die had been cast that would degrade our environment, and especially our water, for the next 170 years and, looking forward, for the foreseeable future.

Glaciers and pre-European settlement erosion have shaped Iowa into eight distinct landforms.[2] The broad Missouri and Mississippi alluvial plains, shaped by torrents of glacial melt water, form the southwest and southeast borders of Iowa. These level floodplains are intensely farmed in the present day and the water table in these cropped fields is often lowered using networks of the porous drainage pipe known as tile. Many of these fields are levee-protected from flooding.

The bumpy spine of Iowa's Loess Hills in the far western part of the state was formed by loose, wind-blown silt picked up mostly from the Missouri floodplain during the Wisconsin glacial period. This highly erosive area is one of the least-farmed places in Iowa and is still home to remnant prairie.

The rolling hills of the Northwest Iowa Plains were wind-shaped during the dry and cold glacial periods. Thick Loess soil provides a fertile base for corn and soybean crops. This is the highest and driest area of Iowa and is also where livestock production is most intense.

The Iowan surface was formed similarly to the Northwest Iowa Plains: howling winds off the Wisconsin glacier shaped this prehistoric tundra. The winds exposed the large granite boulders, carried down from Canada by earlier glaciers, that are characteristic of this area. The land is extensively cropped with corn and soybean, and much of it is tile drained.

The Des Moines Lobe lies where a tongue of the Wisconsin glacier extended south into Iowa before melting 10,000 years ago. This part of Iowa is the southernmost extent of what is known as the Prairie Pothole region, which extends from Des Moines to central Alberta. Thousands of wetlands were left behind by the melted glacier. Insufficient time has passed for nature to form extensive stream networks, so agriculture formed its own drainage system: the networks of field tile and trapezoidal ditches constructed to drain the water away to major rivers like the Raccoon, Des Moines, and Skunk. This lowered the water table, drying out the wetlands and making the soil suitable for crop production. Some of Iowa's most valuable natural resources, the Great Lakes of Okoboji and Spirit, Storm Lake, and Clear Lake, were formed at the hem of the glacier.

The Paleozoic Plateau is the most unusual area of Iowa. Many know this as part of the Driftless Area, which also includes parts of Southeast Minnesota, Southwest Wisconsin, and Northwest Illinois. But the truth is, only the area east of the Mississippi River is completely without drift, the finely ground material pulverized by advancing glaciers. Nonetheless, the influence of glaciers has been far less here than in the rest of Iowa, and deep valleys and bluffs carved into the limestone bedrock form dramatic scenery. Only about half the land here is farmed, and the streams still retain some of their original biological integrity.

The Southern Iowa Drift Plain is the visage of Iowa that many visitors to the state retain, maybe because Interstate 80 lies along its northern edge from west to east. The last glacier was here 500,000 years ago, and an extensive stream network was formed by natural erosion since that time. Loess soils on the rolling hills provided an ideal substrate for the earliest farmers, and all but the portion in far South-central Iowa is excellent farm ground.

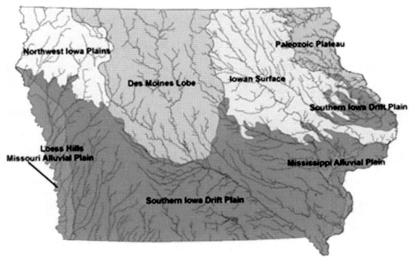

Iowa landform regions. Image credit: Iowa DNR

Conversion of the perennial-plant-dominant native ecosystems to one dominated by ultimately two annual plants required modification of Iowa's hydrology, e.g. the distribution and movement of water across and through the land's surface. This alteration of the natural flow of water took three main forms: field tile to lower the water table; constructed ditches to capture and drain away the tile water; and physical removal of stream meanders. The time a drop of rain would remain on the Iowa landscape was shortened from centuries to mere days in some circumstances, tightening and intensifying

Iowa's hydrology to remove water, and remove it fast. Thousands of miles of meandering prairie streams were straightened and effectively transformed to storm sewers, divorced from their floodplains by the spoils of excavation, which in many cases were used to levee the creek-cum-ditch and protect the now-square fields.

This hydrological modification had dire consequences for our environment. Perhaps the most staggering change has been wetland loss. The wetland ecosystem once occupied as much as 20% of Iowa's area, 7.6 million acres. By 1980, this area had been reduced so that less than 1% (30,000 acres) remained, with only 5,000 acres of prairie pothole and marsh still holding on.[3] This loss occurred mainly due to drainage and filling for agricultural reasons.

Drainage tile lowered the water table so wet fields could be worked and planted. This effectively dried up both perennial (wet all year) and ephemeral (wet part of the year) wetlands, eliminating habitat for waterfowl, reptiles, and amphibians. The drainage tile also became the main loss pathway for nitrate-nitrogen, which would become Iowa's most recalcitrant water pollution problem. Nitrogen from fertilizer, manure, and fertile prairie and wetland soils might otherwise stay on the landscape and out of streams, were it not for tile.

Meandering prairie streams were clear water systems populated by clean water species such as smallmouth bass, northern pike, and redhorse sucker. Removing meanders with steam shovels and dynamite allowed water to rush off the landscape much faster in the straightened streams, causing them to erode downward and form the mini canyons that we see in the present day. Energized water scours vertical streambanks left bare by the downcut, muddying the water and making it unsuitable for clear water sight-feeders. Rough fish like carp and bullhead now dominate these systems. The down-cutting effect is most pronounced in tributaries of the Missouri River, where thick loess soil was easily erodible.

Engineered hydrology and the steel plow allowed the early Iowa farmers to quickly intensify crop production. By 1910, farmers in Iowa and other U.S. states were already producing 1,500 pounds of corn grain per year for every person in the U.S. (it's about 2,200 pounds now). In the 1920s William Berry, a professor at what was to become the University of Northern Iowa, wrote that drained land generated a surplus of grain and "has so upset farming conditions as to threaten the foundations of agriculture" as farmers struggled through low prices and the farm depression of that decade.[4]

Of course, no person is going to eat 1,500 pounds of corn in a year, and after 1910 and until recently, most of the corn that Americans didn't eat was fed to livestock, especially cattle. And as we intensified our agricultural system, we also intensified the way that we eat. From 1929 to 1975, our per capita appetite for beef increased from 50 to 120 pounds and poultry consumption increased from 14 to 40 pounds per year. Total meat consumption now stands at 264 pounds per person per year.[5]

Most of the heavy work on early Iowa farms was done by animals—horses, mules, and oxen. The beasts of burden ate a lot of what the land produced, especially oats but also pasture plants. Iowan John Froelich invented the first gasoline-powered tractor in 1892, but by 1919, still only 1% of Iowa farmers had one and the animals were still doing the hard work. By 1950, however, 1% had grown to 80% and the need for working animals, and the stuff that they eat, had dwindled. Working animals had been powered with plant energy generated that year on the farm; by contrast, tractors were powered with plant energy generated over the eons and stored as petroleum.

Oats had been the "other" crop grown by Iowa farmers in rotation with corn, alfalfa or clover, and Iowa was the top oat producing state for many years. But tractors and fossil fuel drove a wholesale conversion of Iowa's cropping systems. The small grains of oats, wheat, and barley, along with the legume clover and alfalfa crops that provided much of the nitrogen nutrient needed for corn production, were displaced by soybeans. Although a legume like alfalfa and clovers, soybeans fix far less nitrogen for the following year's corn crop and can create a nitrogen deficit in the field. This stands to reason because the bean has a lot of protein—nitrogen-containing organic compounds—and the amount of nitrogen removed in the harvest can exceed what the soybean crop fixes into the soil from the atmosphere. Thus, any corn crop that followed soybean would be nitrogen-deficient, and yields would suffer. But an easy solution to this problem was already at hand.

Before 1910, all terrestrial nitrogen on earth had as its origin either oxidation of atmospheric nitrogen by lightning, or fixation by plants (legumes). The nitrate-containing mineral of saltpeter was also mined for fertilizer. Fritz Haber and Carl Bosch would both go on to receive Nobel prizes in chemistry for the invention and industrialization of a process that produced ammonia from atmospheric nitrogen gas. This new type of fixed nitrogen was first used to make explosives but would also soon create a different explosion—a population explosion ignited by the easy availability of fertilizer for farmers that could afford it.

Following World War II, inorganic fertilizers manufactured using the Haber-Bosch process became a viable alternative to the organic nitrogen generated by legumes. This also coincided with the emergence of soybeans as a desired commodity crop. In the 1920s the food pioneer A.E. Staley (if you are old enough, you may remember Staley baking powder and corn syrup in your grandmother's kitchen) had realized soy protein would be an excellent component of animal feed, and he began promoting soybean production across the Corn Belt. Use of chemical fertilizers for nitrogen-hungry corn went hand-in-hand with adoption of soy as Iowa's second cash crop, because soybeans displaced much of the alfalfa and clover that had been fixing nitrogen for corn. By 1996, oats, alfalfa, and clovers had vanished from most of the Iowa landscape, and our livestock was eating mainly soybeans and corn.

Manufactured nitrogen fertilizer use skyrocketed from 16 pounds per Iowa corn acre in 1960 to 122 pounds in 1968; soybean area increased 213% during this same time. Iowa's water quality cake was baked; diverse, integrated crop and livestock farms began to rapidly disappear. Although modern corn hybrids efficiently use manufactured fertilizers, a greater portion of the nitrogen leaches beyond the roots when compared to the organic nitrogen of legumes. This leached nitrate ends up in aquifers, drainage tile water, and ultimately Iowa's lakes and streams and the Gulf of Mexico, catalyzing a Dead Zone where aquatic life can't exist. In this new and intensified system, fertilizers are often applied long before corn can use it, and some is inevitably lost. The modern quest for the almighty bushel did not tolerate a shortage of nutrients, resulting in overapplication of fertilizer across Iowa.

Manufactured fertilizer, soybeans and tractors displaced small grains (oats, barley, wheat), alfalfa, clover and animals on farms, now simplified to a two-crop rotation. The ease and convenience provided by genetically modified seeds smoothed the transition and enabled farmers to crop more acres with ever-shorter working hours. Livestock went from pasture and barnyards on nearly all farms to concentrated animal feeding operations, CAFOs, on only a few, allowing farmers to intensely focus on only corn and soybean production if they wished.

Demand for meat, eggs and dairy, however, continued to grow with world population and wealth. With fewer farmers wanting or needing livestock, those that continued production greatly enlarged and intensified their operations. This is especially apparent with hogs, Iowa's primary livestock animal. In 1980, 65,000 Iowa farmers raised a total of 13 million hogs; by 2002 the number of hog farmers had dwindled to 10,000, but total hog numbers increased to 14 million.[6] An Iowa hog farmer now raises an average of 4,700 hogs compared to 200 only 40 years ago. And bear in mind that a hog needs only six months to reach market weight, so the actual numbers raised in a calendar year are twice as large. Concentration of hogs in certain areas of the state (mainly northwest, north central and southeast Iowa) allowed buyers, packing houses, feed and equipment suppliers and haulers to geographically align with production. Similar scenarios also played out with cattle and poultry. The devolution from diverse, multi-species farms to ones specializing in intense soybean and corn production, with a subset of the latter raising concentrated livestock, clearly has its efficiencies. This has come at a steep cost, however, to both the environment and the prosperity of small towns across our state.

Iowa comprises 1.5% of U.S. area but is home to 34% of the country's hogs (25 million). The population of Iowa beef cattle actually declined about 50% from 1980 to 1990, but has remained fairly stable since then, numbering about 4 million now.[7] But many of the cattle no longer graze on pasture, and instead grow to market weight in feedlots or covered but open confinements where their manure accumulates, presenting the same sort of environmental challenges as concentrated hog production. The population of egg-laying chickens has flown higher and faster than even that of pigs. In 1997, Iowa had 21.5 million layers; fast forward 20 years, and Iowa was now home to 56.6 million laying chickens. An astonishing 19 out of 20 Iowa layers reside in operations that house 100,000 or more birds.[8]

Millions of animals produce a lot of waste, and manure is a good fertilizer for our corn crop. Fertilizing with manure generated by modern livestock confinements, however, is a much more complicated and management-intensive process compared to use of manufactured fertilizer. First, it's expensive to haul manure. On a pound per pound basis, manufactured fertilizer contains much more nutrient than manure, because much of manure is comprised of water (especially true of hog waste from CAFOs) and organic matter. Water is heavy and hauling it requires fuel, and it's not economically practical to haul hog manure more than about 5-10 miles, depending on the current price of manufactured fertilizer. Beyond that, the farmer may as well buy commercial fertilizer. Secondly, the nutrient content of the manure, and how much of that crops will be able to use in that growing season, can be variable and difficult to quantify. For this reason, many farmers use manure to supplement a fertility plan that includes manufactured products, or vice versa. Often manure rates are determined only by a crop's need for nitrogen, and not also phosphorus and other nutrients. For these reasons and others, it's well-established that nutrient inputs to crops and stream nutrient pollution are higher in areas where livestock is concentrated and when manure is incorporated into the fertilization scheme.[9]

Since 1980, the total amount of corn fed to American livestock has not changed much. Corn exports have also been relatively stable, notwithstanding a modest increase in recent years. Farmers in countries such as India, China, Ukraine, and Brazil have gotten pretty good at growing corn. U.S. corn yields, however, keep steadily increasing and have gone from around 100 bushels per acre in 1980 to about 175 today. That corn had to go somewhere, and that somewhere was liquid fuel for cars. Although Iowans have been able to put gasoline mixed with ethanol (90/10 ratio, E-10) into their gas tanks since before 1980 (known as gasohol early on), use of ethanol blends for liquid fuel did not take off until the Energy Policy Act of 2005 increased the amount of biofuel (i.e., any fuel derived from plant biomass) required to be mixed with petroleum-based fuels. Currently the U.S. Environmental Protection Agency (EPA) requires liquid fuels sold in the U.S. contain in total about 20 billion gallons of biofuels, and advocates of establishment-agriculture are craving and demanding more. Soybean oil is also made into renewable fuel (biodiesel, biomass-derived oil or blends of diesel fuel and biomass oils) and the EPA required 2.4 billion gallons of that stock be blended with diesel in 2020. These required ratios are part of what is commonly known as the Renewable Fuel Standard, RFS. A staggering 20% of Iowa's land area is used to grow corn for fuel ethanol, and more than half our corn is used in this manner.

Vehicle manufacturers have adapted engines on some models so they can run using blends that contain more than the traditional 10% (by volume) of ethanol. RFS requirements would be difficult or impossible to meet without this accommodation. The EPA approved sales of 15% blends in 2011 and now some engines can operate on blends that are as much as 85% ethanol (E-85). Most car owners in the U.S. now routinely fill their tanks with ethanol blends. Iowa's governor Kim Reynolds recently proposed that half of all gas pumps at Iowa filling stations be required to dispense E-15.[10]

The lower price of ethanol blends helps reconcile the lower gas mileage that most cars get when fueled by them. A gallon of E-10 contains 97% of the energy of pure gasoline, meaning a car that could be expected to get 30 miles per gallon will get 29 with E-10. New cars seldom get the predicted mileage shown on the show room sticker, which is based on pure gasoline.

The public has not similarly embraced biodiesel fuels; the reasons for this are complex and likely related to storage, performance, and policy. Some reports show that even Iowa farmers avoid using their own soy biodiesel, with only 8% of on-farm diesel sourced back to renewables.[11]

The RFS also specified amounts of ethanol to be made from the stems and leaves of corn and other plants, known as cellulosic. The technology to produce cellulosic ethanol, however, never developed adequately to meet RFS requirements, which the EPA waived every year of the standard. The last of the commercially sized cellulosic ethanol plants closed in 2020.

Researchers have produced a mountain range of scientific literature on the environmental pros and cons of crop-derived fuels, and the conventional wisdom is that they modestly reduce greenhouse gas emissions when compared to unblended petroleum, although there is new research that shows corn ethanol may produce more emissions than gasoline.[12] Whether the environmental tradeoffs connected to land use and water quality associated with corn production are worthwhile, and how they compare to crude oil extraction, has been left to elected leaders, most of whom have little grasp of the science. It's clear that biofuel policy is being driven by farmers' zeal to continue doing what is done best: produce corn. It's the birthright of the Iowa farmer, and our state has produced as much as we can. We task the rest of the world with figuring out what to do with it all.

But the halcyon days of King Corn may be numbered. Electric cars are emerging onto the transportation landscape and they seem poised to capture much of the vehicle market. Both Ford and General Motors have stated they will soon be all-electric. Reduced demand for liquid fuels in general, and ethanol especially, seems imminent.

Many consider Iowa's biculture of corn and soybean to be the most efficient way to harness photosynthesis and produce usable organic carbon from our productive soils and cooperative rainfall. Reducing the diversity of an agro-ecosystem to two species, however, increases its vulnerability to pests, namely weeds and insects, both of which can in short order devour the system's purported efficiencies.

In a bit of irony, many of the weeds that thrive in Iowa's cropping system were brought here unknowingly by the farmers themselves, hidden in their pockets and belongings. Turf crops like alfalfa crowded out weeds and extended crop rotations that included small grains and clovers which, along with corn, provided weed-suppressing plant diversity. Bare soil was required for growing corn, and weed seeds found this medium favorable during the corn part of the rotation. The remedy was first cast iron and then steel, that is, the implements used to disturb the soil and uproot germinated weeds. This was effective, but a century of prairie winds and rainstorms scraped and scoured Iowa soils from tilled fields. Many of our creek valleys are filled with six feet of eroded upland soil delivered by the plow and the elements.

The post-World War II chemical industry gave farmers another option for weed control. Chemicals such as Atrazine, 2,4-D, Dicamba, and Alachlor used on cropped fields killed not only weeds but also some things we didn't want killed: desirable insects and the animals that ate them. Overall, herbicide use on corn grew from 11% of the acres in 1950 to 95% in 1982.[13]

A new weed-control strategy germinated in 1970 when a team led by Monsanto chemist John Franz synthesized the chemical glyphosate, commonly known now as Roundup. Research showed that the chemical was a broad-spectrum herbicide, toxic to many plant species including the broadleaf weeds and annual grasses that reduced productivity in annual crop production. It was also toxic to crops, too, and did not become an important herbicide until other Monsanto scientists were able to genetically modify annual crops in ways that left them invulnerable to Roundup's killing action. It didn't take long for Roundup to become the neutron bomb of agriculture, annihilating weeds but sparing the crops that had the DNA antidote inserted into their genetic code. Seeds of cotton, alfalfa, sorghum, canola, sugar beets, and most importantly for Iowa, corn and soybeans all soon were available that had the magic genes. Roundup Ready soybeans became available in 1996, and farmers loved the convenience and effectiveness of this weed control formula so much that by 2005, an astounding 87% of all U.S. soybeans were Roundup resistant.

Many farmers found Roundup to be safer and easier to use than the products it replaced, and a lot of evidence showed it to be less toxic to humans and animals than the earlier formulations. Its effectiveness helped reduce the frequency and intensity of weed control tillage, which along with regulations for soil conservation in the 1985 Farm Bill, helped lessen soil erosion. It was so effective, however, that it likely contributed to the decline of milkweed and other plants that provided food and habitat for pollinators like the monarch butterfly. But perhaps its most profound consequence is that it enabled Iowa farmers to intensify the production of the row crops of corn and soybean. More acres of these crops could be farmed in less time, and Roundup Ready soybeans ushered clovers, alfalfa and the once common oats out the door in most areas of Iowa.

The all-cash-crop-all-of-the-time rotation was also vulnerable to insects. The decline in plant diversity allowed the rootworm and corn borer to survive the carpet-bombing farmers' arsenal which included everything from kerosene to sulfur to mineral oil to arsenic. Chemists also formulated potent toxins like organophosphates and DDT to help kill the pests. But they didn't stop there; more than 10,000 new pesticides were registered with the U.S. Department of Agriculture, USDA, from 1947 to 1952.[14] Dead bugs meant more profit for the farmer, with a dollar spent on chemicals producing $4 in more grain. But poisoned bugs also meant poisoned birds, reptiles, and amphibians. And in some cases, poisoned farmers and family members.

As with weeds, DNA pointed to a different approach for insect control. Corn hybrids made resistant to insects by insertion of bacterial DNA into the corn germplasm arrived in the 1990s.[15] The bacteria DNA enabled the corn plant to synthesize its own pesticide that was effective in killing corn borer caterpillars, in particular. Corn attacked by these larvae also become vulnerable to other pests like fungi. The hybrid corn was named Bt to reflect the donor bacterium: *Bacillis thurengiensis*. Bt-corn now accounts for 82% of the U.S. corn crop, and like Roundup, simplified farming in ways that allowed farmers to crop more acres with fewer labor hours.

Genetic modification has not been the technological end of pest control. In recent years corn and soybeans have been planted with a coating of neonicotinoids, toxins that protect the seeds from insects while they lie ungerminated in the soil. This pest control strategy does not come without some consequences for the environment, as these chemicals leave both bees and fish vulnerable to weakened immune systems, and survive long enough in the environment to enter municipal drinking water treatment plants.[16]

While many will say that genetic modification for pest control has been an overall environmental good, there is no doubt that it has also enabled farmers to intensify production of corn and soybeans at the expense of other crops and overall plant biodiversity on the farm. Organic chemicals, many of which are derived from and applied with equipment powered by fossil fuels, have replaced tillage and hand weeding (especially of soybeans) but they have had both direct and indirect consequences for the environment.

Iowa agriculture followed no roadmap traveling from 1840 to 2022. Although almost all production and market decisions were deliberate—genetically modified seeds and ethanol, for example, few could have imagined or planned for them more than a few years before their emergence. One decision led to another, something akin to what is known as the drunkard's walk, where the direction of each step is somewhat random but also somewhat dependent upon the previous step.

Almost none of the decisions driving the current production system were made with the nutritional or caloric needs of human beings in mind. Rather, the system has been designed for commerce, especially since World War II. As the number of Iowa farmers has shrunk from 230,000 in 1951 to 85,000 today (only about half that number are full-time farmers), agribusiness has exploded. This includes not only companies that sell products like seeds, chemicals, fertilizer, and equipment to farmers but also media firms, Ag advocacy organizations, insurance and financial firms, the entire fuel ethanol industry and a whole host of other business enterprises that depend on farmers and the corn and soybeans they grow. These organizations and the people they employ enjoy a symbiosis with farmers that helps maintain the status quo with the ongoing production system and, unfortunately, the condition of water and air.

A cottage industry of consultants, researchers and technical service providers has also emerged to ostensibly help farmers mitigate the pollution, especially that created by soil erosion and nutrient loss, that is part and parcel of the modern production system. A veritable army of county, state, and federal employees stand ready to preach the gospel of soil conservation and water quality to willing farmer congregations. The problem has been that the coalition of the willing has not been able to grow large enough to overcome the fundamental weaknesses baked into the system. These include the desire for tile drainage, the propensity of farmers to over-apply nutrients, lingering devotion to tillage, lack of synchronicity between fertilization and crop nutrient uptake, concentration of livestock such that responsible manure management is impossible, and reliance on fossil fuels.

Many in academia have also built their careers and reputations studying the various aspects of and potential solutions for the pollution generated by agriculture. Because of industry and farmer recalcitrance, researchers are left to parse out the most minute details of a particular best management practice (BMP), year after year, published paper after published paper, hoping that someday something will change that will catalyze farmer adoption. Most of this research is done at taxpayer expense with little to show in terms of improved water quality.

The third rail solution for Iowa's environmental problems has always been regulation. Folks in the conservation world say the word only in whispers and only among their closest confidantes. Agriculture has effectively sold the narrative that regulation won't work, and can't work, because Iowa farms and farmers are too diverse and need license to be creative when deciding what is best for their farm in terms of conservation. And Iowa agriculture still clings to the outdated image of the farmer as the rugged individualist, eking out a living from what the earth and the atmosphere will allow. Property rights rule, and if downstream people want clean water, they can pay for it, or travel somewhere else to find it.

Many people earning their living from farming and agribusiness hold an intense hostility toward regulation. Since conservation professionals and university researchers need land and the people who farm it to conduct their work, they only rarely, and at great risk, advocate for regulation.

The truth is that Iowa farming is not very diverse and could hardly be more homogeneous than it is: land lying within two degrees of latitude and three degrees of longitude; almost exclusively two annual crops of corn and soy; livestock in confinements raised by a small subset of farmers; the vast majority of farmers white males in the second half of life.

And regulation *has* worked in the past to improve environmental outcomes—most notably conservation compliance in the 1985 federal Farm Bill which required farmers on highly erodible land (HEL) to adopt soil conservation BMPs if they wished to be eligible for farm subsidy payments. This almost immediately reduced soil erosion and improved the clarity of Iowa streams.[17] There is no reason to think that similarly designed rules wouldn't help reduce other types of agricultural pollution, such as that caused by nutrient and manure runoff.

So, the $64,000 question is, why don't we make stronger attempts to regulate agriculture's pollution? Neither political party strongly advocates for it in Iowa, and prominent national politicians such as Democratic USDA secretary Tom Vilsack openly dismiss it as a credible option. Republicans tend to be hostile to regulation in general, but overall Democrats have gone along with this approach for agriculture, as the Vilsack example illustrates. Many professional conservationists owe their jobs to Iowa's voluntary approach to farm conservation, in that they serve as technical service providers on conservation projects and liaisons among farmers, NGOs, and academia. Donors contribute funds to NGOs that target communication and cooperative projects with farmers, with the objective of enhancing voluntary adoption of BMPs. University researchers are funded through agencies like the USDA, EPA, Iowa Department of Agriculture and Land Stewardship, Iowa Department of Natural Resources, [DNR] and many others, all of which are largely controlled by anti-regulation politicians.

Our state's featured water quality improvement policy is the Iowa Nutrient Reduction Strategy (INRS). The strategy considers that we have two general types of water pollution: point source (PS), which originates from municipal and industrial wastewater discharges; and non-point source (NPS), the vast majority of which is sourced to agriculture. The policy was created from 2010-2012 and was released to the public in 2013. The nutrients nitrogen (N) and phosphorus (P) are the focus and the stated objective is to reduce loss of each to the stream network by 45%, which aligns with goals set by the Gulf of Mexico Hypoxia Task Force, a consortium of government agencies and tribes coordinating work to reduce the size of the Dead Zone to pre-1996 levels.[18]

Although the federal Clean Water Act of 1972 compelled point sources to clean up their act, it failed to reduce by much the nutrient content of their discharges. The INRS addresses this through a regulatory approach targeting wastewater treatment plants permitted under the National Pollution Discharge Elimination System (NPDES). The Clean Water Act almost completely ignored pollution from agriculture, and the INRS addresses this through a non-regulatory, voluntary approach. In Iowa about 90-95% of stream nitrogen pollution and 85-90% of phosphorus pollution is from NPS, i.e. agricultural, sources. Nothing compels farmers to adopt BMPs and there are no improvement milestones, deadlines, or consequences for non-adoption or failure to meet the water quality objectives. Farmers *are* eligible for cost share (public) money to help pay for approved practices.

Farmers who want to adopt these practices often need assistance to navigate the bureaucratic maze to get to the cost share funds, and many practices require technical assistance. And water quality projects coordinated within a geographical area targeting groups of farmers require coordinators experienced in engaging and connecting the various stakeholders. Meaningful regulation could effectively cancel the need for these types of jobs. Agribusiness, farmers, and political conservatives are predictably anti-regulation. But many who don't fall into that group, i.e. environmentalists, liberals, and academics, who might otherwise be pro-regulation, aren't, not only because they fear backlash but also because their living is derived from the industry I call Big Pollution.

What follows in this book are 60-odd essays on Iowa's current agricultural production systems and how they relate to our environment, especially the disturbed quality of our lakes and streams. Although these perspectives are informed by science—my own and that of others—I've tried to write the essays colloquially and creatively, this in order to reach the only audience with the power to demand the changes needed to improve our water: the masses. If I'm still floating your boat after those 60 essays, I finish with "Downstream," a concluding chapter that summarizes my thoughts on what has to happen if Iowa is to have something none of us has ever seen at the state scale. CLEAN WATER.

IOWA'S REAL POPULATION

This essay has been read by more people than anything else I have written, and this by a long shot. There is no doubt in my mind that most people were drawn to the piece by the map, created with the help of my friend and colleague Dan Gilles. The basic idea here, that Iowa's livestock waste is enormous in comparison to human waste, has been well-understood by most people who study Iowa agriculture and the environment for a long time. But the image of the map resonated with people in a way that completely took me by surprise. I also must give some credit for the map to Iowa State Geologist Keith Schilling, with whom I discussed the idea prior to creating it. As it turns out, I underestimated the total amount of waste, and this was corrected in the companion piece, "Fifty Shades of Brown," which was written a few months later and follows this essay.

Iowa has around 3 million people, a total that has not changed much over the last 80-90 years. People are large animals, and as such, our bodies produce a lot of waste. That said, we produce much less waste than the animals that we eat. Take hogs, for example. A feeder pig is about the same size as a human being, but it excretes 3 times as much nitrogen (N), 5 times as much phosphorus (P), and 3.5 times as much solid matter (TS-total solids). Some of this is because of the pig's diet and some it is because modern hogs grow really, really fast (these things relate to each other, obviously). A pig weighs about 3 pounds at birth and about 250 pounds at slaughter a mere 6 months later, so it is gaining more than one pound per day. By comparison, a human infant gains a pound about every 20 days. There's a reason we use the word "hog" metaphorically and pejoratively because they consume anything and everything in sight virtually non-stop, which is one reason why they make for a good food animal.

Everybody knows Iowa has a lot of livestock. If you're like me, maybe you have heard from time to time that our state has enough animals to effectively be as populous as California, using one common example. As you will soon see, it's bigger than that. Much bigger.

Exactly how many of each livestock species that we have at any one time is a difficult thing to quantify. I'm going to present some watershed-by-watershed numbers for the following analysis and I do not claim that they are on-the-money, but I have consulted with a couple of experts and I am confident they are in the ballpark. Anyway, statewide, we have around 20-24 million hogs, 250,000 dairy cattle, 1.8 million beef cattle, 80 million laying chickens, and 4.7 million turkeys. I did not consider sheep, goats, horses, broiler chickens or scapegoats (e.g. wildlife, often blamed by people in agriculture for our water pollution problems).

When I sum up the N, P and TS values of the waste from these animals, what would be the equivalent-sized human population that would generate such waste is staggering:

> Iowa hogs: equivalent to 83.7 million people
> Dairy cattle: 8.6 million people
> Beef cattle: 25 million people
> Laying chickens: 15 million people
> Turkeys: 900,000 people

In total, these five species generate the waste equivalent to that produced by about 134 million people, which would place Iowa as the 10th most populous country in the world, right below Russia and right above Mexico. (Caveat: obviously Russia and Mexico have their own livestock that I am not counting.) And in terms of population density in the context of N, P and TS waste, Iowa would come close to the country of Bangladesh. Managing the waste from these animals is possibly our state's most challenging environmental problem. Of course, we do have a lot of cropland to apply this waste to, but the time windows in which farmers have to do this without damaging the crops with equipment are usually not large. Wet, cold and hot weather can all limit application. As a result, there are only a precious-few weeks in a year when this Mt. Everest of waste can be applied to corn and soybean fields. And there can be no doubt that the sheer amount, and the logistical complications of hauling and handling it, have consequences for water quality.[1] Watersheds with the highest density of livestock frequently have some of the highest stream nitrate concentrations (North Raccoon, Floyd, and Rock River watersheds, for example).

My colleague Dan Gilles, a Water Resources Engineer at the Iowa Flood Center, was able to derive the human population for Iowa's 56 major watersheds. Dan has been a great collaborator and most days he could run circles around me. Anyway, our most populated watershed, the Middle Cedar, has 294,000 people. Even in that watershed, the human-equivalent livestock population (3.6 million) dwarfs that of actual people. I added the human population to this human-equivalent livestock population for each of Iowa's HUC8 watersheds and this is illustrated in the map by relating it to a city or state that has a similar human population.

To finish up, I present this illustration not to make any value judgments on the livestock industry. Clearly it is an important part of our economy. I think we can and should, however, objectively and dispassionately ask ourselves how many livestock animals we can accommodate while still being able to achieve our desired environmental outcomes. Denmark and the Netherlands both have livestock densities on the scale of Iowa. As a result, both countries have in the past suffered environmental consequences similar to our own, but both country's governments have intervened in more forceful ways than ours. I'm not saying this is good, bad, or in between, it's just true. I think even livestock industry advocates would say there is not much that limits further expansion in Iowa, except perhaps available land in certain areas of the state to apply the waste to. Is it reasonable to think about what's possible when trying to reconcile our desired environmental outcomes with the economic and regulatory considerations the industry wants? If we are going to be honest with ourselves, then I think the answer to that question is yes.

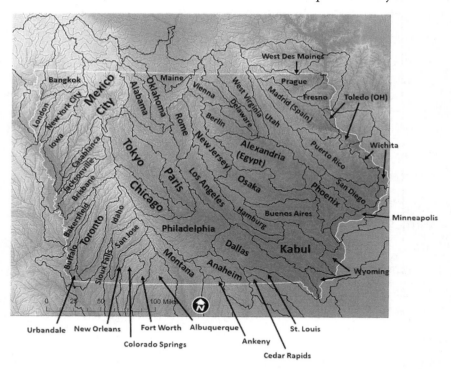

This map shows the human waste equivalent of the people, hogs, laying chickens, turkeys, and dairy and beef cattle with the city or state that relates to it with its human population only. Reflected is an average of N, P, and TS waste. Only the population of the city proper is reflected, not the overall metropolitan area.

FIFTY SHADES OF BROWN

I wrote this about two-and-a-half months after "Iowa's Real Population" be-cause Larry Weber, director of IIHR-Hydroscience and Engineering at the Uni-versity of Iowa and co-founder of the Iowa Flood and Nutrient Centers, kept asking me how Iowa compared to other states when it came to livestock waste. This piece evidently was a bridge too far for some Iowa Ag people, and one of them made what I thought were some veiled threats toward me in a guest ed-itorial run in The Des Moines Register. *That prompted me to write, "The Swine Republic," which became the title for this book. That essay follows this one.*

Some of you may recall the map from the previous essay titled "Iowa's Real Population" (see the facing page) that quantified the amount of fecal waste generated by Iowa's people and livestock. I then related that to the equivalent human population of various places around the U.S. and world.

Since that time, some folks have been asking me what Iowa looks like relative to other states in this regard, so here goes.

First, my method. I harvested livestock population data for each U.S. state from the recently updated Census of Agriculture using the National Agricultural Statistics Service Quickstats website.[1] These animal populations were queried: beef cattle, dairy cattle, hogs, lay-ing chickens, food chickens (broilers) and turkeys. I looked at refer-ence values for the amount of nitrogen, phosphorus, and total solids generated by each type of animal and converted that to a human equivalent. I then added that number to the human population to get a "fecal equivalent population," which I will call FEP for brevity from here on out. Since US states vary in size from 1,545 (Rhode Island) to 665,000 square miles (Alaska), I divided the FEP by the states' areas to get a FEP density, if you will.

In "Iowa's Real Population," I had an FEP for Iowa of 134 million. With the updated USDA data, it's now 168 million. The number of people commenting on that map following the blog post took me by surprise and actually was unnerving, causing me to fear that I had over-calculated. These updated numbers were a relief.

After I divided that number (168 million) by Iowa's area, and did the same for every other state, the table at the end resulted. So just to ensure clarity, in Iowa we are generating as much fecal waste in every square mile as 2,979 people. For reference, my home of Iowa City is the 2nd-most densely-populated city in Iowa and has 2,775 people per square mile. So, imagine an Iowa-sized Iowa City. That's how much fecal waste we are generating.

Now it must be said that some other states do have a lot of live-stock animals. The tiny state of Delaware (2nd on the FEP/square mile list) has 52 million chickens; the huge state of Texas has 12.5 million beef cattle and 170 million chickens. Arkansas has more than 200 million poultry birds, although its 930,000 beef cattle still produce more waste than the poultry.

The hog manure generated in Iowa floats our state to the top of the FEP/square mile list. Iowa is home to one out of every three U.S. hogs, with 23 million residing here at any given moment, a number that has increased by 64% since 2002.[2]

In only six states are human beings the top fecal producer, these all on the east coast except for Alaska. The map shows the animal producing the most fecal material in each state; for simplicity purposes, the chicken in the map represents the total of all poultry birds (layers, broilers, turkeys).

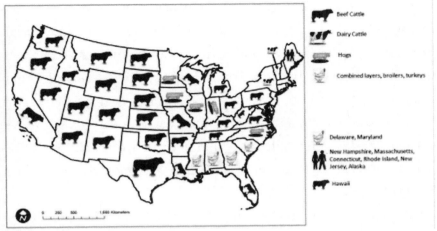

Largest generator of fecal waste in U.S. states.

What does this mean for us? We clearly have a lot of crop area to apply that manure to, and it must be said that manure is a good fertilizer and can promote healthy soils. Manure has value beyond just the macro-nutrients of nitrogen and phosphorus. The organic carbon contained within manure is especially beneficial to crops and soils. Manure is a much more difficult fertilizer to manage, however, compared to synthetic chemical fertilizers, and manure almost always needs to be accumulated and stored for long periods of time before application to crops. Manure fertilization also presents a lot more uncertainty to the farmer when it comes to precisely determining the necessary amounts commensurate to crop needs. This is why watersheds with dense livestock populations tend to have higher stream nitrate levels.[3, 4, 5]

I also want to say that we should not ignore the fact that livestock production has a very real beneficial effect for rural Iowa's economy—transportation, equipment, construction, and meat packing are just a few of the industries that benefit. Read Art Cullen's book, *Storm Lake*,[6] if you don't believe me.

But if you think our meat appetite comes without profound environmental consequences, read Elizabeth Kolbert.[7] (For the record, I am not a vegetarian.) In the modern era, the biomass contained within our bodies outweighs that of Earth's wild mammals 8:1, and when we add in our domesticated food animals, that ratio jumps to 23:1. Imagine what this last ratio must be for Iowa. It's got to be staggering. Not much of Iowa, America, or Earth for that matter remains untouched by the feet and the crap of human beings and our horde of animals.

I'll finish here on a tangent by saying that I get a fair number of comments relating to the blog that fall somewhere along the spectrum of a) courteous envy that I am able to post my thoughts; b) astonishment that I would do so; and finally c) "Do you still work there?" I'm always consciously guarding against sounding pretentious, and I proceed here at the risk of doing that.

First and foremost, I am trying to put credible (and almost always publicly-available) information and data into an understandable context. In my view, to do that effectively requires adding a perspective. So yes, I add perspective, most often my own.

Second, and last, I worry about the current state of affairs if people are astonished by the mere existence of this type of expression. I can hardly believe we have gotten to this place. I firmly believe that if we are to solve problems, we all ought to be able to talk about them openly, especially when they involve things we hold in common like our lakes, streams, air and wildlife.

Fecal Equivalent Population (FEP) per Square Mile of U.S. States

State FEP/Square Mile

Iowa 2,979
Delaware 2,371
Wisconsin 1,554
Nebraska 1,463
Pennsylvania 1,452
North Carolina 1,410
Indiana 1,334
Maryland 1,280
Ohio 1,260
Kansas 1,258
Oklahoma 1,254
Missouri 1,227
New York 1,150
New Jersey 1,092
California 1,090
Kentucky 1,062
Minnesota 1,058
Illinois 930
Arkansas 909
Georgia 896
Texas 892
Vermont 892
Virginia 891
Connecticut 887
Tennessee 882
South Dakota 868
Alabama 829
Florida 771
Rhode Island 749
Massachusetts 743
Idaho 679
Mississippi 649
Colorado 527
South Carolina 520
Michigan 509
Washington 487
North Dakota 483
Louisiana 364
West Virginia 361
Hawai`i 310
New Mexico 281
Oregon 267

Arizona 255
Montana 255
Utah 244
New Hampshire 242
Wyoming 197
Maine 99
Nevada 96
Alaska 1.5

THE SWINE REPUBLIC

Following the companion essays of "Iowa's Real Population" and "Fifty Shades of Brown," the Iowa Farm Bureau Federation submitted a guest editorial to the Des Moines Register *that implied (at least in my opinion) that I needed to shut up about livestock production and manure. As a result, I wrote this one in anger; at the time I felt it was important to show that I wouldn't be intimidated by the Ag establishment. It's short (about 500 words) and doesn't present any new information or insights. But the title of this book was taken from the essay and I felt it was important to include it here. So, this should be read as the 3rd essay in a series that includes the two aforementioned ones.*

I have written some things about manure lately. If you were able to make it to the end of those essays, you found these points were made:

> We have a lot of livestock animals in Iowa

> These animals produce a lot of waste

> This waste is used to fertilize crops

> Manure is a good fertilizer

> Sales of commercial fertilizer are not affected very much by the availability of manure

Furthermore, these conclusions culled from the scientific literature also were highlighted in the essays:

> When farmers use manure, they tend to apply nutrients well beyond the agronomic needs of the crop

> Livestock density correlates with degraded water quality

For the most part, these are uncontroversial positions in my world. Almost mundane, really. University researchers know this, commodity organizations know this, agency people know this, politicians know this, farmers know this. However, most of those folks are afraid to talk about those last two bullets in public.

When I throw some words at those bullets and put the information in relatable maps, the industry responds not with ideas to better manage the situation, but rather with this (it's a web link):

FOR THE LOVE OF GOD WE NEED MORE HOGS[1]

So, the argument goes like this: our cropland has the capacity to handle twice as much manure and therefore twice the number of hogs. Ok, that's cool. Do our streams have the capacity to handle more nutrients assuming we don't reduce commercial fertilizer inputs by commensurate amounts? Of course, we don't know because our agencies take the industry position and actively oppose nutrient standards for the *public's* water. Some guy named G. Orwell once said, "So long as the public is not permitted to have standards of comparison, they never even become aware that they are oppressed." Amen, brother, amen. Whatever happened to the common good?

I'm really hesitant to make certain distinctions in my writing, but when somebody does it for you in public, what the heck. As the saying goes, don't look a gift hog in the mouth:

Me: Cleaner Water.   Industry: Double the Hogs.

Folks, there are people who look at a green lake or a brown stream and say, "What's the big deal? After all, BACON!!" As if civilization just figured out how to cure pork.

I know this is an agricultural state and a great place to raise corn and soybeans and a great place to concentrate the animals that will eat that stuff. I also know these things are important to our economy and our identity and that we will always do them at some level.

What I don't understand is why the public is expected to indemnify those activities AND tolerate (or pay to remedy) the current level of pollution that comes with them. I want the industry to explain THAT in the pages of the *Des Moines Register*.

RANSOM

When I go back and read some of my earlier essays like this one, I see that they are denser than my more recent work. One of the reasons I write now is to have fun; three years ago, that was not part of the equation. I was really happy with this one when I wrote it and was a little taken aback that a former colleague from the Ag side of my career didn't like it. The overriding theme here is that water quality in Iowa has been taken hostage, and if the public wants better water, then we better be prepared to pay a ransom. I decided there was more to say on this, so I also wrote "Ransom, the Sequel," which follows this one.

One thing that I see real essayists do when beginning a piece is start with a quote from someone famous. I guess that's what you're supposed to do when you can't think of soaring words on your own. It occurred to me that I might want to try this. Thus:

"I grasp the hands of those next to me, and take my place in the ring to suffer and to work, taught by an instinct, that so shall the dumb abyss be vocal with speech."—Emerson

Just so you know that I am consciously trying to be unpretentious here, that is literally the only thing of Emerson's that I am certain that I've read. But, I like it, and so here we are. Sometimes I think we're lucky that people like Emerson didn't have Twitter and whatever else because they might have gotten satisfied (and lazy) just tossing out tiny gems like the one above, and many of the great works might never have been written.

Speaking of Twitter, a few weeks ago I saw a post from an Iowa farmer commenting on the Lake Erie Bill of Rights, which passed on February 27th, 2019.[1] The bill garnered 61% of the vote. The measure would allow Ohio residents to sue on behalf of Lake Erie, which if you don't know, suffers from nutrient-driven harmful algae blooms. This particular farmer commented this was an example of why farmers needed to engage with farm policy and commodity organizations, because "the threat was real." I found the choice of words here interesting, especially *threat*. Someone unknowledgeable about water quality issues relating to agriculture might wonder just what threat could be posed by people wanting clean water. Although this farmer didn't really want to say it, I don't think I am going out on a limb by saying that what is threatened is agriculture's license to release unregulated amounts of nutrients beyond the farm field and into the surrounding environment, and the ability to farm in ways that result in that outcome.

This comes on the heels of former Ohio governor John Kasich's late-term attempt to institute protections for Lake Erie by declaring through executive order eight watersheds that flow into the lake as distressed. The Ohio Soil and Water Conservation Commission, the farm lobby, and state legislators squashed that idea and blocked it. For many, there was something therapeutic about Kasich's efforts, even if it was done without much risk (Kasich was a lame duck). Finally, a politician who seemed serious and fed up with the pace of progress on nutrient pollution.

The new Ohio governor, Mike DeWine, recently proposed a $900 million "protection fund" that would focus on Lake Erie and other Ohio waters and would use at least part of it to "focus on farm runoff and sediment from bleeding into waterways." (Kasich proposed spending $3 billion.) "Land management and wetlands creation would also be a target," DeWine said. "There also has to be incentives that are built in to help farmers, so they don't bear the entire

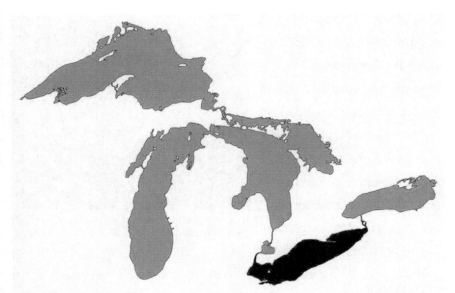

Lake Erie in dark blue. Image credit: By Phizzy at the English Wikipedia, CC BY-SA 3.0, https://commons.wikimedia.org/w/index.php?curid=4502187.

burden of doing this," he said to reporters. "I would make sure they are farming in a manner which does not cause as much of the nutrients to flow into the lake as are currently happening." (Emerson, he's not.)

Make no mistake, Kasich's executive order was a threat. DeWine's approach here is very much old school, that is, providing public dollars as cost share to farmers in an effort to entice them into adopting practices that will reduce nutrient runoff, without compulsory measures that agriculture sees as regulation. This is pretty much the history (with a few exceptions) of how this country has dealt with nutrient pollution. There have been some limited successes with phosphorus pollution, but this strategy has been ineffective in reducing nitrogen pollution.

Meanwhile back in Iowa, very few farmers I talk to or read about are getting the economic outcomes they want and feel they deserve. Compared to the capital investment required to farm in the

U.S. Midwest, there is good reason for them to feel this way. A thousand acres of land in Iowa (probably close to the minimum needed to operate profitably) is worth $10 million or more. Equipment, buildings, and the rest, probably another couple million at least. To plant a crop on that land probably requires upwards of $400,000 in seed, chemicals, fertilizer, insurance, etc. Maybe more. If the farmer makes $100/acre at harvest, that's $100,000. Not a bad income, but certainly not what one might expect with a $12 million investment. And we know with certainty the $100k would be less without government assistance and immunity from regulation and many forms of taxation.

Lake Erie algae bloom. Photo credit: Ohio State University.

At the same time, many (most?) Americans are not getting the environmental outcomes, like good water quality, that they want from our food production system. So, farmers aren't getting the economic outcomes they want, and the public isn't getting the environmental outcomes that we want. At the same time, the taxpayer indemnifies the system with publicly supported crop insurance, usually unknowingly. This begs the question, who is getting the outcomes they want from our policies, and in particular, the old school policies targeting improved water quality?

I think the answer to my question is those who benefit from cheap commodities and maximum agricultural land use, what I call Max Acres. If we were to design a system that would produce a huge abundance of anything without bankrupting the producers, how would we do it? Well, of course, we would incentivize the activity with government policy and subsidies while not putting any controls on supply (the current situation in the US with corn and soybean production). This virtually guarantees overproduction. Therefore, farm subsidies like crop insurance are in effect a subsidy for the commodity buyers and those whose livelihood is connected to them and Max Acres, and this goes far beyond just agribusiness. You could even make the case that I am one of them.

In the current scenario, the farmer is continuously encouraged to produce more bushels, and increased production without a concomitant increase in demand drives the per bushel price down. In this situation, the only way for the grain farmer to increase his income is to produce more bushels, and the spiral continues. Excessive pollution, especially nutrient pollution (more bushels, after all), is a predictable outcome in this scenario, especially when government policy is designed to keep nutrient prices low. An example of this is the taxpayer-subsidized fertilizer plant that was recently built in Weaver, Iowa.[2]

Now the taxpayer, after already having been asked to indemnify this system, is told that the only way to reduce the resultant pollution is to contribute more public funds so farmers aren't financially burdened in their efforts to improve water quality. Advocates of this approach exist on both ends of the political spectrum and rationalize it with the idea that the public benefits from the farmers' private actions, and thus we should have skin in the game. In my view, water quality is taken hostage by this old school policy, while at the same time, we do little to address the underlying methods and economics of crop production that drive the pollution problem in the first place. And the beneficiaries of low commodity prices and Max Acres are relieved of any responsibility for degraded water quality.

I'm doing more pontificating here than I should, so I need to finish up and to do that I will talk about another famous writer, Wendell Berry. Wendell is not my favorite writer. I find his essays to be lots and lots of long words and sentences, with gems buried within, but the gems are truly precious. Anyway, he has talked about how each generation finds contempt and disgust with previous generations (think slavery), and we are crazy if we think our generation will be immune from this. One thing I believe future generations of Iowans will think about is this: we knew our water was degraded, we knew what caused the degradation, we had ideas on how to fix it, but we didn't fix it. And the reason we didn't fix it is because we lacked the courage to confront the forces that kept us locked into a status quo preferred by only a few.

So, there is today's effort to fill the dumb abyss with some words.

RANSOM, THE SEQUEL

I got a little pushback on my first ransom essay, which is okay and to be expected in Iowa. I don't expect anybody to swallow this stuff without chewing.

Because I feel like I only have about 1,000 words to make a point before losing most of you, I divided "Ransom" in two, and here is part two.

You might recall from part one I said we do little to address the underlying methods and economics that are driving the stream nutrient pollution. I feel strongly that this is true.

There is an Ag policy writer named Bryce Oates. I have learned some things from him:

> All productivity in the U.S. has increased 77% since 1973. However, real wages have increased only 12%.[1] Thus, the investor class has siphoned off most of this increase. (Although I do think this is a problem, I don't mean to use "investor class" in a hostile way; many of us fall into that category.)

> Things are not that different in agriculture. In 1973, farmers got $0.40 of the consumer food dollar. In 2017, this was slightly less than $0.15[2] which is worse than it sounds because half of that $0.15 was actually spent purchasing products from other industry groups (think livestock producers buying feed grain).[2]

> In 1973, average Iowa corn yield was about 90 bushels per acre. Last year it was 196 bushels per acre, thus, the productivity increase for corn production is basically on par with the economy as a whole, and maybe even a little bit better. Some of that increase may be due to more favorable weather, but who cares, a big increase.

Many want to understandably celebrate the productivity and innovation of the Iowa farmer. So why aren't we compensating them accordingly? Where are the financial benefits of this productivity increase going? The answer of course is corporations and agribusiness.

I've come to believe that what I just described is part and parcel of the water quality and other pollution problems associated with corn and soybean production. As I said in "Ransom," farmers operate within a more bushels/lower price spiral. We've rewarded their productivity increases with less money per bushel, just like wage earners in our society.

Someone once told me the definition of an agronomist is a person who never ceases to be amazed by a plant's response to nitrogen. Now, that increase from 90 to 196 bushels per acre owes more to crop genetics and weed and pest control than to nitrogen, but the farmer needs *enough* nitrogen to reach the yield potential conveyed by these other factors. And make no mistake, farmers want to reach that yield potential because of the *more bushels* world they live in, and because of the inherent satisfaction that comes with improvement. To that end, we have underlain our landscape with drainage tile to construct what is essentially the largest storm sewer on earth to lower the water table, and then we keep the landscape saturated with nitrogen, much of it in the loss-vulnerable and water-soluble form of nitrate. People who study these things even have a saying for this engineered creation: *the leaky system,* a term I think coined by Jerry Hatfield at the Agricultural Research Service of USDA. Most of the approaches we have for reducing nitrate loss and improving water quality also focus on maintaining the storm sewer and nitrogen saturation. One of the problems we have here, however, is in nature, you don't get something for nothing, no matter how hard you want that to be true.

Up to this point, I think you may be able to make the case for public participation (i.e., $$) in these approaches. The bridge too far for me to cross is that we also are asked to indemnify the whole kit and caboodle with publicly supported crop insurance, which inherently incentivizes environmentally suspect practices. I just cannot square these things in my mind, along with a license to pursue whatever means necessary to maximize crop yields, with a rational approach to better Iowa stream water quality. I just don't know how you do it, and my sense is that many of our institutions have not thought this through very well, or that they are in denial about it.

Planting corn in the modern day. Photo credit: Deere and company.

Farmers often shoulder the blame for poor water quality, which they understandably hate. I would just ask, where are the major beneficiaries of these productivity increases and Max Acres policies when it comes to water quality? Currently we rely on the altruistic instincts of farmers to improve water quality and we try to inspire those feelings with public cost share for best management practices. But I think farmers are like the rest of us. We're not all driving Priuses or putting solar panels on our roofs.

What is mysterious to me is why farmers have gone along with it all. What I mean by that is this: Why have they gone along with largely relinquishing the benefits of increased productivity while being forced to absorb the blame for the water quality problems connected to this increased productivity? Maybe some would say they had no choice. I don't know. A few months ago, I was on a water quality panel with two farmers. One operated a crop-livestock operation in eastern Iowa with her husband. She very clearly and movingly articulated the financial struggles her family was forced to confront in keeping the operation viable. I asked her later on if she and other farmers were not getting the economic outcomes they felt they deserved, why did they so tenaciously defend the system? The answer was that she felt farmers were committed to providing cheap food to America (cheap was not meant to be a derogatory statement about food quality). I don't feel qualified to dive into her response any further and will just let it stand on its own.

INPL
(Iowa Needs Public Land)

More heartbreaking than the condition of our water is the dearth of public land we have in Iowa. And in the years since I wrote this essay, the Iowa legislature has made it more difficult for the state to purchase land and for people to donate land. The reason: they think more land is needed for farming. In my view our lack of natural spaces will have consequences for the state as young people, many now wanting experiences rather than the things of previous generations, will leave the state. My own three children have left—one to Oregon and two to Colorado. Nothing makes me sadder about Iowa than the near absence of public land and natural spaces. It's shameful and a travesty.

You've probably heard, like me, that Iowa does not have much public land and that we are pretty low on the totem pole in this regard. But since it is risky to just go by things you've heard, I did a little digging. There are a couple of ways to look at this: (a) the total amount of public land area and (b) the percentage of the state's total area that is in public hands (local, state, and federally held lands).

In terms of the total public land area,[1] Rhode Island has the least: 23 square miles. Rhode Island is the smallest U.S. state at 1,555 square miles, or about the size of three Iowa counties combined. All of Rhode Island's public land would fit into a square of about 5 miles by 5 miles, which is roughly the size of Ames.

Iowa has 1,576 square miles of public land, which is 8th smallest of all the states. Six of the states that are below us (RI, DE, CT, MA, MD, and VT) are all small states, the biggest of which, Maryland, is about the size of 22 Iowa counties combined. The very small states of New

Hampshire, Hawai`i, and New Jersey all have more public land area than Iowa. Hawai`i and New Hampshire did not surprise me but New Jersey did, considering that most people have a vision of New Jersey as a concrete-covered metropolis. The other state that is below Iowa in public land area—Kansas—is bigger in total area, about 1.5 times bigger. An agricultural state like Iowa, Kansas has 13 square miles less public land than we do. In terms of the percentage of state area in public hands, Iowa fares worse. We are 3rd lowest after Rhode Island and Kansas, with 2.8% of our land in public hands.

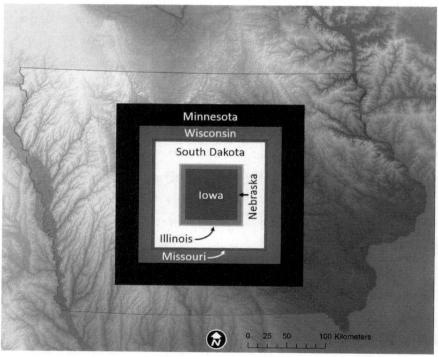

Each square represents the public land areas in Iowa and its bordering states, and is scaled to Iowa's total area. For reference, Iowa's land fits into a 40-mile square; Minnesota into 143-mile square.

An important question is, what do your public lands look like? You, like me, might have guessed a lot of it is in state parks, but in fact

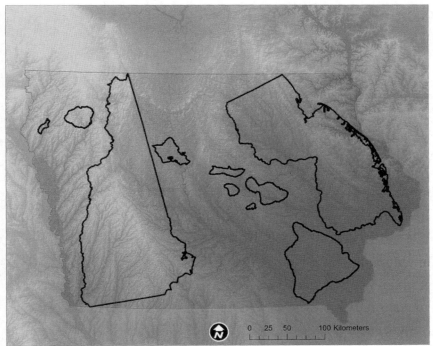

New Hampshire, Hawai`i, and New Jersey each have more public land than
Iowa. All are to scale. Dan Gilles helped with this map.

only about 6.7% of our public land lies within state park boundaries
(about 68,000 acres or 106 square miles). Thus all our state parks
would about fit into a square 10 miles by 10 miles, about the size
of the cities of Des Moines and Urbandale combined. A much larger
area of public land, about 585 square miles, comprises Iowa's Wildlife Management Areas. The balance of our public land lies within
city and county parks, state forest land, land that is home to public
buildings, and road easements. And farmland. Yes, you read that
right—farmland. Of the state's land holdings, about 29,000 acres
are in the DNR's land lease program. Of this, about 17,000 acres are
in row crop, 10,000 acres in other crops, and about 2,000 acres are
currently idle. If it were all in one place, this farmed, state-owned
land would be more than three times larger than our largest state

park (Yellow River Forest Camp). In total, state-owned land managed by the DNR comprises less than 1% of the state's area and surprisingly (to me anyway), 8% of this DNR land is farmed.

You might wonder if and how this all relates to water quality. In the Iowa Nutrient Strategy Science Assessment, land retirement is the most effective strategy for reducing nutrients (nitrogen-N and phosphorus-P) in the state's streams, with an expected reduction of 85% for N and 100% for P. We also know that the fraction of land in row crop production relates very strongly to stream nitrate levels, something we call the Schilling equation, named after my colleague, state geologist Keith Schilling. He and the previous state geologist, Bob Libra, published a paper[2] almost 20 years ago that demonstrated multiplying a watershed's row crop fraction by 10 would roughly estimate the stream N concentration at the outlet, thus 50% (0.5) in row crop would produce a nitrate concentration of 5 ppm. This applies statewide as well, with about 67% of the state's land in row crop and the long-term statewide average stream nitrate in the neighborhood of 6-7 ppm. Granted, retiring crop land to a more natural state does not necessarily or even commonly make it part of the public holdings. But this does illustrate the potential of returning land to a more natural state for improving water quality.

Another thing to remember here is that natural lands have a halo effect in that they enhance environmental conditions in areas around them. This is clearly noticeable to the physical senses when you travel to places like Minnesota and Colorado, both of which have nearly double the population of Iowa but far more public land. Natural lands restore hydrology, moderate climate, store carbon, reduce flooding, provide habitat and all sorts of other visible and invisible benefits to the areas where we live and work.

To finish, this might be a good time to mention the long-forgotten Iowa Open Spaces Plan.[3] In 1987 the Iowa legislature addressed the perceived need for additional open spaces in Iowa. They directed the Iowa DNR in House File 620 to "prepare a statewide, long-range plan for the acquisition and protection of significant open space lands" such that 10% of the state's area (5,600 square miles) be included under some form of public open space protection by the year 2000 (that would make our square about the size of South Dakota's in the map). Then Governor Branstad, in his second of six terms, signed this bill. As the maps show, it didn't come close to happening.

DRUNK DAD

In March of 2019, an anomalous climatic event occurred over the Great Plains that meteorologists called the Bomb Cyclone. Copious amounts of rain fell upon frozen ground and a deep snowpack, causing the Missouri River to flood like never before in recorded history. Levees failed along Iowa's southwestern border with the Missouri, flooding farm fields with water and sand. This came only eight years after another devastating Missouri River flood caused by Rocky Mountain snowmelt. Many blamed mismanagement by the U.S. Army Corps of Engineers for both floods, and that inspired this essay.

William Blake said, "you never know what is enough unless you know what is more than enough." I think about this ever-more frequently as the years fly by. I am at the point in my life where I want to call it when more than enough becomes maddeningly obvious. Enough of more than enough.

The latest episode in this series is the idea reported in the *Des Moines Register*[1] and elsewhere that the U.S. Army Corps of Engineers (the USACE, or the Corps) favors endangered species over people, especially with regard to the recent Missouri River flooding. I don't claim to be an expert on the inner workings of the Corps, but I've been up and down the river enough times to know that this is not an agency staffed with radical environmentalists. I find this idea to be a crystallization of the obstacles before us as we try to make Iowa's landscape more resilient, sustainable and ecologically sound.

Permit me to step back for a moment and take a look at this country's history with the Missouri River. Although people all over the world identify the Mississippi as the American river, the Missouri is longer and drains a larger area (when you subtract the Missouri watershed from the Mississippi's). From the continental divide in Yellowstone Park, a droplet of water travels 3,902 miles down the Missouri to the Mississippi at St. Louis, and from there finally to the Gulf of Mexico. That's the world's 4th longest river stretch and would be the longest were it not for the work of the USACE and others shortening both of the great rivers hundreds of miles to facilitate shipping and navigation. I challenge you to stand where Sacagawea stood with Merriweather Lewis atop the hills overlooking the start of the Missouri's main course at the Madison, Jefferson, and Gallatin river convergence at Three Forks, Montana, and not be in awe of the natural grandeur of America. Or look at the lower falls of the Yellowstone River, the Missouri's once awesome tributary, now sometimes sucked nearly dry by irrigation before joining the Missouri in western North Dakota. Imagine what this country's great rivers were once like.

Confluence of the Gallatin, Madison, and Jefferson rivers at Three Forks, MT, to form the Missouri River. Image credit: Jim Harris, *Outdoor Bozeman.*

For the Missouri, everything changed with the Pick-Sloan Flood Control Act of 1944 that authorized management of the Missouri River basin for navigation, flooding, water supply, hydroelectricity and recreation. "Pick" was General Lewis A. Pick, head of the USACE. Over 50 dams were constructed as a result, and the Missouri channel was straightened up to Sioux City to facilitate movement of barges. The largest earthen dam in the world (until 1975) was constructed on the Missouri at Glasgow, Montana, and was actually finished prior to the Pick-Sloan Act. Five more Missouri dams were constructed in the Dakotas: Garrison, Oahe, Big Bend, Fort Randall, and Gavins Point. As part of this, 202,000 acres of Native American land were transferred to the USACE. Imagine the outrage today if 202,000 acres of Iowa farmland were ceded to the federal government.

Lower falls of the Yellowstone River. Image credit: USGS.

Although many people would likely say the hydrological transformation of the Missouri basin benefited the American economy, in my view it was also an unmitigated environmental disaster on par with the loss and degradation of the Florida Everglades. Most of the sediment transported by the Mississippi River came from a wild Missouri slithering back and forth across its erodible floodplain over the millennia. Trapping the sediment behind dams and divorcing the river from its floodplain largely ended sediment delivery, contributing to the erosion of coastal wetlands in Louisiana and imperiling species that evolved to use the unrestrained river and its floodplain. Furthermore, this transformation caused the Missouri to erode downward, destabilizing many of its Iowa tributaries in the Loess Hills area of our state. This has resulted in massive streambank erosion and water quality degradation of our own inland streams.

Secretary of the Interior Julius Krug signs the Pick-Sloan Act as tribal leader George Gillette sobs in grief. Image credit: Department of the Interior.

Control of the river helped populate the lower Missouri valley and make it into a highly productive agricultural area. In doing that, we followed in the footsteps of the ancients. Since the dawn of agriculture, our species has been lured by highly productive floodplain soils, and in fact civilization arose in such situations in Mesopotamia and Egypt. Native Americans also used floodplain agriculture to obtain food security. Despite the risk of devastating floods, rich soil along with easy access to irrigation water from the river has been too tempting to resist.

In the present time, we clearly do not need to live and farm in the Missouri floodplain to achieve food security. That activity does arguably contribute to Iowa's prosperity, but when things go wrong, boy do they go wrong, as the tragedies of 2011 and last month remind us. The thing that bothers me is that we refuse to admit this tragedy is the result of periodic natural forces and instead blame human errors, especially, the errors of our government, specifically the errors of the USACE. When the Nile flooded the Egyptians' land, did they blame the pharaoh? I don't know, but I tend to doubt it.

In the outstanding chronicle of the USACE effort to control the lower Mississippi River, *Atchafalaya*,[2] John McPhee explored some of these ideas. McPhee describes how a bend of the Mississippi River near the Louisiana/Mississippi border flowed perilously close to the Atchafalaya River and actually started leaking water to the Atchafalaya about 500 years ago. The Atchafalaya is now what is known in hydrology as a distributary, which is a stream that branches off and flows away from the larger river, usually near the delta at the bottom of a large watershed. Following the huge 1927 Mississippi River flood, people began to realize that the great river might someday cast a wandering eye over to the course of the Atchafalaya, 10 feet lower and 150 miles closer to the Gulf of Mexico than the Mississippi's current course. In such a circumstance, Baton Rouge, New Orleans, and the American petrochemical industry would be left without a navigable river and the mouth of the Mississippi would be shifted 100 miles to the west. The laws of physics being what they are, the flow of the Mississippi is eventually going to be captured by the Atchafalaya. Such a course change happens once a millennium on average, with the last time being around A.D. 1000. In 1950, the USACE was ordered by Congress to preserve the current hydrologic condition of the Mississippi River forever by preventing such a natural calamity.

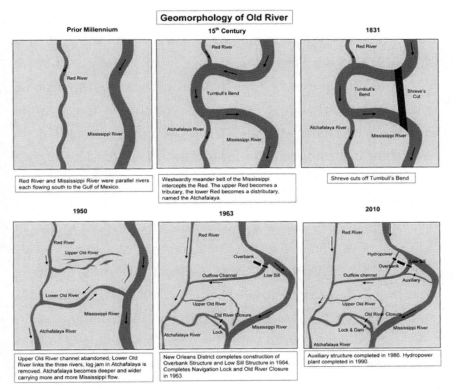

Evolution of the Red, Mississippi, and Atchafalaya river connections. Image credit: By United States Army Corps of Engineers—http://www.mvs.usace.army.mil/arec/models_old_html.html[dead link], Public Domain, https://commons.wikimedia.org/w/index.php?cu.

Now, I might say it is common for us to designate a motherly personage to nature. When it comes to hydrology, however, nature is not Mother. Nature is the father. A brooding, angry, and vindictive father. Drunk Dad, I will call him.

The USACE made the very bold decision to construct a control structure right at the spot where the Mississippi-Atchafalaya nuptials were most likely to occur. The resulting structure, completed in 1963 and called Old River Control, gently allows about 20-30% (but no more) of the Mississippi's flow to detour away from the Mississippi main channel to the Atchafalaya and then to the Gulf at

Morgan City, LA. Better to lose a managed 30% than lose it all. A bloodletting of sorts. Everything was copacetic until the Next Great Flood (1973), when Drunk Dad woke up with a hangover and was on the brink of taking the Corps to the woodshed. But the structure held, and the Mississippi remains in its 1950 channel today. An auxiliary structure was added after 1973 to bolster the system.

An interesting component to the McPhee tale is that seemingly everyone he interviewed (except Corps VIPs) expected the structure to fail at some point in the future. This included everyone from college engineering professors to the people sweeping the floor in the control room of Old River Control. They knew the Mississippi. At the time (1989), McPhee wrote: "People suspect the Corps of favoring other people. In addition to all the things the Corps does and does not do, there are infinite actions it is imagined to do, infinite actions it is imagined not to do, and infinite actions it is imagined to be capable of doing, because the Corps has been conceded the almighty role of God."

A thousand miles north in Iowa, Missouri, Kansas, and Nebraska, we also conceded what we thought was divine power to USACE, to break and tame the wild Missouri River. Not because we had to, mind you, but because we wanted to. How has that worked out for us? Well, sure enough, we did safeguard some good farm ground and urban infrastructure most of the years by having the Corps put the river in a prison. But shipping has been a complete flop. In fact, not a single barge made the trip up to Sioux City from 2003 to 2014. I don't know how you make the case that channelization was worth the resulting ecological disaster. Much of the shipping that has occurred in recent years ironically has been to haul materials around to create shallow water habitat for the endangered pallid sturgeon, in addition to some short-distance (less than 10 miles) movement of sands and gravels mined from the river for road projects. And as far as the flood? Well, in my view all this talk of bomb cyclones and climate change and endangered species is really a distraction from an uncomfortable idea: we have chosen to set up shop on a precarious piece of real estate.

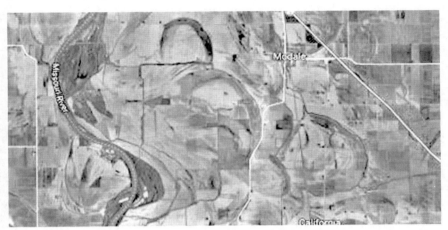

Google Earth image of the Missouri River floodplain in Iowa, showing river bends of the past.

We're angry, but not because we wrecked of one earth's great rivers. No, we're mad because every once in a while, Drunk Dad gets to missing his rowdy teenage son Missouri, and busts him out of the prison the Corps built just for him, and then the kid goes on a crime spree. And despite our displeasure with the Corps, I have little doubt that we will ask them to bring the wrath of God down on the Missouri River and call on them to build an even bigger and tougher and meaner prison. Such is our wisdom.

And that's more than enough for now.

HELLO, DARLING

One evening in early 2019, I gave a presentation to a civic group in Fairfield, Iowa, a town that lies just to the south of Lake Darling State Park. For good reason, these folks felt helpless to protect the water quality in the recently restored lake. I thought the story of Lake Darling needed to be told.

You might recall that I've written about how little public land Iowa has—8th-lowest of the states in the total amount of public land and 3rd-lowest in the percentage of our land area that is in public hands. This made me wonder about water, specifically, how much water we have relative to other states.

It turns out Iowa has 416 square miles surface water area, which is 6th-lowest of all the states.[1] The country as a whole is about 7% surface water area, ten times higher than Iowa. Depending on how you define a lake, Iowa has about 160 public lakes, including four Silver Lakes but remarkably no Green Lake, at least in name. A handful of these lakes were here when Europeans first arrived, formed 12,000 years ago by the melting Wisconsin glacier. We drained a bunch of stuff left behind by the glacier, most of which would now be thought of as wetlands and might not fit our current definition of a lake. But some clearly were lakes. Captain James Allen and his Dragoon explorers were some of the first Europeans to lay eyes on the marshy Des Moines Lobe area of north-central Iowa in 1844. In his journal Allen remarked that "then comes a series of lakes, many of them connected by slues and straits to form chains, almost impossible to go around or to cross, and extending from the Des Moines to the northward and eastward. This kind of country continues on the river about 35 miles, giving the greatest embarrassment to the traveller, who must frequently betake himself to a raft or ponton wagon to make his progress through it." Also, "From the waters of the Missouri, we next come in about 30 miles to the upper branches of the Raccoon. Approaching these branches the prairie is flat and wet; and much filled up with marshes and grassy ponds, through which it is difficult to find a practicable route."[2] (Spelling errors are his.) Our great-grandfathers drained about 3.5 million acres of standing water in this area of Iowa, which is more than 10 times the area of our existing surface waters—think about that for a minute.

Because we have so few lakes, and because so many of them were constructed (and for several, restored) at taxpayer expense, a reasonable person might think we should pull out all the stops to protect them. That's what I thought anyway, when I agreed to be on the Iowa DNR's Lake Nutrient Science Advisors (NSA) committee in 2007.[3] There were ten other committee members, most if not all more distinguished and knowledgeable about lake science than me. Most of the group are now retired. The committee set out to evaluate the existing lake water quality science from Iowa, surrounding states, and other countries, with the objective of recommending water quality standards for the nutrients nitrogen (N) and phosphorus (P). This was not an easy task because there are not direct cause-effect relationships between the N and P drivers and the response variables important to Iowa lake visitors, the most important being water clarity. This is not to say that N and P aren't important for water clarity—they are. What we know is that high levels of one or both increase the likelihood of poor lake water quality. Think of nutrients like they are high blood pressure. Having it doesn't mean you will have a stroke, but....it's a risk factor. Based on the information available to us, we recommended standards of 35 parts per billion (ppb) for P and 900 ppb for N. The existing data strongly suggested that these were thresholds for increased likelihood of nuisance algae blooms and reduced water clarity.

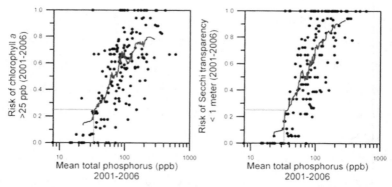

Figure 3. Risk of Chl-*a* exceeding 25 ppb and Secchi depth < 1 m related to TP in Iowa Lakes. Horizontal red line represent 25% risk of exceeding criteria and vertical red line is the intercept with the TP axis.

Example of the data used by the Lake Nutrient Science Advisors to develop a recommended phosphorus standard of 35 ppb.

To my knowledge, there have been two petitions for rule making to adopt the standards made to DNR and the Environmental Protection Commission (EPC), which is a governor-appointed citizen group that provides policy oversight over Iowa's environmental protection efforts. Both were denied. The most recent petition was heard just this year (2019). Now, I wish to say that I do not know if Iowa lakes would be any cleaner if these standards had been adopted following our report in 2008, but I believed then, as I do now, that water quality standards represent a starting point for improvement and build some accountability into the efforts to improve Iowa's water resources. It was painful for me to see the DNR explicitly state in its recent memo to EPC that our work was not supported by science, especially after many months of work on this project. I can assure anyone interested in this issue that that statement is not correct. I never heard this said in 2008.

By now you may have anticipated from this essay's title that at some point I would cannonball into Lake Darling, which is in southern Washington County. Here goes nothing. Lake Darling is a constructed lake (1950) that is the focal point of a state park of the same name, named after the Pulitzer Prize-winning (twice) Iowan Ding Darling. Darling was an important figure in the early conservation movement and would no doubt weep if he saw some of our lakes in their mid-summer, algae-choked condition. A $16-million lake restoration project was completed for Lake Darling in 2014[4]. As part of the project, about 80% of watershed landowners installed erosion and nutrient runoff controls. At the time, DNR State Park Bureau Chief Todd Coffelt said, "the key to a good state park is a good body of water."

Lake Darling has a relatively large watershed compared to its lake area (41:1). Knowing what it now knows about Iowa's landscape, the DNR would not build a lake with that large of a ratio. Like other constructed lakes, Darling is a flow-through system and water flowing in from a large area captures a lot of pollution which can then degrade the condition of the lake. In the case of Lake Darling, however, we must wonder if a smaller watershed would be much of a benefit.

Within 1.5 miles of the lake in its watershed are 19 fields where hog manure is being applied. Some of these fields are within ½ mile of the lake. A person knowledgeable of the situation told me those 19 fields are included in 35 manure management plans (MMPs). To confirm, I asked the DNR field office and was told that those numbers "could be accurate." The DNR "doesn't track how many plans are in each field because the MMP is a plan and is subject to change at any time." Nor does DNR know how much N and P is being applied to those fields. Thinking that I don't need to be any more diligent than our regulatory agency, I'm going with that and please forgive me if you think that's less than earnest. This all should not be a surprise to anybody, and I don't write this to indict DNR staff. It is the state of affairs in Iowa and has been for a long time. There are 346 concentrated animal feeding operations (CAFOs), 32 open feedlots, and close to 500,000 hogs just in Washington County[5] where Lake Darling State Park is located. There are four staff people in the local Iowa DNR field office who work on CAFO issues in Washington and 15 other counties, but none of them focuses on CAFOs exclusively. There are about 1,600 CAFOs in total within the jurisdiction of that field office.

Does the above scenario put the lake at more risk than others without such a stressor? The scientific literature says yes. I and others,[6,7,8] have documented how crop rotations that include manure fertilization oftentimes receive nutrient inputs far above recommended agronomic rates. The manure management plans should in theory restrict what the high-end fertilization rates should be, but not many people I talk to believe that is the case, at least statewide. I want to emphasize that I'm accusing no one of anything illegal or untoward when it comes to Lake Darling. However, I think any reasonable person would conclude the lake is in a risky spot.

Ok, back to the nutrient standards for lakes. Following the restoration, a DNR fisheries biologist was quoted[4] as saying Lake Darling "will be clear to depths of 4 feet, greatly enhancing the environment for both aquatic species and people." This was exactly the situation that the proposed nutrient standards were designed to protect! In the Lake Nutrient Science Advisors report,[3] we stated "The consensus of the NSA (committee) is that a Secchi depth less than 1.0 m (about 3.3 feet) in lakes is not compatible with primary body contact recreational use (Class A)."

Ten years after the NSA report, the DNR stated in its memo to the EPC that nutrient standards would create an untenable economic burden for local communities forced to confront degraded or impaired lakes. Is that the case here? I'm not an authority on economics but I do know the current DNR seems to be ignoring some of its own information in making that statement, specifically on the economic benefit lakes provide to the surrounding area. In their assessment of Lake Darling, the lake and park were found to contribute $8.5 million/year to the local economy, and this before the restoration. In a county with only 22,000 people, that's about $400 per person per year. Lake Darling is not anywhere close to a municipal boundary and is not used for municipal water supply nor does it receive point source discharges. The lake's economic impact may be dwarfed by that of livestock, I don't know. But let's cut the crap here. It seems pretty clear who will be economically burdened by protecting the taxpayer-funded water quality enhancement, at least when it comes to Lake Darling, and that's the people raising hogs. For crying out loud, let's be honest with ourselves.

I believe this is the truth: the real threat of nutrient standards in lakes or any other water body is that they bring accountability to the system, both to the regulated and the regulators. The livestock industry adamantly asserts that they are regulated. Well yeah, sort of. They are regulated in the same way driving is regulated. You get a driver's license, you license a car, you get insurance, and the paved world is your oyster. There are speed limits, but if you've ever driven I-80 between Des Moines and Iowa City, you can see what they're worth. In the unlikely event you screw up and get caught speeding or crash, then yeah, you're "regulated." We have an analogous system for non-point source water pollution. The present system enables the livestock industry to essentially not comply with any nutrient regulations because the DNR really has nothing it can regulate in any meaningful or effective way. A lot of people like it like that because the public goes to bed at night thinking the whole thing is regulated when it really isn't. As a result, our lakes and streams suffer. It's taboo in many situations to talk about this, but I've seen and heard more than enough and I'm done with taboo.

When evaluating the most recent petition for rule-making, the EPC received eight public comments. Seven were yea and one was nay. The nay carried the day. Considering the current state of affairs, it likely could have been 10,000 yeas with the Almighty being one of those, begging the EPC to have mercy on His creation, and the lone nay still would have prevailed.

I'm never sure how to end these things. Iowans have paid $16 million to restore Lake Darling, and a bunch more for a bunch of other lakes. I, for one, would like to know that somebody is guarding that investment of the public's money. I'm not convinced that there is, and I think some people like it that way.

STOP SAYING WE ALL
WANT CLEAN WATER

I wrote this on a whim sitting at my kitchen table in Iowa City one dreary April Sunday afternoon. Now I look at this one as a manifesto of sorts; a scream born out of frustration about the condition of Iowa's water, which has been somewhere between substandard and terrible my entire life. If clean water is something we all want, why don't we have it?

If you're reading this, you've probably heard or read the phrase "we all want clean water." In all likelihood, the words came from someone of stature or someone knowledgeable about water quality issues. Today I had the idea to shake the Google tree and see what fruit fell to the ground when I entered the phrase "we all want clean water." It turns out one of our politicians, Iowa Senator Joni Ernst, has been quoted saying this so many times that I had a hard time figuring out who else had said it, so I started plucking names out of my head and attaching them to the phrase. What resulted was an impressive list, a veritable Who's Who of Iowa politics and agriculture. I did my own name as well, on the off-chance I had been recorded saying it (I didn't find anything). Two events in particular seemed to unleash a deluge of weallwantclean water, the first being the Des Moines Water Works lawsuit, the second being Waters of the United States (WOTUS) rule. I began to wonder, if all these important people genuinely believed their own words, why don't we have the water quality that we want?

Clearly, we do not *all* want clean water, at least not in any meaningful way. Yeah, I get that nobody wants to drink poisonous water.

But is that what we are talking about here? When it comes to our lakes and streams, we may all agree that the concept of clean water is a good one, but a critical mass of someones or somethings is holding us back from getting it. Either the sacrifice to get it is thought to be too large, or the idea that our water quality is substandard is considered to be incorrect.

This critical mass has managed to successfully thwart the will of the public. In 2010, 62.6% of voting Iowans voted yes for the Iowa Outdoor Recreation Trust Fund Amendment. If funded, the resulting revenue would pay for lake restoration and watershed protection, among other things. The legislature continues to decline our invitation. In 2016, 74% (!!) of Linn County, Iowa, residents voted for a $40 million conservation bond that will help address water quality. The Des Moines Water Works (DMWW) lawsuit targeting 13 northwest Iowa drainage districts for elevated nitrate concentrations in the Raccoon River was considered to be highly controversial. Even so, 63% of Iowans were found to support the position of the waterworks.[1] More recently, 81% of Polk County residents voted to tax themselves for water quality projects. And yet our government and many other of our institutions, at least in my view, lack a collective urgency to address the public's wishes, especially when it comes to nutrient pollution. How do we explain this?

While researching some things for this essay, I came across an article[2] about the DMWW lawsuit written by Mark Muller of the McKnight Foundation in 2013. In the article he states that "Iowa farmers are feeling unfairly persecuted for following well-established farming practices. Most of the corn and soybean farmers of northwest Iowa are adhering to agronomic guidance and business advice provided by bankers, crop advisors, and university professionals." Ok! I think we might be getting somewhere!

Let's look at statewide nitrogen loss. Using University of Iowa and Iowa DNR monitoring data, I calculated this to be 626 million pounds in 2018, with a 20-year average of 580 million pounds. That average loss (580M pounds) is worth about $232M to the fertilizer manufacturers and retailers. There are people who toss out the red herring that a lot of this lost nitrogen is from the soil. But in landscapes where this is true, farmers will replace it with their own inputs, so I wish people would just give this duplicitous argument a rest.

Farmers can and do survive the loss of nitrogen quite nicely, which is one of our obstacles to improved water quality. But let's just say they were able to reduce their nitrogen loss to zero. By my calculations that would reduce nitrogen fertilizer sales 23% over the last 20 years. Hmm. I'm no economist but I tend to believe that would result in some industry contraction at both the production and retail level. One perverse response to this has been the emergence of inhibitors, chemicals co-applied with the fertilizer to help keep the fertilizer in place until the corn needs it. Of course, these don't come free and the farmer must buy them from a retailer, and in fact farmers have been able to get public money to help defray the cost. While these products make some sense intuitively, the evidence that they've improved water quality is sketchy at best. But they do seem to increase corn yields, at least in some situations, so everybody's happy with this taxpayer contribution to the machine. I oftentimes wonder how many wetlands we could've built with the money that's been spent on these products. At least a few. But then again, you can't grow corn in a wetland.

Back to the Muller piece. We arrived at this place through an evolution of agronomic science and the resulting economic infrastructure created around it. Rome was built while most people still had not realized that nitrogen pollution was a bad thing, and a whole lot of people still don't think it's all that bad. And the people who built Rome are definitely not Nero; they are not going to burn it down and start over. There's too much at stake for them, regardless of what the public wants for water quality.

Fall tillage. Image credit: Iowa State University.

Iowa's dysfunction when it comes to water quality and the inability of policy to connect with what the public wants, are two consequences of this evolution. Wealth, careers and reputations (both individually and institutionally) have been built in lockstep with The Evolution, across all sectors of our economy—public, private, NGO, and academia. There's no grand conspiracy here, just a bunch of people, a lot of them smart and powerful, acting in their own self-interest. This was not done with any ill will, but degraded water quality, at least in terms of nutrient pollution, has been the result.

A symptom of the dysfunction is the maddening paralysis associated with our institutions' inability to stigmatize bad practices. Year after year, things continue to happen that we know beyond a shadow of a doubt degrade the environment and are not necessary in the current production system. It seems that many of our institutions think if they criticize a missed layup or free throw, the homecoming king will get them thrown off the cheerleading squad. Some of these things include continued tile installation, fall tillage (especially after soybeans are harvested), corn and soybean production in the 2-year floodplain, and, my personal un-favorite, manure application to snow. An example of what I am talking about is Iowa State University guidance[3] guidance on this last issue. To condense that one for you: heroin is dangerous, so at least use a clean needle.

Manure applied to snow-covered hillslope in Iowa.

If I hope to accomplish anything in what remains of my career, that thing would be we start talking about this water quality issue honestly. A lot of people don't, or can't. I'm reminded of that whenever I hear "we all want clean water."

In the public lands debate in this year's legislature, I read where a legislator was quoted as saying "I'm not opposed to clean water." Although that was likely a spontaneous comment, I do think it is a much more accurate description of where our politics resides on this issue, and I can at least respect the candor.

I love reading about the famous physicists of a century ago, Einstein, Bohr, Curie, and others. Anybody that can put a metaphorical cat in a metaphorical box (Schrödinger) and become famous for it—that's true genius! One of these people was Wolfgang Pauli, he of the famous exclusion principle. Reportedly he told a graduate student that the student's paper was so bad, it didn't even rise to the level of being wrong. That's where I feel like Iowa is with nitrogen pollution. It's not like we haven't given it an effort—we have. But thus far the effort has been so feeble and futile that it doesn't even rise to a level where we can at least say that we've failed.

Wolfgang Pauli, 1900-1958. Image credit: Bettina Katzenstein / ETH Zürich [CC BY-SA 3.0 (https://creativecommons.org/licenses/by-sa/3.0)].

FROM GOLF TO GULF?

Mark Twain famously (and accurately) said a lie will fly around the world while the truth is still getting its boots on. We deal with this all the time in Iowa with our water quality, and one of the myths that just won't die is that fertilization of turf grass is a driver of our degraded water. There's just no evidence that this is the case, and if a reasonable person took a second to think about the area of Iowa covered by corn and soybean crops compared to turf grass, the absurdity of the notion would become apparent. But yet, apparently in an effort to put a salve on industry feelings while also distracting the public, important people still peddle this hogwash.

If you've followed the issues connected to Iowa agriculture and water quality, you likely know some things about Gulf of Mexico hypoxia, otherwise known as the Dead Zone. This is the low-oxygen condition that develops off the coast of Louisiana that is driven by nitrogen (N) and phosphorus (P) entering the Gulf in the Mississippi and Atchafalaya Rivers.

Do golf courses contribute to this, and do they degrade local water quality?

Iowa DNR has this information: "Nutrients, especially nitrogen and phosphorus, are our main nonpoint pollutants in Iowa. Nutrients can come from fertilizers (both on agricultural land and on residential lawns, golf courses, etc.)."[1]

Former Iowa Governor and USDA secretary Tom Vilsack had this to say,[2] with regard to nutrient pollution: "Farmers' voluntary conservation efforts are a unique story in America. Other people aren't doing these things. The golf course guys aren't doing it. The lawn care folks aren't doing it."

Former Iowa Secretary of Agriculture Bill Northey[3]: "While I support a clean responsible environment, we must also maintain Iowa's

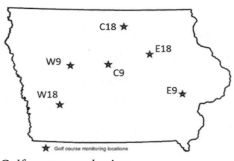

Golf course study sites.

productivity and thriving Ag industry. Runoff from urban lawns and golf courses should be included."

Bill Northey again[4]: "I don't like going into the city and seeing large amounts of nutrients being applied to lawns and golf courses."

And it's not just Iowa. Minnesota State Senator Mike Goggin said in an interview[5] that the Minnesota state government was singling out agricultural fertilizer use while not applying the same scrutiny to urban sources of pollution. "Where does it end? Do we go after the golf courses? Do we go after the lawn-care companies?"

So, golf courses are an important component to Iowa's stream nutrient problem. Myth or reality?

Some actual science on this topic exists[6]. Native Iowan and current Johnson County hacker, State Geologist Keith Schilling, is perhaps the number one expert on the subject. When he's not trying to break 100, Keith does some excellent research in hydrogeology and water quality and while his name appears on no golf trophies, it does appear on more than 160 published scientific papers. As part of his research, he recently led a study of nutrient (nitrogen-N and phosphorus-P) loss from Iowa courses.

There are over 400 courses in Iowa and at least one in each county, and compared to many other states, there are plenty of places to golf in our state. As part of his study, he randomly selected six courses

(3-18 hole and 3-9 hole) spaced across Iowa. The studied courses are representative of Iowa's landforms and ecoregions. Monitoring wells were installed in a tee, fairway, and rough location at each course and soil samples were collected. Quarterly groundwater samples were collected and monitored from the wells for two years, and surface water samples were collected from ponds and streams where they existed.

Groundwater nitrate concentrations averaged from undetectable to 2.8 mg/L (ppm) at five of the courses and 7 mg/L at the western Iowa 18-hole course (W18 on the map). At the West 18 course, the tee and rough wells contained low levels of nitrate (average about 3 mg/L), but the fairway well averaged about 15 mg/L. Some evidence emerged late in the study that this well may have been installed at or near a barn location when the course land was used as a farm, thus there likely was some legacy nitrate associated with the accumulation of livestock manure. As a reference, nitrate was measured in nearby private drinking water wells and these are shown in Table 1 below, and you can see that groundwater under the golf courses was lower than private well water at all locations.

Course	Average Groundwater NO3-N	Nearby Private Well NO3-N (average)	Average Groundwater P	Nearby Stream P
W18	7.0	8.3	0.14	0.18
W9	1.0	5.0	0.11	0.18
C9	<1.0	<1.0	0.15	0.21
C18	<1.0	9.1	0.11	0.10
E18	1.5	10.7	0.10	0.10
E9	2.8	7.4	0.16	0.12

Table 1: Water monitoring results from gulf course study. All units are mg/L (ppm).

Groundwater loading rates (average concentration multiplied by the groundwater recharge rate) were found to be about 2.5-3 pounds of N per acre, close to what the pre-settlement condition would have been and only about 1/10th of the nitrate loading occurring within the respective watersheds. Conditions at the Central 18 (C18) course were unique in that golf course groundwater could be compared with tile water draining an adjacent row crop field. In this case, tile water had nitrate concentrations of 13.1 mg/L, whereas golf course groundwater had nitrate values < 1 mg/L. Considering both sites have the same soils and were monitored during the same climate regime, differences in subsurface water concentration can only be due to differences in land use and fertilizer management.

Groundwater phosphorus (dissolved) at the golf course wells averaged 0.10 to 0.16 mg/L. These levels were similar to the rivers draining the respective golf courses (0.10 to 0.21 mg/L). Data for dissolved phosphorus were not available for the nearby drinking water wells. Table 2 shows the average groundwater dissolved phosphorus at the golf course locations versus those measured at other groundwater studies around Iowa.

Study	Dissolved P concentration (mg/L)
Farmed Wetlands	0.42
Clear Lake Outwash	0.21
Okoboji Region	0.15
Golf Courses	0.13
Western Iowa Deep Loess	0.12
Rock Valley Alluvium	0.09
Fractured Glacial Till	0.09
Clear Lake Fractured Till	0.09
Story County Fractured Till	0.07

Table 2: Groundwater phosphorus from various Iowa studies.

Interestingly, turf grass has similar nutrient requirements to that of corn. But there is very little evidence that much nitrogen is lost from turf, and in fact scientists have investigated the potential of turf grasses to scavenge nitrogen when used as a cover crop

Installing water monitoring well on Iowa golf course.

and as a living mulch to grow between corn rows. One problem with the latter scenario: turf grasses can out-compete corn for the nutrients.

Don't think I am giving you license to fertilize your lawn with any amount of N and P that you please. There is evidence that the phosphorus in turf fertilizer can degrade local water quality, especially when applied to properties adjacent to natural lakes. As such, Minnesota and Wisconsin restrict phosphorus application to residential lawns. While such regulations don't exist in Iowa, phosphorus should only be applied when a soil test has indicated a need for additional amounts. The Iowa Professional Lawn Care Association has placed a self-enforced restriction on the use of P fertilizers on lawns surrounding lakes and other waterways.

In researching this piece, I found that Iowa is a golfing state (I, however, have never golfed a round in my life, even though I've seen the 19th hole a few times). In terms of golf courses per square mile, Iowa is 19th, even ahead of Minnesota where golf is hugely popular. Still, the total golf course area in Iowa relative to row crop area is very small. In the nitrate-famous Raccoon River watershed, golf courses occupy 0.14% of the area (i.e. 14 out of every 1,000 acres) but contribute (according to Keith's research) only 0.1 out of every 1,000 pounds of the nitrate load. If the entire Raccoon River watershed were a golf course, the stream's nitrogen load would decrease by more than 90%.

THIS IS WHY WE CAN'T HAVE NICE THINGS

Trump's trade war with China would've hit Iowa farmers pretty hard, were it not for relief payments from the federal government. About one-half of Iowa soybeans had been going to the country prior to the Trump presidency, and I never once heard a cross word about China during my four years at the Iowa Soybean Association. Of course, soybean farmers' attitude about their biggest customer changed quite a bit after Trump was elected. This essay was written to highlight how the resources we spend on water quality are dwarfed by what we spend on agriculture as a result of stupid politics.

You may have heard that our country's administration is in a trade dispute with China. The US has imposed tariffs of 10 to 50% on a variety of Chinese goods including steel, aluminum, solar panels and clothes washing machines. China responded by imposing a 25% tariff on US soybeans and some other US products. China had been the biggest buyer of US soybeans, purchasing $12 billion-worth in 2017. Soybeans traded as high as $17.40 per bushel in 2012. They are trading for $8.70 per bushel as I write this and have been as low as $7.91 only two weeks ago.

As input prices (seed, fertilizer, fuel, chemicals, etc.) did not decline along with grain prices, farmers are getting pinched. In response, the federal government in 2018 offered about $12 billion in relief known as MFP—Market Facilitation Program—payments. Farmers growing soybeans were by far the largest recipients of the MFP payments. About a week ago, the administration announced that another $18 billion would be made available to farmers, again focused largely on soybeans but more widely distributed to other farm commodities compared to the 2018 program.

As you read this, be aware that I am not judging the propriety of the MFP payments. In fact, I would say that farmers deserve relief under the circumstances. I am going to try to put these MFP payments into the relative context of water quality and conservation. Since Iowa produces 13% of US soybeans, I'm estimating Iowa's MFP portion to also be 13%, which amounts to $3.5 billion over the two years. What would $3.5 billion do for water quality?

> First, we know that land retirement reduces nutrient loss better than other any practice. According to Iowa State University.[1] Iowa farmland now averages $7,264/acre. Iowa's MFP payments would pay to retire 482,000 acres of Iowa farmland, about the size of the Boone River watershed upstream of Webster City.

> Iowa farmers plant crops in about 250,000 acres lying within the 2-year flood plain, where input losses are disproportionately high. Assuming a generous profit margin of $200 per acre, we could pay farmers that amount ($200/acre) to not farm those acres for 70 years.

> Cover crops are perhaps the best hope for stabilizing water quality in the corn-soybean system. Assuming cover crops cost $30 per acre to plant, $3.5 billion would pay for cover crops on every single Iowa corn and soybean field for the next five years.

> CRP stands for Conservation Reserve Program, a federal farm bill program that essentially allows the public to rent the land (almost always environmentally sensitive or marginal land) from the landowner. In return, the landowner agrees to plant and maintain species that will improve environmental health. Contracts are usually from 10 to 15 years in length. The current rental rate for Iowa averages $221/acre.[2] Iowa's MFP payments would pay for 10-year

CRP contracts on 1.6 million acres, or about 7% of Iowa's cropped acres, assuming that many acres would be eligible.

> Denitrifying woodchip bioreactors are a cost-share-eligible practice under the Iowa Nutrient Reduction Strategy. Assuming they cost $15,000 each, $3.5 billion would pay for 233,000 of them (about 2400 per county). Currently we have fewer than 100 statewide.

> Constructed wetlands are another cost-share-eligible practice. Assuming a $250,000 construction and design cost, $3.5 billion would pay for 14,000 of them. Currently we have about 90.

> Looking at the downstream end of things, the Des Moines Water Works (DMWW) is the state's largest municipal drinking water utility. Their annual operating budget is $46 million.[3] Iowa MFP payments of $3.5 billion are equivalent to the DMWW operating budget for 76 years. At a nitrate removal cost of $1 million/year, MFP payments would cover that for 3,500 years.

I could go on with this exercise, but I think you probably get the picture.

We oftentimes hear that sufficient money doesn't exist to fund all the practices we need to improve water quality. The total needed to fully-fund the Iowa Nutrient Reduction Strategy has been estimated at an amount eerily similar to the Iowa MFP total: $4 billion.[4] Senate Water Bill 512, which became law last year, only provides up to $282 million for water quality improvements over 20 years, an amount (in total) that is a mere 8% of the MFP payments.

Which brings me to my main point here. Whether or not overall water quality has improved over time (stream clarity has improved since the 1970s, while nitrate has gotten worse), the public has said that it wants something better than what they have now and is willing to pay for it. In fact, the public is practically begging to be taxed to raise money for water quality improvements.[5,6] I say this with a certainty—water quality fails to meet our expectations NOT because we lack the collective wealth to improve it. This just cannot be true. Something else must be at work here. In my estimation, that something is that good water quality is bad for business. The evidence that this is a zero-sum game is in plain sight. To illustrate that, I'll return to the MFP.

To be eligible for the MFP payments, farmers must plant a crop. Anyone who has eyes in their head can see that is one tough nut to crack in Iowa this year because of spring moisture. Thus, late planting farmers are faced with decisions that have absolutely nothing to do with producing food, fuel and fiber. Plant a crop with greatly diminished chances of reaching maturity and take the MFP payment or choose to apply for "prevent plant" insurance payments. Farmers who want to plant but are being delayed by wet weather could end up in a trap where they are too late for an insurance claim but also ineligible for the MFP payment.

A very good summary of this was written by the Illinois Ag writer Stu Ellis.[7] In that piece he states: "The requirement to plant a crop for eligibility for the trade mitigation payment should please agribusiness. It ensures that every seed, fertilizer and crop input supplier will have as much business as possible. It ensures that every grain elevator and grain processor will have as much grain to handle and process as possible. And it ensures the U.S. grain trading industry has as much volume as possible to trade."

I write this today on May 29th, 2019, looking out at some bad, bad water in the Iowa River. Two visitors from India briefly accompanying me today even remarked at the appearance of the water. When I estimate some things from water quality data being collected right now, the Iowa River at Wapello will carry 170 million pounds of sediment and 2.6 million pounds of nitrogen to the Mississippi River,

TODAY. The Des Moines River moving past Keosauqua today will carry 1.2 billion pounds of sediment, along with 3.5 million pounds of nitrogen. The Raccoon River, draining only 6% of Iowa's area, will deliver over a million pounds of nitrogen to its confluence with the Des Moines River. TODAY.

Yes, I know we are having an unusual weather condition right now, and it is a factor in those numbers. But the fact of the matter is, we made weather a factor by wiping out the ecosystems that provided weather resilience. The landscape has no resilience to extreme weather. We see this year after year after year. Heck, when it comes to nitrogen loss, it has no resilience to even average weather.

Clumsy ending: I think we deserve better.

WHO WE ARE

I purchased a pickup (slide-in) camper just prior to writing this, and the first weekend I owned it, I drove to nearby Lake Macbride State Park to try it out. I also brought my boat, hoping to do a little fishing. One look at the lake changed my mind. A few days later, Erin Jordan of the Cedar Rapids Gazette *wrote a story about the beach advisory the Iowa DNR posted for the lake because of the ongoing harmful algae bloom that was occurring in the lake.*

I've always wanted a pick-up camper and finally got around to buying one last week, and I wrote most of this from that humble abode. I made the trip to Platteville, Wisconsin, to buy this one of unknown age for $1,500,  which was a steal considering its near-mint condition. I like camping, but I don't want to sleep on the ground anymore. Plus, if writing my blog is as risky as some people seem to think it is, I figured some backup housing options might be prudent.

I brought it and my boat up to Lake Macbride Friday evening, thinking some solitude and an Iowa lake might provide me with some inspiration.

I was soon inspired.

Despite the prediction of heavy rain, which proved accurate, the campgrounds were packed, and I was lucky to get a spot. Macbride is

Iowa's 6th-most-visited state park (out of about 60), with more than 500,000 visits in 2018. I find the lake, like many of the constructed lakes in our parks, to be quite scenic. You would be hard pressed to make a distinction between Lake Macbride and a lake embedded in the hardwood forest of central Wisconsin.

Until you get to the water's edge, that is.

The dynamic nature of our rivers tells us who we want to be, and who we don't want to be, depending on the day. It's way too often the latter because we've turned many of our streams into outdoor plumbing.

Lakes, on the other hand, store our transgressions for us and tell us who we are.

I backed down the boat launch near the Lake Macbride beach on Saturday morning, and was saddened, but not shocked, to find the water was disgusting pea soup as far as the eye could see. This was not an obstacle for some, however, as people were on the beach, paddling kayaks and paddle boards, and fishing from boats and shore. I decided to take my boat over to the muddy waters of Coralville reservoir, where I caught no fish.

Forced with another boat-launching choice of mud or soup on Sunday morning, I chose instead to walk from the campground to the waterfall where Macbride empties into the reservoir. The air was so wet it dripped water like a boxer. Two or three monsoon downpours highlighted the walk, and I got to the waterfall in a pouring rain.

A strange effluvium, like something from a painter's palette, formed where Macbride's soup pooled out onto the reservoir's coffee.

This is who we are.

It doesn't have to be this way.

The green and brown of our land are now the green and brown of our water, and the taxpayer has invested a lot of money trying to correct this. The DNR has spent at least $100 million of your money on lake restoration since 2007, including some money spent here at Macbride.

We're not very good at guarding our investments. As far as I can tell, Macbride is not included in future restoration plans, so what we see here is what we get, at least for the time being.

Green water caused by mega-blooms of algae does present hazards to people. It was recently in the news that our DNR will not follow an EPA recommendation to impose stricter hazards on Iowa lakes because they "do not agree with the formula and science used to develop the 8 micrograms per liter for cyanotoxins microcystins standard," according to an Iowa DNR spokesman. It's interesting the DNR also did not agree with the lake nutrient standards proposed by their own assembled science team. The DNR says adopting these standards will not make our lakes any safer for recreation. I guess that's probably right, if we don't have enough desire, or courage, or determination, or whatever it is we lack, to make the fundamental changes on the landscape necessary for clean water.

Endnote: The DNR later adopted the EPA microcystins standard.

QUASKY

I wrote this one immediately after fishing with one of my heroes, semi-retired newspaper columnist Orlan Love. Orlan and I still correspond and occasionally he sends me pictures of huge smallmouth bass that were foolish enough to share the same water with him. An interesting (and unfortunate) part of that day was that I stumbled into an old outboard motor while wading the stream, apparently left there by the Delhi Dam breach during a huge rainstorm in July of 2010. I banged up my shin pretty badly; it got infected and took months to heal.

The sport of angling has spawned thousands of writers from Jeremiah (Old Testament, 1000 BC), to Izaak Walton (*Compleat Angler*, 1653), to Ernest Hemingway (*The Old Man and the Sea*, 1952), and Norman Maclean (*A River Runs Through It*, 1977). That last one has stayed with me since the day I finished it. While trout fishing in the Rocky Mountains of Montana is the story's centerpiece, the book is about coming to grips with not being able to make a difference.

This post today was inspired by "angling," which of course sounds so much more noble than "fishing," because it is. It's the highest form of fishing, fooling something into biting something it shouldn't. I love doing that.

Tragically, I've only fished (or angled) twice since spring but one of those times was yesterday and if you're only going to fish twice in five months, you're super lucky if one of those times is with Orlan Love. I was super lucky yesterday.

Orlan is a semi-retired newspaper columnist who spent most of his career at the *Cedar Rapids Gazette* writing about Iowa's environment and agriculture. I've corresponded with him for a few years on various topics.

Orlan's favorite stream is the Wapsi, which runs right through his hometown of Quasqueton, where he still lives. According to Orlan, it's sort of a good news/bad news story with the Wapsi. The good news is the fish are far bigger now than when he grew up (1950s-60s). He says the fish got bigger all over eastern Iowa following the implementation of the Clean Water Act in 1974, which pretty much ended human sewage-caused fish kills. The fish now have time to grow up. The bad news is that in many recent years the stream has become nearly unfishable using his preferred method: wading and casting. More rain and more drainage tile combine to keep average flows on the Wapsi too high for safe wading on many more days compared to yesteryear.

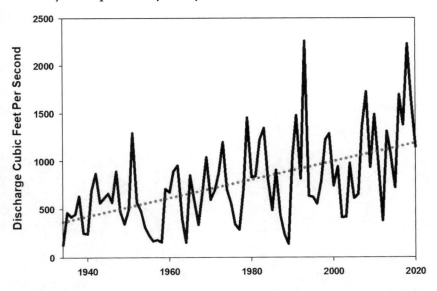

Annual average discharge for the Wapsipinicon River at Independence, Iowa. The dashed line is the trend.

We didn't fish the Wapsi yesterday because Orlan thought algae had the water a little "off" and he knew smallmouth bass were active on the Maquoketa River, about 30 minutes from the Love shack in "Quasky." So at 7AM we headed over there in Orlan's pickup.

The Maquoketa stretch we fished is downstream of the Lake Delhi dam, an unnatural landscape feature that ironically keeps the exiting river in a natural state. Much of the sediment and nutrients that would degrade stream water quality are held back by the dam. The Maquoketa's rocky and sandy stream bottom remain relatively silt-free, allowing smallmouth bass and other clean water species to thrive. One of these clean water species is the redhorse sucker. While the redhorse doesn't provide many angling opportunities, it is a pollution-intolerant species and we saw hundreds of them quivering in current buffered by big rocks. As a boy, Orlan handfished the bony redhorse out of the Wapsi at the Quasky dam, where they congregated while spawning. His mother ground their flesh into fish patties, a process that pulverized the maddening bones and made them edible.

We waded upstream from our entry point and fished likely-looking pools as we went. Orlan generously gave me first crack at spots, and even with that enormous advantage, I couldn't outfish him, and believe me, I ain't no slouch when it comes to catching fish (and

Orlan Love and a redhorse sucker.

bragging about it). There's a theory out there that whoever has his lure in the water the most will catch the most fish, and if that is true, no one on earth will out-fish Orlan. His style is a relentless cast/retrieve/cast/retrieve which is only interrupted by a hooked fish. In total we caught about 35 "smallies" in four hours of fishing. Not fantastic fishing, but very good for Iowa in my experience.

On the ride to and from, we talked about the newspaper business and Iowa angling. I have nostalgic feelings about newspaper outdoor columnists. Back in the days when I fished a lot, urgently-necessary garage clean-out or lawn work was weekend torture because it cut into fishing time. If you knew you couldn't make it out to the lake or stream, you could always read about it in the Sunday morning paper thanks to guys like Orlan and Larry Stone at the *Des Moines Register*. It all seems so long ago now.

Driving from Quasky to Delhi and back, we saw countless spools of drainage tile sitting in farmyards and on truck flatbeds rolling down US 20. We wondered, where does it end. In Orlan's home turf of the Upper Wapsi, our research at the University of Iowa shows about $6.6 million was spent on new agricultural drainage tile in just one year (2016), and who knows how much since then. This dwarfs what is spent on water quality in the watershed, even with an ongoing watershed project.

I'll finish with a few words about Quasqueton. Although Quasky is small, it seems to be holding its own and the town looks good. It's small enough (population ~550) that there are no house numbers and that Orlan's garden can provide enough tomatoes for everyone attending the annual Historical Society Fish Fry. I should say that his is no normal garden—79 tomato plants. He also is a no-till gardener and plants an oat cover crop following harvest.

Unscientific observation: these small towns in eastern Iowa seem to be faring better than their counterparts to the west. I don't know why, except that maybe they are within commuting distance of good jobs in population centers.

Thanks, Orlan.

DEMAND CLEAN WATER NOW

Some time ago, I wrote an essay for the Iowa Ideas Magazine, *which was published in the* Cedar Rapids Gazette. *That piece forms the bulk of this essay. That is reproduced here with their permission; the title for the essay is mine and not the* Gazette's. *As to the title: I am 61 years old, grew up in Iowa, and have lived here most of my adult life. Although some things have improved and exceptions can be found, for the most part the state's water quality has never been good or even adequate during the span of my life. Some of this connects to decisions made 100+ years ago by our great-great-grandparents, including my own. But some or most of it is because of recalcitrance and the insistence that we tolerate the status quo. I reject that.*

Iowa's most talked about water quality problem is stream nitrate pollution, and I spend roughly half of my research hours studying the issue. The problem is not new and the drivers of it have been known for 50 years: fertilization and the altered hydrology of Iowa crop fields. Google Scholar is a search engine researchers use to quickly scan the scholarly literature. "Iowa stream nitrate" generates 28,000 hits in Google Scholar, about 1,400 of which pre-date 1970.

Although I and others continue to study the details, the problem boils down to this: when the amount of nitrogen applied to fields exceeds crop needs, and that excess can find an easy pathway to the stream network, elevated levels of stream nitrate result. That pathway is usually tile drainage—networks of porous pipes used to lower the water table in the northern two-thirds of Iowa. In far northeast Iowa, nitrate can also quickly penetrate thin topsoil and enter streams through the porous limestone bedrock known as Karst.

Iowa stream nitrate levels have increased approximately 10-fold over the past century and possibly a lot more than that in some rivers.

The nitrogen atom of the nitrate molecule may cycle through soil particles, bacteria, fungi, plants and animals multiple times over months or even years before entering a stream. Or less commonly, the applied commercial or manure fertilizer may directly enter a stream in the weeks or months after application. In either case, the fundamentals remain much the same. We saturate the landscape with this water-soluble nutrient and then in our haste to dry out the soil, provide it with a first-class ticket to the Missouri and Mississippi rivers.

The resulting stream nitrate impairs our drinking water, catalyzes nuisance and harmful algae blooms, and kills off part of the Gulf of Mexico when the Mississippi River unloads our baggage every summer.

Our government's main strategy to address this and many of the other negative environmental consequences related to agriculture has been to offer cost-share (public) money to entice farmers into adopting best management practices (BMPs) thought to reduce the pollutant de jour. Every American that has ever lived since 1930 has contributed on average around $700 to farm conservation programs.[1] There have been some successes, most notably with soil erosion, but thus far progress toward solving nitrogen pollution has been agonizingly slow, and in fact the problem may be getting worse. My own research shows nitrate loss in Iowa has increased more than 70% since 2003.[2]

Iowa farmers can receive cost share funds for a variety of nitrate-reducing practices including wetlands, saturated buffers, cover crops, woodchip bioreactors and others. Unlike BMPs for soil erosion, those designed to reduce nitrate loss offer the farmer very little or nothing in enhanced crop yields or farm value, with the possible exception of cover crops in some circumstances. In the absence of regulation, we are relying on farmers' altruistic instincts for BMP adoption.

What is the path forward to solving this problem?

In my view there are a couple of elephants in the room. One is the amount of fertilizer farmers are applying. Extra fertilizer (both commercial and manure) is cheap insurance when it comes to growing corn. People who study these things know that on average, farmers are applying nitrogen fertilizer in excess of the rates recommended by Iowa State University. And this is before we consider nutrients excreted by livestock. To give farmers license to apply however much fertilizer they want or feel they need, and then ask the public to pay for practices to trap the excess at the field's edge with wetlands or bioreactors or whatever, is not a logical road map for water quality improvement. To top it off, the taxpayer indemnifies the system with publicly supported crop insurance. Government policy helps keep fertilizer cheap, and government policy makes sure that the public shoulders the burden for the resultant pollution. I find it difficult to reconcile these policies with the concept of cleaner water. (I make that last statement mildly).

Elephant number two is the group of individuals and companies that purchase commodity crops and benefit most from the super-abundance of corn and soybeans and the low prices that come with that abundance. *We ask nothing of them when it comes to water quality*. This needs to change.

Most Iowa farmers are conducting their businesses as any rational person would do under the circumstances. They're operating within a system that most of them had no part in creating and feel powerless to change. Although I think it's fair to expect certain things from farmers, I also think it's unfair to expect them to solve this.

Going forward, we need to recognize this is a continental scale problem and solutions will need to address complex socio-economic factors that cross state lines. There are very few problems of this scale and magnitude that have been solved through individual actions. Better water quality will only result if Iowa voters demand it and then hold their elected leaders accountable to the development of solutions that engage everyone benefiting from the exploitation of our natural resources.

MIDDLE OF NOWHERE IS DOWNSTREAM FROM SOMEWHERE

You don't have to take my word for it to know the quality of Iowa streams and lakes is poor—you can see it for yourself firsthand. I see it for myself quite often as I try to catch a fish or two around the state. The Lower Iowa River is one of our most disturbed large streams. It's the subject of this essay.

I have been trying to get out with my fishing boat lately and last Friday evening I launched it from the Sturgis Ferry access in south Iowa City. Even though the water was treacherously shallow, I motored up to the graffiti-decorated railroad bridge near the Iowa City Dairy Queen and caught a few channel cats.

Later on in the weekend I made the decision to go further south a ways, thinking there might be more water to float my boat. Eighteen miles south of Iowa City on Gilbert Street, which morphs into Sand Road at some point, puts you at the River Junction Park Access. The park is so named because the English River marries the Iowa River nearby, in the boot heel that makes Johnson County non-rectangular. That's where I went first thing Labor Day morning.

River Junction Park is literally and figuratively "at the end of the road" (Sand Road) and driving in I found the park to be quiet and the campground cozy. It's the proverbial "middle of nowhere," at least for Iowa.

Unfortunately, one look at the boat launch made me yearn for the scenic beauty of the Iowa City DQ and the amateur art of the nearby railroad bridge.

Now I just have to say this is sloppy, angry, stream of consciousness writing here, but I just looked at this launch and said to myself, what the hell. I don't know for a certainty where the mud comes from, but because of the upstream sediment trap that is Coralville Reservoir, most of it must come in from either Clear Creek or Old Man's Creek. Here's a bone for everybody who thinks weather causes bad water quality: there was scattered rain between 0 and 0.5□ in this area Saturday evening, otherwise known as a gully-washer (in Phoenix).

I just cannot comprehend why we tolerate water features such as this in what would otherwise be a splendid little park.

I went ahead and launched my boat and headed upstream where I saw a couple of miles of shoreline and rip rap so ugly that it made a row of '49 rusted Buick car bodies look positively scenic (yes, we used to use car bodies for rip rap). The water was brown and foamy and smelly and again I thought, what the hell.

Like all states, Iowa has surface water classifications based on their designated uses. The Lower Iowa River is a "Class A1" water meaning it is designated for primary contact recreational use, i.e., "waters in which recreational or other uses may result in prolonged and direct contact with the water, involving considerable risk of ingesting water in quantities sufficient to pose a health hazard. Such activities would include, but not be limited to, swimming, diving, water skiing, and water contact recreational canoeing."

Ok, so I don't have any water quality measurements to give to you from Monday, but I think mine is an informed opinion and my opinion is that no human being should've been in contact with that water (there were kayakers).

In 2007, the American Rivers conservation group named the Iowa River one of the 10 most endangered American Rivers[1] because of livestock pollution and communities without proper sewage treatment. Kevin Baskins of Iowa DNR said at the time that "there's definitely some need for improvement there."

According to Iowa DNR water quality resource coordinator Adam Schnieders,[2] Iowa as a state is moving forward with stricter wastewater treatment plant rules. In 2018 alone:

> 154 wastewater treatment plants have been required to assess nutrient removal capacity

> 125 have been issued new, stricter permits (what a concept)

> 82 have submitted feasibility studies

> 24 have met targets of removing 66 percent of nitrate in wastewater discharge

> 11 have met targets of removing 75 percent of phosphorus in wastewater discharge

> 27 have committed to upgrades

Also I should say that since the 2007 "Most Endangered" designation, the number of hogs in the Iowa River watershed has increased from 2.2 million to 2.7 million (as of 2018),[3] with the increase alone generating the untreated waste equivalent of 2 million human beings, which is only the combined population of Iowa's 109 largest cities (everything bigger than Waukon).

But wait a minute, by that last measure, the Iowa River should be as pristine as a mountain stream, at least if you believe the farm media.[4]

I have to tell you folks, if you think there is hope for a stream like the Iowa River, then you're more of a dreamer than I am.

People try to gaslight our lakes into Tahoe and our streams into the Blue Danube, but I encourage you to see for yourself.

Swine manure can protect water quality

IT'S THEIR WAY OR THE HIGHWAY

Minnesota has a state law that prohibits row crops within 50 feet of a stream. This is a no-brainer for water quality: less chemical fertilizer gets into the stream during minor flooding and streambank soil erosion is reduced. Riparian corridors vegetated with perennial plant species also provide valuable wildlife habitat. When Iowa conservation districts pushed for a similar law here, they were told to get lost.

Soil and water conservation districts (SWCDs) are government units established under state law to help implement natural resource management programs at the local level. There are 100 of these districts in Iowa (one in every county; Pottawatomie County has two) and they are led by a 5-member elected panel of commissioners. SWCDs are staffed by USDA-Natural Resource Conservation Service (NRCS) and Iowa Department of Agricultural and Land Stewardship (IDALS) professionals, as well as watershed project coordinators. In my county (Johnson) there is a District Conservationist, Conservation Assistant, Soil Conservationist, Soil Technician, Urban Conservationist, and Watershed Coordinator on staff.

These offices are the focal point and information centers for farm and urban conservation. Staff salaries are paid through the agencies and grants, while the district and commissioners have nominal budgets of $2,000 per year or so to conduct business. The districts have taxing authority in Iowa, although to my knowledge, that option has never been exercised. Commissioners help prioritize conservation policies and increase local awareness of natural resource concerns and opportunities. The commissioners come from all walks of life, but many are farmers, especially in the rural counties. They are people who donate time and energy for the betterment of Iowa's air, soil, and water.

Conservation Districts of Iowa (CDI) is a statewide association of the 500 elected commissioners. Each year, CDI meets to discuss issues important to soil and water improvement. They propose and vote on resolutions that are then forwarded to the state soil committee at IDALS. If the state soil committee agrees with a resolution, a process begins whereby the resolution may become state policy or law if the legislature and governor also agree.

This year, CDI passed a resolution with a super majority to require 30☐ buffer strips on either side of Iowa streams, similar to a law passed a few years ago in Minnesota requiring 50☐ buffers. It reads as such:

Title: Require Permanent Buffer Strips to Protect Streams (Resolution #5)

Statement: Some farmers plant crops up to the edges of streams, even though nearly every Iowan can understand that water quality would benefit if stream banks were protected. Permanent vegetation along streams reduces the risk of the bank collapsing, and vigorous plant roots filter dissolved nitrogen as water seeps downhill toward the stream. Thick plant growth also slows the flow of excess runoff across the surface, allowing suspended soil particles to be deposited on land rather than in the bottom of the stream. Even though a few streams are protected every year with voluntary installation of buffer strips, many more miles of stream edges become vulnerable following brush and timber clearing. To meet the goals of the Nutrient Reduction Strategy (Iowa's policy for dramatically improving our surface water quality) we should protect our stream banks from further degradation.

Action: CDI should work with the SCC, IDALS, ISU and the Iowa Legislature to develop, introduce, and lobby for legislation similar to Minnesota's buffer law. This legislation prohibits crop farming within thirty feet of a stream and would require permanent buffer strips to be installed to protect water quality.

We have known for a long, long time that stream buffers are one of the most logical and fundamental of all conservation practices. If you're reading this, however, I'm sure you've seen crops planted right up to the stream edge and perhaps even corn sloughing off into the stream. There are glaring examples along I-80 between Des Moines and Iowa City.

Corn planted to the edge of the Des Moines River southeast of the City of Des Moines.

In response to the soldiers at CDI, the generals at IDALS issued a statement[1] that included this: "… incentive-based approaches to delivering conservation practices that are tailored to the landscape—instead of mandatory regulations—are the best way to achieve our state's water quality goals."

Is this objectively true? There is plenty of evidence that says otherwise.

The Ag industry's main claim to environmental improvement relates to reductions in soil erosion. While it is easy to make the case that it is still too high, it's undeniable that improvements have occurred in Iowa, especially since 1985. Hmm. *What happened in 1985?*

The 1985 Federal Farm Bill included a provision for "conservation compliance." If farmers were cropping highly erodible land, they were required to adopt certain soil retention practices if they wanted to participate in commodity programs (e.g., be eligible for public assistance through price supports and now, crop insurance). This had an immediate positive effect on water quality.

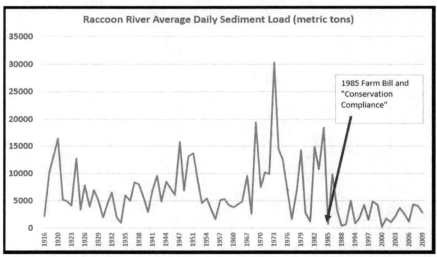

Sediment loading in the Raccoon River of Iowa. Note the dramatic improvement following the 1985 Farm Bill.

The industry is also touting its achievements in reducing phosphorus pollution. In fact, water quality data[3] shows phosphorus loads have increased some but not nearly as badly as nitrogen loads. Why have we made progress on phosphorus in some areas? Well, phosphorus attaches tenaciously to soil particles and when you mandate soil conservation in Farm Bill programs (e.g., 1985 Farm Bill conservation compliance) you also reduce phosphorus loss.

And let's look at Monarch butterfly preservation efforts. It must be said that the industry and others have responded forcefully to the species' decline these past few years, and there are signs that efforts are working. I applaud these efforts. Of course, a cynic might also add that the industry was looking skyward for a falling anvil with *"ENDANGERED SPECIES ACT"* stamped on the bottom. That regulation can float like a butterfly AND sting like a bee, in Muhammad Ali fashion, by restricting activities on private lands.

I have to wonder, where were all the Monarch-come-lately cheerleaders when we were spraying, mowing, and plowing ditches into corn-soybean oblivion over the past 40 years, something virtually every conservationist knew was horrible? Heaven forbid the industry would have supported a rule or a regulation or even a mild suggestion of "DON'T DO THIS."

Better to wait for the anvil, I guess.

Back to the 30' buffer proposal. Would it improve water quality? Yes, it would, and I know of no person that would say otherwise. Would it cost some farmers some money? Again, yes it would, at least without easement or set aside payments. By my estimates about 1% of Iowa farmland would fall into the 30' category, but a fair amount of that is already unfarmed and buffered.

What is maddening here for me is that our institutions can't bring themselves to say that some practices are disproportionately destructive to streams and the environment and that they should be restricted or banned. Rather, the industry prefers to obstruct common sense laws, but they will be more than happy to take credit for the environmental benefits once the obstruction is overcome.

I've always wondered if the industry opposes environmental laws precisely because they know they will work, and fear this will invite all sorts of future shenanigans from the lunatics who want cleaner water.

I'd like to find a way out of this by mentioning a recent article in the *Washington Post*.[4] The thrust of that article is the $30 billion relief package for farmers affected by the ongoing trade disputes, which includes about everybody farming in Iowa. The article stated that "The bailout was created by the Trump administration as a way to try to calm outrage from farmers who complained they were caught in the middle of the White House's trade war with China. In an attempt to pacify farmers, the Agriculture Department created an expansive new program without precedent."

So yes, I get that farmers are outraged that their markets have been disrupted, if not out-right destroyed. So, we're going to pay them for that. Ok. We are also going to pay them to help insure their crops against weather calamities and price declines. Ok. We are also going to politely dangle more money in front of them (incentive-based approaches, after all) in the hope they will not do profoundly unwise things like plowing and planting up to the edge of the stream. Whew. Does anybody get dizzy riding this merry-go-round, and does the public ever get to have any expectations when it comes to water quality?

Farmers shouldn't be the only ones with the right to get outraged. I'm outraged that the water quality of Iowa streams has been substandard my entire life. I'm outraged that the Iowa and Cedar rivers stink. I'm outraged that we help kill off part of an ocean. I'm outraged that people from India tell me our rivers look bad. I'm outraged that the water supply for our state's largest city has been impaired for half of a century.

And yes, I'm outraged that the industry makes society worship the cult of "no regulation" when it comes to the water resources that belong to us all.

If you want better water, it's their way or the highway.

FISHING IN THE RAIN

There's an old saying that says the two best times to fish are when it's raining, and when it isn't raining. Yeah it's a kind of groaner, but there's nothing like a sweet summer rain to make the fish bite and put your mind at rest. And a restful mind is what I need to come up with ideas.

I've always liked fishing in the rain for several reasons, not the least of which is that the fish bite. But it can't be just any rain; a slow and steady warm rain with no wind and no lightning is best. Fish won't bite if there's lightning, and besides I'm terrified of lightning and if you've forgotten what it's like to wear a soiled diaper, try being 10 miles from the dock on Lake of the Woods when a lightning bolt comes out of nowhere to strike the island 50 yards to starboard. Sorta takes the fun out of fishing in the rain.

While fishing in the rain Saturday morning, it occurred to me that many other species seem to not mind a slow steady rain. The blue jays still were taunting each other with their blue jay obscenities, and wood ducks seemed to be playing chicken with their dare-devil flying amongst the one million trees that have been planted in Johnson County's Kent Park.

While trying to catch a meal's worth of bluegills, I thought about how to work into an essay a presentation that I had heard the previous day, this by Dr. Kim Van Meter. She is an Iowa native (Gilbert) and Ecohydrology professor at the University of Illinois-Chicago. Kim has multiple degrees from the University of Iowa, including a BA in English, a MS in Chemistry and PhD in Engineering, and you can hear them all in her voice and her words. Some of her recent work has looked at "legacy" nitrogen (N) in the Mississippi River Watershed. By legacy we mean N accumulated in the soils and groundwater of farmed landscapes. This accumulation is the result of A > B where A = manure and fertilizer N inputs, and B = N harvested in the grain.

The Van Meter work has shown that as much as 40% of the stream N in the Mississippi Basin is a result of farming activities and surplus nitrogen that was applied 20 or more years ago.[1] This might be considered a bit of good news, if we were reducing this surplus. There's not much evidence, however, that we are doing that here in Iowa. In fact, when I look at statewide N budgets for Iowa, I think the surplus is increasing.

Our main inputs of N are commercial fertilizer, hog manure, and fixation by soybeans. Soybeans are a legume and they "pull" nitrogen out of the atmosphere and "fix" it in the soil. This is why corn grown after soybeans needs less nitrogen than corn grown after corn. When I look at these inputs over the last 20 years, along with the amount of nitrogen harvested in the grain crop, it's pretty clear that all are increasing, but, the amount of input N is increasing faster than the amount of N leaving in the crop. Under this circumstance, we would expect the amount of N leaving in our rivers to be increasing. This is in fact happening (see graph of my data; bear in mind this graph does not include beef, dairy or poultry manure).

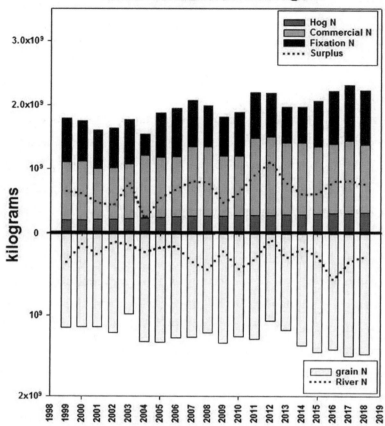

Summary of nitrogen inputs (top) and outputs (bottom) for Iowa, 1999-2018.
Notes on the data sources are at the end of the essay. The idea for the graph
format I got from the Van Meter presentation.

What I am doing here with the graph is N Budgeting, i.e., quantifying inputs on one side of the ledger and outputs on the other. I recall
attending an Environmental Protection Commission (EPC) meeting
about 10-15 years ago and watching DNR staff person Calvin Wolter,
who had recently created some statewide nutrient budgets, get aggressively challenged by an Ag industry advocate on the work he had
done. At the time, I found this somewhat curious.

Now I know these budgets are a threat. They open up the curtains on a little shop of horrors, mainly by eroding much of the industry rhetoric of the last 20 years on fertilization. Some of that has included catch phrases like "spooning it on," "agronomic rates," "manure is a resource" and insistence that rate reductions (i.e. reducing the amount applied) will not improve water quality.

In my view, the industry has painted itself into a corner with its rhetoric. If indeed farmers are applying at agronomic rates, then we must be:

a) losing a far larger percentage of the inputs to streams than what the industry wants to admit, or

b) mining soil fertility in destructive ways that could be of crisis proportions, or

c) both a and b.

The other more logical explanation here for our increasing stream nitrate is that we continue to apply nitrogen in amounts that are substantially larger than what is being harvested in the grain, and of course the industry is not exactly excited about admitting this either.

Thus, the wet paint and the corner.

When I do a very basic linear regression of the data shown in the chart, these are the increases I get from 1999-2018:

> Nitrogen excreted by hogs: +59.8%

> Purchased commercial nitrogen: +35.3%

> Nitrogen fixed by previous year's soybeans: +29.4%

> Nitrogen harvested in the grain (corn and soybeans): +11.2%

> Input surplus (Hog N + commercial N + fixation N—grain N): +55.1%

> Nitrogen transported by Iowa rivers: +82.9%

That 55.1% number is what Kim Van Meter is telling us will be in our children's and our grandchildren's water 50 years from now. If she's right, there's not much hope in solving things in my lifetime, especially if there's nothing to compel the industry to get its arms around this, and there isn't. Now I know their rhetoric is that it's the soil, or weather, or point sources, or golf courses that are the problem. That rhetoric is unserious.

The other thing at work here is that the industry wants to continue expansion of hog production.[2] Well, ok. You can't very well make a sincere argument that Iowa can absorb more hogs unless you're going to reduce inputs of commercial nitrogen. That is not happening. People want to sell nitrogen.

Yes, N removed in the grain is increasing with improved crop yields, but it is not keeping up with the inputs, at least not in Iowa. Clearly the industry's goal when it comes to inputs is not perfection; rather their strategic goal is a consistent surplus of N on the landscape, and your water is the collateral damage.

Now we hear from time to time that Iowa has exciting momentum when it comes to water quality. But when I look at the N data, it sure appears the momentum lies with our efforts to squeeze every last bushel and hoof of productivity from the landscape. From an environmental perspective, those last few bushels are going to come with a heavy price in terms of water quality, if history is the indicator.

I don't really like the phrase "factory farm" because nearly all farms have by necessity specialized and adopted certain methods of the industrial revolution. The phrase doesn't really say much to me. On the other hand, I do believe Iowa is a "factory state." Iowa is one giant photosynthesis factory, one that we keep fueled with a super-abundance of nitrogen and phosphorus and one that has very few limitations on what it can emit to the surrounding environment.

Can that factory be retooled to produce the environmental outcomes that we want? The industry would have us believe that it can, provided the taxpayer ponies up sufficient money and they are given sufficient time, usually on the order of decades or generations. Ok then. This is probably a billion dollar per year problem, at least for a while, unless the system can be transformed to something different, something like Matt Liebman (Iowa State Univ.) has been proposing for a long while.

I will wander toward an end with a return to fishing, this on Sunday, again in the rain. This time for channel cat, a species that tolerates the worst in us. As I looked at a muddy Iowa River, I thought about Dr. Van Meter's comment that rivers are "integrators." In the disturbed and managed ecosystems of Iowa, these rivers are "us." Do we like what we see? I don't.

How do we change this? I read recently that change happens with push from the outside and leadership from the inside. We need a lot more of both.

MMPS ARE CRAP

About everyone knows Iowa is a big hog state, and in fact it is the biggest. One-third of all the hogs in the U.S. call Iowa home, about 25 million at any one time. Fertilizing crops with manure in lieu of commercial formulations has benefits, but management of manure from large, concentrated animal feeding operations (CAFOs) is a colossal challenge. An average hog confinement in Iowa now houses about 5,000 hogs, and managing their excrement is akin to managing the waste of 20,000 people. This "management" has been made easier by lax regulation of the livestock industry, which in turn has attracted more hog production to the state. Part of the "regulations" require the creation of manure management plans (MMPs), which are in effect a state-endorsed overapplication of nutrients to Iowa crops. This is one reason why we have the water pollution that we do in Iowa.

An article authored by Anna Jones recently appeared in the U.S. on-line version of *The Guardian* about Iowa and our struggle with nitrate pollution. One thing in particular about the article caught my eye and it was the description of a Marshall County farmer's management of hog manure. He and his brother borrowed $1.5 million to build two hog confinements with a third still under construction. Ten thousand weaned pigs (18 days old) are raised in the two buildings and one brother finishes (hogs fed until they reach market weight) 2,500 hogs at the site.[1]

In a process governed by Iowa "law," manure is stored in an 800,000-gallon pit beneath the confinement which is emptied once per year and applied to a 200-acre corn field.

Please permit me a few moments to take a deep dive into this pit.

According to the most recent nutrient budget created by the Iowa Geological Survey,[2] those hogs will produce 73,000 pounds of nitrogen. Per Iowa DNR CAFO rules, 25% of that can be expected to evaporate from the pit, thus reducing the total nitrogen (N) to 54,750 pounds. Another 2% can be expected to be lost during application if it is injected (more than ¾ of Iowa hog farmers inject manure with the rest applying to the surface). This further reduces the amount to 53,655 pounds. Applied to 200 acres, that effective N application rate is 268 pounds per acre, about double the ISU recommended rate for corn grown after soybean and about 1.4 times the recommended for corn following corn.[3]

Why do our "laws" permit this overapplication of nutrient?

The technical reason is because the rules written in Iowa Code Chapter 65 Animal Feeding Operations are based on a strategy for nitrogen management known as Yield Goal or 1.2 Rule, first advocated by the University of Illinois agronomist George Stanford in 1966, before we had a Gulf of Mexico Dead Zone and the world's largest nitrate removal facility at the Des Moines Water Works. It works like this: if you think the corn yield potential of your field is 200 bushels per acre, then multiply 200 by 1.2 to get the pounds of nitrogen you will need, which in this example would be 240 lbs/ac.

This is how manure management plans (MMPs) work in Iowa.

Manure management plans are not protective of water quality.

The easy-to-understand 1.2 formula quickly and unfortunately became the conventional wisdom in agriculture and the environmental wreckage it has wrought is nearly incalculable. In his first published paper on the subject, Stanford made a statement almost unheard of for a scientist: "Future progress (in agriculture) demands that less empirical means be developed for predicting and meeting the N needs of crops."[4]

In other words, if you're growing corn, don't bother yourself with a bunch of stupid evidence.

We have known since at least 1987 that this approach to nitrogen management is flawed.[5] A more recent paper[6] stated "yield-goal based N recommendations are not useful" when deciding how much nitrogen to apply.

In the example from the *Guardian* article, the Marshall County farmer must have demonstrated to DNR that he had the potential of producing 223 corn bushels per acre on his field. While the average 2018 Iowa corn yield was 204 bu/ac, 223 is very possible. Marshall County was #1 in 2018 with an average of 226 bu/ac.[6]

The problem we have is that a field does not always or even commonly reach its yield potential (bugs, disease, rainfall etc.). In those circumstances, excess nitrogen is lost to the environment and the public shoulders the burden for the environmental consequences. Your tax dollars are paying for conservation practices that help trap these excess nutrients on a small subset of farms.

So, you might ask yourself why industry advocates tenaciously defend this manure management approach here in Iowa.

The answers are obvious. If we enlarge the area required for manure application by reducing the allowable application rate, not only do we increase hauling costs for the manure, we also in effect constrict the expansion of the hog production industry. In fact, some counties and watersheds are now so nutrient-rich as a result of intense livestock production, you would have to remove confinements and/or restrict sales of commercial fertilizer to get inputs aligned with crop needs. And to repeat, your tax dollars are paying for conservation practices that help trap excess nutrients, in effect enlarging the area into which the industry can expand.

Remember this when people tell you they want to double Iowa's hog population.[7]

And as bad as this story sounds up to this point, it gets worse. We have nearly non-existent enforcement of manure management plans. Fields get included in multiple MMPs, which is not illegal, but our DNR allows farmers to work it out between themselves on who gets to apply where in such situations. The growth of the industry has far outpaced DNR's ability to monitor and regulate it.

And this last shoe drops with a thunder: we still sell almost as much commercial fertilizer in areas that are livestock-dense as in areas that aren't.

Thus, we've had a return of nutrient-fed algae blooms in places like Lake Darling, which was restored only six years ago at taxpayer expense ($16 million). Is it any wonder we have water quality problems?

Tragedies abound in the story of hog industry expansion. One is that farmers filling out their paperwork and following their MMP understandably think "it's all good." And why wouldn't they? Our government has given them license to think that.

It's not "all good," at least when it comes to our water.

IOWA IS HEMORRHAGING NITROGEN

A large part of my job is aggregating and analyzing data as I help manage the Iowa Water Quality Information System, a network of water quality sensors deployed in streams around the state of Iowa that measure stream conditions in real time. The bulk of the data is for nitrate-nitrogen, which is a regulated drinking water contaminant and enters the stream network mostly as result of row crop and animal agriculture. Nitrate has contaminated thousands of private drinking water wells around Iowa, and many municipal supplies as well, including the water provided to 1/5th of Iowa's population by the Des Moines Water Works. Nitrate in drinking water causes blue baby syndrome (methemoglobinemia) and is a suspected carcinogen for adults who consume high nitrate water. Nitrate from Iowa also helps drive Gulf of Mexico Hypoxia—a Dead Zone that forms off the coast of Louisiana every year where fish, shrimp and other aquatic life can't live. Nitrate is Iowa's most talked about water quality problem. This essay summarizes water quality from the sensor network for 2019, when stream nitrate was particularly bad. The reader should know that the costs for nitrogen and corn shown in the essay are not current.

Someone once told me, "For god's sake, start at the end" when giving a presentation, and since there is a lot to unload with this one, I'll give you a couple of nuggets, if you don't have time to read the rest:

> For the 2019 Water Year (10/1/18 to 9/30/19) Iowa stream nitrate load was 980 million pounds.

> Since 2003, statewide stream nitrate loads have increased 100.4% (i.e. doubled), as measured by the 5-year Running Annual Average.

Ok, here goes:

A "water year" (WY) is a convention used in hydrology to describe the period from October 1 to September 30. Scientists use this when evaluating hydrologic data because autumn and early winter precipitation accumulates in the soil as liquid water or on the surface as snow, and thus doesn't reach rivers until spring.

Today I am going to present some nitrate-nitrogen (NO3-N) data for the 2019 WY along with similar data accumulated since 1999. This analysis didn't all happen at once; much of this was aggregated and analyzed a couple of years ago and published in two scientific papers.[1,2] This blog post is just an update. Notes on data sources are at the end.

Herein I look at the state in three ways: areas draining to the Missouri River Basin (31% of Iowa, abbreviated as IAMoRB), areas draining to the Upper Mississippi River (69% of Iowa-IAUMRB), and Iowa as a whole (IATot). There are objective reasons for dividing Iowa in this way—soils, climate, hydrology, and some other things.

Water from all Iowa streams eventually makes it to the Gulf of Mexico, where a "Dead Zone" develops every year as a result of Midwest nitrogen and phosphorus loss from farmed fields.

The amount ("load") of NO3-N leaving the state during WY 2019 was 980 million pounds. This was the second-highest load since 1999 (2016 was the biggest—1.25 billion pounds). Of this total (2019), 39% left the state in the Missouri and 61% in the Upper Mississippi. One caveat here: the statewide load includes 2,300 square miles of Minnesota that drain into Iowa, about the size of four Iowa counties.

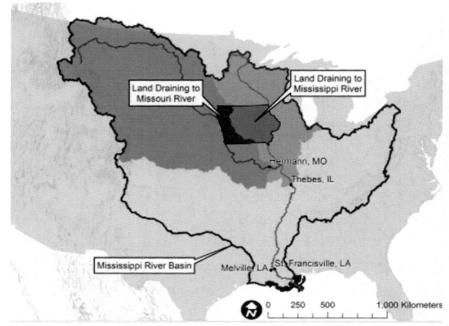

Iowa areas draining to the Missouri River, Upper Mississippi River, and the Mississippi River watershed draining to the Gulf of Mexico.

When comparing watersheds, we often look at load per watershed area: NO3-N yield. In 2019 this was 34.2 pounds per acre (lbs/ac) for areas draining to the Missouri; 24.0 lbs/ac for areas draining to the Mississippi; and 27.2 pounds statewide.

Since greater than 90% of stream nitrate is from agricultural sources in Iowa, we also look at load per cropped area. These values are shown in the map below. Using a current price of $0.31/pound for anhydrous ammonia and with corn at $3.79/bushel, recommended nitrogen application rates[3] range from 145-197 lbs/ac, so you can see that the losses are substantial relative to corn nitrogen needs.

I don't have precipitation data aggregated, but 2019 was a wet year and river discharge was well above normal. When we calculate water discharge, we often use a convention called water yield. This is water volume per watershed area. Water yield normalizes discharge data and allows us to compare apples to apples when looking at watersheds of varying size. Average water yield for Iowa since 1999 is 11.1 inches; in WY 2019 it was 20.7 inches. These values for Iowa areas draining west to the Missouri are 8.7 (average) and 18.8 (2019) inches and east to the Mississippi, 12.0 (average) and 21.4 (2019) inches. Take home: eastern Iowa is wetter than western Iowa.

It's a good idea not to put too much stock into one individual year when looking at stream pollutant loading. Weather does play a role in year-to-year variations. It's not the driver of the problem, but it is important because we've removed all the natural resilience from the landscape. To account for anomalous years, we often look at the 5-year Running Annual Average (5YRAA), which as the term implies, is the average of the current year and the previous four.

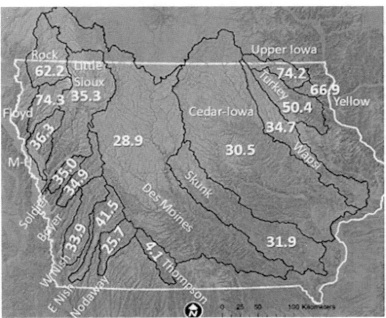

2019 nitrate losses in pounds per crop acre.

The 5YRAA is at its highest level since 2003 for Iowa as a whole (my dataset begins in 1999; the first year I can calculate the 5YRAA is 2003), and for the two sub-regions draining to the Mississippi and Missouri.

Nitrate loading to the Missouri is increasing far faster than areas draining east toward the Mississippi. The 2019 5YRAA is about three times larger for western Iowa than in 2003. For areas draining east to the Mississippi, the increase is 74%, and statewide, 100.4% (i.e. doubled).

Assuming 2013 as a starting point for the Iowa Nutrient Reduction Strategy, the 5YRAA for IAMoRB, IAUMRB, and IATot has increased 77%, 34%, and 46% since then, respectively. That 45% reduction goal? It's 65% now, if we are to use actual water monitoring data as the metric. This illustrates the folly of trying to measure success by cataloging implemented practices.

I also look at where a raindrop has its biggest impact—i.e. where does it dissolve the most nitrogen? Here I use the metric of Flow Weighted Average Concentration (FWA). This is the total N load

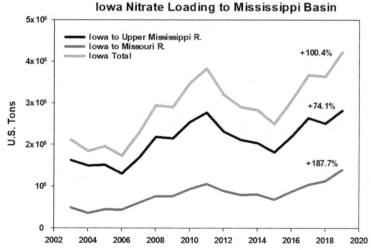

Five-year running annual average nitrate loads for Iowa areas draining to the Missouri River (brown), Upper Mississippi River.

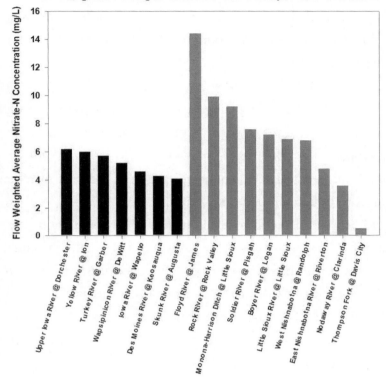

Flow Weighted Average Concentrations for Major Iowa Rivers-2019

Flow weighted average nitrate concentrations in WY 2019. Streams draining to the Upper Mississippi River are denoted by black bars on the left;
streams draining to the Missouri River by gray bars on the right.

divided by the total water discharge. Units are mg/L (ppm). This
is shown the graph on next page. The NW Iowa watersheds of the
Floyd and Rock usually are at the top of the heap, and 2019 was no
exception. I tend to think this is because livestock concentration.

PERSPECTIVES

The WY 2019 stream nitrate load was just short of a billion
pounds. Is that a lot? A billion to us seems like a big number but I
can increase or decrease it by changing the units, which are a human
construction. So we must put these things in perspective:

> A human being excretes about 10 pounds of nitrogen per year. Thus the fecal and urinary waste of Iowa's 3.2 million people in 2019 included about 32 million pounds of nitrogen, which is about 3.3% of the total stream load.

> A billion pounds of nitrogen spread out among 85,000 Iowa farmers is ~12,000 pounds per farmer. 12,000 pounds is enough to fertilize about 80 acres of corn (if grown after a previous year's soybean crop).

> You would need 236,000 thousand-gallon anhydrous nitrogen nurse tanks to hold a billion pounds of nitrogen.

> A billion pounds of anhydrous nitrogen is worth more than $300 million at current prices (note: anhydrous is usually the cheapest N form of many that farmers buy). Think about what that number might be extrapolated across the several Corn Belt states. This is an objective fact: companies are making money selling this lost nitrogen, and taxpayers are asked to shoulder the burden for the resultant pollution.

I will be surprised if we ever have enough cost share (public) money to address the problem of water quality degradation from nitrate loss. Farmers can buy it for $0.31 per pound but it can cost $2 per pound (or more) to keep it out of our streams. I've calculated that reaching water quality goals for nitrogen using cover crops would cost at least $175 per Iowan per year. Walk down your street and ask a household of four to fork over $700 every year to mitigate nitrate pollution. Something tells me people aren't going to run to get their checkbook.

One last thought. Why have things degraded so much more in western Iowa in the last 20 years? This is an interesting question. I have some ideas but I don't really have the answer.

NOTES ABOUT DATA

Stream nitrate data from 1999-2016 is from the Iowa DNR ambient monitoring database. Since then, that data has been supplemented

with IIHR-University of Iowa[4] and USGS[5] real time water quality sensor data. I use linear interpolation to estimate nitrate levels on days without data. This method has been shown to be reasonable.[6] Stream discharge data is from USGS.

The contents of 236,000 of these left Iowa in its rivers in 2019.

Individual site loads are calculated by multiplying actual or estimated daily nitrate concentrations by stream discharge data.

Region and statewide loads are calculated by looking at overall N yields for the measured areas, and then multiplying that yield by the actual areas of IAMoRB, IAUMRB, and IATot.

Sites do change some from year to year based on data availability. One important watershed—Maquoketa River—dropped out of the monitored areas in 2019.

In total, 79.5% of Iowa is included in the monitored areas; 62.1% of IAMoRB and 89.2% of IAUMRB.

Crop area data is from USDA-National Agricultural Statistics Service.[7]

CRY ME A RACCOON RIVER

I conduct a fair number of presentations and one was at the Whiterock Conservancy near Coon Rapids, Iowa, in November of 2019. Whiterock is a 5,500 acre non-profit land trust that occupies the former Garst family farm and seven miles of the Middle Raccoon River valley. Soviet premier Nikita Khrushchev visited the farm during a trip to Iowa in 1959. The program I conducted and some other events of the day inspired this essay; I have to credit Iowa conservationist Elizabeth Hill with the title.

I suppose we all experience certain days when events crystallize our ideas in ways such that the day and the ideas will both go unforgotten. November 14 [2019] was one of those days for me. That day I conducted a presentation at the "Future of Agriculture" meeting at the Whiterock Conservancy near Coon Rapids. My slides included a variation of the graph shown below.

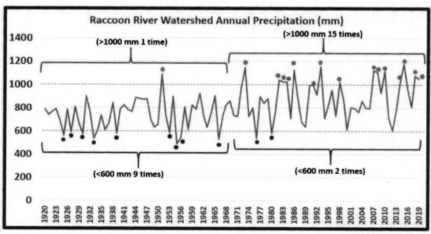

Raccoon River watershed precipitation, 1920-2019, divided into two 50-year halves.

These data show annual precipitation for the Raccoon River Watershed over the past century. When I divide the record into two 50-year halves (1920-1969 and 1970-2019), you can see some striking differences. Prior to 1970, annual precipitation exceeded 1 meter (1000 mm or 39.4 inches) in only one year: 1951. Since 1970, annual precipitation tops 1 meter in 15 years (even though there is a month left this year, I am including it here because 2019 precipitation is already over 1 meter through November 30). The year of 1990 was also very close to the 1-meter threshold (996 mm). Incredibly, 1 meter of precipitation has been exceeded in seven of the last 13 years (2007-2019).

Conversely, annual precipitation was below 600 mm (23.6 inches) nine times from 1920-1969 but only twice since 1970 and not a single time since 1980. The drought year of 2012 is etched in the memory of many Iowans as the worst of their lifetime; it doesn't even make it into the last century's top 10 driest years in the Raccoon watershed.

If you follow the discussion surrounding climate change in Iowa and its potential consequences for agriculture, perhaps these data don't surprise you. My observation is that the industry and its practitioners have been reluctant to come around to the idea that this is a human-caused phenomenon. There's already been quite a lot of social science that examines this, but overall farmers seem to be about ½ to 2/3 as likely as the general population to agree that human beings are a driver of climate change.

This is not to say that farmers aren't adapting to changing weather. The same day as the Whiterock meeting, I happened upon this recently published paper: "Farmers' Perceptions of Climate Change" in *Social Context: Toward a Political Economy of Relevance*.[1] Farmers from Iowa (53) and Indiana (51) were interviewed to explore how the

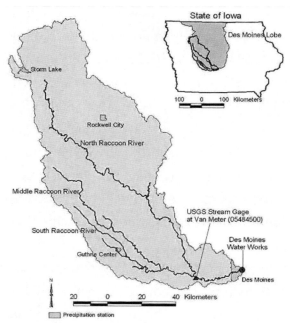

Raccoon River watershed showing the location of the precipitation stations where data were gathered.

political-economic structural context of climate change influenced their perception of and response to heavy rain events.

The adaptive step farmers were most likely to embrace was modifying their application of nitrogen fertilizer. Below are some farmer quotes from the paper regarding changing rainfall patterns and fertilization:

> "With the amount of rain that we had following our side-dress application [of nitrogen], experience told us we were going to run out [of nitrogen]. At the most critical time that that corn plant needed nitrogen, we were going to start running out. We knew that it would have a drastic effect on yield" (IN).

> "Yeah I think we've gone to more extremes...when you get these heavy rains it's harmful. We lose our nitrogen that we all spend money to put out there, it's not cheap" (IA).

> "Boy you can really lose a lot of yield fast if that corn goes short on nitrogen" (IA).

> "I never want to be short on nitrogen, let's put it that way. You don't want nitrogen to be your limiting factor" (IA).

> "Somebody was saying the day after this five-inch rain, 'Is there any nitrogen left?'" (IA).

> "We've had a couple of situations where we had yield loss just out of…You know, we applied the nitrogen and we came in and we planted and it rained and it rained and then it rained some more" (IN).

> "If it keeps raining and it's warm, we're going to lose nitrogen, big time lose nitrogen, and that's when you've got to come back in and put some more [nitrogen] on or you're going to lose the crop, and there's 'why did you lose the crop?' when with another 10 to 15 gallon of [liquid nitrogen fertilizer] you can fix it" (IN).

> "We usually put [a little extra nitrogen on] just to make sure if we have a really wet year, like we had last year and how this year is turning out, that we still have some nitrogen left over [to ensure sufficient yields]" (IA).

> "If it rains a whole lot, that nitrogen, some of that, will wash away and go down in the dead zone of the Gulf of Mexico" (IA, same farmer as previous comment).

I should point out that the paper's authors were sympathetic to the farmers. As such, they make this comment in the paper: "Our work is meant to shed light on how structural forces are shaping actors' actions and modes of thinking and in this way to reveal how individual farmers are not at fault for the ills of modern agriculture" (my emphasis with the underline). Nonetheless the researchers arrived at this cold conclusion: "However, even among farmers who saw agricultural N loss as the key contributing source to water pollution issues, they generally argued that this was an inevitable consequence of heavy rain events and the system of agriculture and thus not something they were significantly concerned about."

During my Whiterock presentation, there was one audience member insistent that because climate change is caused by all of us, we should all shoulder the burden for farmer adaptation, and that these adaptive changes should focus primarily on the dynamics of climate change-driven hydrology happening in real time all around us. I am not, nor have I ever been, against public money (cost share) for farm conservation, if it is spent to produce environmental outcomes beneficial to the public. That being said, I think our state desperately needs a discussion about cost share that also includes a dialog about the ills of modern agriculture. Does anybody reading this think the industry is ready to have that discussion, at least when it comes to nutrient pollution?

Finally, something else happened on November 14 that I think helps illustrate my point. On the way to Coon Rapids, I took the photo below about 5 miles west of the North Raccoon River. If you don't know, those round objects are spools of drainage tile. You might also note the mountain of harvested corn in the background.

Tile spools in the North Raccoon watershed.

To cope with increased rainfall, farmers are not only using more nitrogen; they're also installing more drainage tile to better dry out the soil. Tile is the getaway car for excess nitrogen wanting to bolt the scene.

The Raccoon River serves as the municipal water supply for the Des Moines metropolitan area. Des Moines is the country's (if not the world's) largest city removing nitrate (since 1992) from its source water to comply with safe drinking water regulations.

I posted the photo on my Twitter feed with the only comment being that this was west of the town of Perry, in the Raccoon River watershed. A staff member of the Iowa Department of Agriculture and Land Stewardship replied with the challenge "…and your point is?"

My point is this: if we want clean water (and I'm not sure that we do), let's have the honest dialog we desperately need.

DON'T P DOWN MY LEG
AND TELL ME IT'S RAINING

*A constant source of frustration for me is the never-ending gaslighting on
Iowa agriculture and water quality. Some of this can be quite creative while
a lot of it is downright moronic. A commonly gaslit topic is water quality
trends. People get really fixated on whether the water is getting better or
worse over time, conveniently neglecting the fact that the current state is
substandard at best and terrible at worst, regardless of which direction it's
headed. The title, a country euphemism for "don't lie to me", was particularly
appropriate for this essay because it is about phosphorus pollution.*

Plants require nutrients for growth and agronomists divide these
into macro- and micro-nutrient groups, depending on the quantity
needed. Most important for both crop production and water pollution here in Iowa are the macronutrients of nitrogen (N) and phosphorus (P).

Nitrogen is the beer of the nutrient world. We drink a lot of it, spill
a lot of it, and maybe get a little sloppy in the process. Phosphorus,
on the other hand, is more like tequila. A couple of shots and before
you know it, you're dancing on the table and trading your clothes for
beads. When Mother Nature gets too much P, or starts chasing her P
with some N, watch out; harmful algae blooms result.

The Iowa Nutrient Reduction Strategy (INRS) Science Assessment[1] determined that 79% of Iowa's stream P comes from non-
point sources (NPS, agriculture, for the most part) with the remain-
der originating from point sources (PS) like wastewater treatment

plant discharge. To meet the state's 45% reduction goal, the load reduction from each source needed to be 29% (NPS) and 16% (PS).

To reach a percentage improvement goal, you need a reference point. For the INRS, this is the annual average stream load for the period 1980-1996, which was estimated to be 21,436 tons.

Earlier this year, the Iowa Nutrient Research and Education Council (INREC), an affiliate of the Agribusiness Association of Iowa,

This lake got the worm from the tequila bottle. Photo credit: Ohio State University.

released a report saying that the annual average non-point source P load had dropped 22% from the 1980-96 baseline, and that "Iowa Agriculture has nearly met the 29% non-point source reduction goal." This conclusion was "attributed to fewer acres under intensive tillage and significant increase in no-till acres." Interestingly, the report failed to mention that this presumed improvement also linked back to a decline in soil phosphorus content, but that's a story for another day. Most importantly, the conclusion did not rely on any water monitoring samples or data. At any rate, the report states that the annual P load now averages 16,800 tons.

That INREC report was like a warm spring rain falling on seeds lying within the detritus of my keyboard. But I had to wait several months for the harvest, which was this week. The harvest coincides with a manuscript being accepted by the *Journal of Hydrology* on Iowa stream P loading.

The authors of this paper, "Total Phosphorus Export from Iowa Agricultural Watersheds: Quantifying the Scope and Scale of a Regional Condition,"[2] are Keith Schilling, Matthew Streeter, me, and two other fellows. If you want to read it and are unable to access it at the link, get in touch with me via email and I will send it.

We evaluated water quality data at 46 Iowa stream locations over 18 years (2000-2017) from 4,000 samples in total. Although 4,000 samples are much better than zero samples (i.e., INREC), 4,000 still isn't really enough to definitively pinpoint P loads. So we used an established hydrological model to estimate P levels on days that were absent of data.

Our results show that from 2000 to 2017, annual average P load delivered by Iowa streams to the Mississippi and Missouri river basins was 27,326 tons, about 62% higher than the INREC estimated total and 27% higher than the 1980-1996 baseline total identified by the INRS. The P load for the first nine years of our study (2000-2008) averaged 27,839 tons while the last nine years (2009-2018) averaged 26,812 tons, so we don't see the statewide total changing much over the past couple of decades, and we certainly do not see a 22% improvement.

We recommend holding off on printing the "Mission Accomplished" sign.

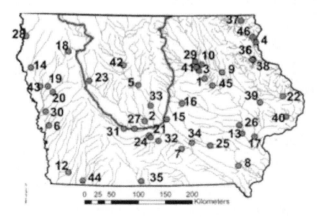

Sample locations used for the *Journal of Hydrology* phosphorus paper.

If you're interested, geographical variation in P loads is shown in the map below. The higher-loss watersheds tend to be the ones with the greatest slope. Phosphorus strongly attaches to soil particles and soil erosion is greatest in hilly landscapes; thus the flat areas of north central Iowa lose relatively small amounts of P while the hilly areas of southern and western Iowa lose far more.

Our analysis also compares Iowa P loads with those entering the Gulf of Mexico. Long-term, we contribute about 15% of the P entering the gulf (we contribute 29% of the N [3]). We occupy about 4.5% of the land area in the Mississippi Basin and deliver about 5.9% of the water. As a whole Iowa loses about 1.5 pounds of P per acre per year. This is about double the rate in the neighboring state of Illinois that has a crop production area and system like ours. It should also be said that Illinois has four times as many people and therefore a much larger point source contribution, but it also has far fewer livestock compared to Iowa.

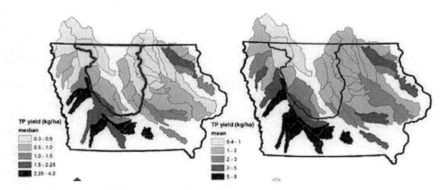

Map showing geographical distribution of P loss in Iowa. 1 kg/ha = 0.9 lbs/acre.

So why the difference between our and the INREC results?

In the conservation business, we tend to measure outputs and outcomes. Everybody does this. They both are important to know. Outputs are things like the amount of money spent, the number of wetlands constructed and so forth. Outcomes in this case means one thing: is the water any better? In a perfect world these things would track together; but you know the rest of that sentence.

The argument exists that there are lag times between implemented conservation and improved water quality. You can lean on that one if you are making progress on reducing inputs (i.e. fertilizer and manure) and/or the imbalance between inputs and crop needs. We aren't.

I want to finish up with a few comments on the Nutrient Reduction Strategy. Like it or not, it is the main tool we have right now for addressing nutrient pollution in Iowa. It's fair to say that it has received substantial criticism from some but also benefited from a tenacious defense provided by some others. Many people forget (or don't know) that the Obama administration green-lighted the voluntary nutrient reduction strategies of Iowa and other states.

Having observed events connected to the INRS these past seven years or so, I think the most serious threats to it do not come from its detractors. What puts it at most risk are inaccurate claims about its success or progress that imperil its credibility in the eyes of the public. It bewilders me when I read statements like "Iowa Agriculture has nearly met the 29% non-point source reduction goal" that go unsupported by water quality data.

We have a massive socioeconomic problem here at the continental scale. Trying to gaslight a way out of it will end badly.

FREE IOWA NOW

Time after time the Ag advocacy organizations mindlessly say things that just aren't true about Iowa's water quality, and almost always these falsehoods go unchecked and unanswered. I've been told many times that I should just ignore the industry rhetoric; that it doesn't mean anything and it's just a salve for people who know the truth but can't admit it. I disagree; any look at America over the past 10 years shows that rhetoric has consequences, and I believe it has had consequences for Iowa's water.

The California-sized Black Sea is bordered by Russia, Ukraine, Bulgaria, Romania, Georgia, and Turkey. It receives freshwater from several major European rivers (especially the Danube) but Mediterranean Sea saltwater also intrudes through a hydrological connection known as the Bosphorus. Thus, Black Sea water is saltier than a lake but fresher than the ocean, producing a diverse ecosystem and productive fishery. Resorts along its shoreline have promoted Black Sea water as therapeutic for at least two centuries.

In the 1960s, USSR agricultural policy increased use of chemical fertilizers and establishment of huge animal production systems in Soviet-bloc countries.[1] One Romanian CAFO reportedly had more than a million hogs. By the 1970s, the Black Sea beaches of Ukraine and Romania were graveyards of fish, clams and crabs doomed by a hypoxic Dead Zone created by Danube River discharge and its baggage stuffed with nitrogen and phosphorus.

Now it must be said that industrial and municipal discharge carried by the Danube from as far away as Germany helped degrade

The Black Sea is shown in the middle of this map. Image credit: By Kamel15, CCBY-SA 3.0, http://commons.wikimedia.org/w/index.php?curid=5623711.

the Black Sea. Budapest, Vienna, Belgrade, Munich, Bucharest, and many other large cities lie within its watershed.

A curious chain of events followed the fall of the USSR in 1989. Many of the huge CAFOs closed and use of chemical fertilizers declined. Only six years later in 1995, it was apparent that the Black Sea was recovering. By 2002, sensitive mussel beds were reestablished, and other ecological indicators were improving.

Similar European dead zones are ongoing in the Baltic and North Seas of the northern part of the continent. Agricultural waste is a strong contributor there also, as both the Netherlands and Denmark (12 million and 28 million hogs, respectively) have animal production systems similar to our own here in Iowa, which we know supplies hypoxia-driving nutrients to the Gulf of Mexico.

Danube River watershed. Image credit: Geology Page, http://www.geologypage.com/2014/11/danube-river.html.

So speaking of the Gulf of Mexico, an article titled *Reviving the Gulf of Mexico's Dead Zone*[2] came my way last week. I was particularly interested in this comment in the article from the Iowa Pork Producers: "The Iowa Pork Producers Association believes there is no science to support that pork farming has any relation to the dead zone in the Gulf."

Mmm hmm.

I have to wonder what catalyzes such a brazen statement. It was far enough out there in la-la land that I felt compelled to confirm its accuracy with one of the article's authors (they did confirm).

If rebuttal was the objective of this essay, I would plow into that weed-infested sod and try to turn it over on itself, but explaining that gravity exists is boring to me, and it would probably be boring for you to read. Instead I will just go broad spectrum on the statement and say that when I search manure + Gulf of Mexico Hypoxia in the Google Scholar search engine, I get 1,800 results, and a lot of those papers are from Iowa including this one: *Effects of liquid swine manure applications on NO3–N leaching losses to subsurface drainage water from loamy soils in Iowa.*[3]

The Iowa Nutrient Reduction Strategy "is a science and technology-based framework to assess and reduce nutrients to Iowa waters and the Gulf of Mexico."[4] On the Pork Producers' own website[5] it states that the voluntary strategy "has been developed in response to the 2008 Gulf Hypoxia Action Plan that calls for the 12 states along the Mississippi River to develop strategies to reduce nutrient loading to the Gulf of Mexico." Furthermore, IA Pork (along with IA Corn Growers Association and IA Soybean Association) was a founding member of the Iowa Agricultural Water Alliance, whose stated objective is to "accelerate the pace and scale of quantifiable water quality improvements in Iowa."

If the Pork Producers Association doesn't think they're part of the problem, then a reasonable person could wonder (and speculate) about why they would want to be part of these other things.

I think these are reasonable questions for folks in agriculture: How is the public to know what rhetoric is serious, and what isn't? What is truth, what is window dressing, and what is being said behind closed doors? Is the industry tailoring the rhetoric for an intended audience one day, and a different audience the next day? These are serious and fair questions for an industry indemnified with billions of public dollars.

Every day, Iowans are being asked to allow the Ag industry to self-solve Iowa's non-point source water pollution problems on their terms and on their time schedule, whatever that might be. Believe it or not, I do understand how reasonable people can rationalize this approach, but herein lies the issue: when a major commodity organization is telling its members that they aren't the cause of the problem (and it stands to reason that they are telling them this, if they're bold enough to say it in public), then volunteer conservation all of a sudden doesn't sound like a smart option, from several different perspectives.

It makes the grown-up inside of me suspect the cute "voluntary but not optional" rhetoric we frequently hear from the industry and our agencies is unserious. If you don't think you're the cause, it seems to me you're probably going to wait for the people who you think are the cause to volunteer.

Like golf course operators, I suppose, whom the aggies are fond of blaming for Iowa's stream nutrient problems.

Ok, so it would be wrong for me to use that one Pork Producers' comment to tar the entire agricultural industrial complex (AIC). I know there have been some good faith efforts at water quality improvement out there in commodity land. But I just have to say this: the Iowa Pork Producers Association is not some fly-by-night organization. What they say has repercussions for ALL IOWANS, and not just their members, who raise one out of every three hogs in the U.S. and are responsible for managing the fecal waste equivalent of three Californias.

Now I have been told in the past that I should ignore the outrageous industry rhetoric and accept it as an anomaly when it inevitably reappears. I think this is a mistake. I think the outrageous is the problem in Iowa.

I believe rhetoric matters. The platitude people sure know this. Why else would we hear so much of it? Sometimes I think "voluntary but not optional" is the roll-in-the-hay progeny of "feeding the world" and "we all want clean water." My advice to them: get a thesaurus already.

I believe rhetoric has consequences. I once thought I'd rather drink Drano than to ever be forced to answer another question about Des Moines Water Works discharging waste brine from their nitrate removal facility. Two jobs and nine years later, I'm STILL answering questions about that. At a recent meeting, I heard a university professor say he was scheduled to conduct a presentation at some hinterland location to dispel the idea that turf grass was the cause of the nitrate problem. I'm sure there are a few agriculture people who will read those last couple of sentences and smugly smile in satisfaction. And those things are nothing compared to the rhetoric-driven foot-dragging that has plagued Iowa water quality over the past 40 years.

Since I'm making the case that rhetoric matters, I'm going to finish this mess by proposing my own:

FREE IOWA NOW

It's short, easy to remember, and doesn't rely on bizarre conflation of synonyms.

So, somebody, anybody, please, Free Iowa Now from this taxpayer-subsidized curse of polluted water and the malignant propaganda that continues to excuse it.

FOOL ME ONCE ...

We're led to believe by some in agriculture that nutrient pollution is a new thing and as such, the public should cut them some slack and give them time to get it figured out. This is a load of bull. We have known the causes and potential solutions for nutrient pollution for decades, at least since 1970. The foot dragging is a classic response by industry to environmental problems in the U.S.: Deny, Deflect, Distract and Delay.

This morning I read for the second time in two years that our state's agriculture department is "just getting started" on addressing Iowa's problems with nutrient pollution.[1,2] As my favorite 1960s TV star Jerry Mathers would say, "gee that's swell," since this pollution has been around since *Leave it to Beaver* was still a thing. You've probably noticed the problem if you've made more than a few trips to an Iowa river or lake over the past 60 years.

Jerry Mathers as the Beaver. By ABC Television—eBay itemphoto front-photo back, Public Domain, https://commons.wikimedia.org/w/index.php?curid=18738253.

This got me to thinking that maybe there's hope that my 30-year old daughter will finally clean up her room. Better late than never. Keep trying, honey.

Maybe we should have grounded her when we had the chance.

Honestly there are days when I wish that the justgettingstarted people wouldn't get me started. This is one of those days. Serious question: Am I crazy to wonder who is writing copy for Ag spokespeople?

Reading today's (2/12/20) "just getting started" tweet[1] from the Iowa Agricultural Water Alliance, a consortium of the Iowa Corn Growers Association, Iowa Soybean Association, and Iowa Pork Producers, the last of whom still denies contributing to the nutrient pollution problem[3] (I know, I know, you can't make this stuff up), returned all sorts of memories to what's left of my mind. Firstly, it made me think of this paper, "Nitrate-Nitrogen in Tile Drainage as Affected by Fertilization,"[4] published in 1981 by Iowa State University Researchers using data from as far back as 1970. Here's a quote:

"The large leaching losses of nitrate measured (from Iowa farm fields) are of environmental, economic, and energy concern. The quality of tile drainage water is important because this water can be a significant portion of total stream flow."

The tweet also made me think of my days spent at the Des Moines Water Works (DMWW) Fleur Drive Treatment Plant. If you don't know, DMWW has been removing nitrate from Des Moines drinking water since 1992. Poking around the scientific literature using Google Scholar generated this gem, published in the 1996 *Journal of Soil and Water Conservation*: "Agriculture and Drinking Water Supplies: Removing nitrates from drinking water in Des Moines, Iowa." Here's an excerpt:

L.D. McMullen, general manager of DMWW, says that nitrate removal concerns in Des Moines go back a long time. "Back in the early eighties [1980s, if you were wondering] we started to notice an upward trend in the nitrate levels found in the rivers," he said.

To improve both water quantity and quality, Des Moines decided to build a new intake in the Des Moines River to supplement the existing intakes from the Raccoon River and other sources. The dual-river system worked for a while, he said, because the rivers were "out of sync," that is, when nitrate levels were high in one, they were low in the other—the treatment plant could flip-flop back and forth between them. That was only a temporary solution, said McMullen, because they soon realized there were going to be times where the levels were high in both rivers at the same time.

Memories of a piece on ISU's digital repository,[5] "Agriculture: environmental problems and directions" (1990), also came to me today. I gotta tell you folks, the zingers in this thing have been preserved like a 40-year-old Twinkie. Here are some of 1990's (the year, not the decade) greatest hits:

Des Moines Register Vault
@DMRegisterVault

From 1992: Des Moines Water Works Director L.D. McMullen shows off his utility's new $4.5 million nitrate removal system.

1:01 PM · Apr 30, 2017 · Twitter Web Client

> Agricultural practices which contribute to nutrient-related water quality problems include: excessive soil erosion; use of fertilizers in excess of crop needs; failure to account for nutrient contributions of legumes and animal manures; and failure to coordinate timing of fertilizer applications according

Cresco, Iowa farm boy, L.D. McMullen, then and now. Larger image credit: Des Moines Register.

to crop needs. (Yes basically the same stuff we're talking about 30 years later).

> The public has a right to expect that Iowa's surface and ground waters will be maintained at such a quality that they can be used as a source of drinking water, for recreation, and for other uses.

> Iowa has established a number of programs designed to encourage voluntary adoption of farming practices...the state is likely to continue its support of this voluntary approach, including providing continued funding for the various programs now underway. However, it is important to recognize that success of this voluntary approach in developing, demonstrating, and adopting such "Best Management Practices" is by no means assured, and failure of this approach may well lead to increased regulation.

> Will farmers, agribusiness, and other groups in the agricultural community support and work to implement these voluntary water protection initiatives? Past history suggests they may not. (You don't say, hmm.)

> Recent sociological research also suggests that the voluntary approach may not be highly successful. Iowa farmers characterized Iowa agriculture as "highly dependent on external inputs, and one where strong motivations toward changes are not pre-existing."

> While it is likely that the ongoing voluntary programs will be given a reasonable period to work before a more regulatory approach is adopted, this period will certainly be far shorter than the 50-year period given for voluntary soil conservation programs to work. (Reminder: as of this morning, they're just getting started.)

> At this point, the challenge is clear. Will the agricultural community voluntarily take the actions necessary to protect and improve Iowa's water quality? There are many who say this will not happen.

Ok, I've gone on long enough with that, if I haven't made my point by now, I never will.

Do Iowans deserve better than to be told that this problem will take a long time yet to solve, even when known solutions are out there? That's for you to decide. It's your water. Although I think we deserve better than to be told by agency staff to not expect instant gratification, all available evidence shows that we should take them at their word on that.

Orwell said to never use a saying or a metaphor in your writing that you heard or read somewhere else. But right now, I can't resist the temptation.

Fool me once, shame on you. Fool me twice, shame on me.

THEY BREAK IT, YOU BUY IT

There are a lot of third rails when talking about Iowa agriculture. In fact, there are probably at least 33rd rails. One is how we fertilize corn with nitrogen fertilizer. Everybody in my world knows farmers use too much when we consider the state as a whole. Every nugget of data that I know of shows this. And yes, people on the Ag side know this, as this essay illustrates. Yet we fail to confront this as a driver of water pollution in Iowa, and an entire school of red herrings has been created by the Ag communication shops to distract from this fact. Getting farmers to align their nitrogen inputs with Iowa State University recommendations would improve water quality and would cost the taxpayers nothing. But there is no industry motivation to do this—farmers think they need extra and the Ag retailers are only too happy to sell it to them.

Last Thursday (2/20/20) the Iowa Soybean Association (ISA) released the results of a study[1] showing Iowa farmers could save up to $99 million per year by better aligning their fertilizer amounts with corn requirements. Among other things, their data show that surveyed farmers were applying about 34 pounds per acre more nitrogen fertilizer than ISU recommendations (140 pounds per acre) for corn grown after soybeans.

The content of the report was not a surprise to me and likely not to anyone that has spent much time studying issues related to nitrogen fertilizer and nitrate pollution in our streams and lakes. The Iowa Nutrient Research and Education Council (INREC), an arm of the Agribusiness Association of Iowa (AAI), reported[2] in June that their survey data showed nitrogen rates to corn following soybean (c/sb) averaged 169 pounds per acre, similar to the ISA data (174 pounds per acre). For corn grown following corn (c/c) the previous year (usually about 1/10th to 1/5th of Iowa crop acres) rates are typically higher.

Using sales data, I've estimated that the overall rate to corn is 189 pounds per acre, and this includes both c/sb and c/c combined. With this analysis I make an admittedly fragile assumption that all commercial nitrogen fertilizer is being applied to corn. Some is probably applied to soybeans and pasture, but until somebody coughs up some credible data on this questionable practice (at least in the case of soybeans), I think I am being as fair as I need to be.

Bear in mind that so far none of this data considers manured fields, where rates are substantially higher. In a paper[3] published four years ago, my coauthors and I used farmer reported data from 768 Raccoon River Watershed fields to calculate the rates shown in the table below, all higher than ISU recommendations.

Crop Rotation	N Rate (pounds per acre using commercial fertilizer)	N Rate (pounds per acre using manure
c/sb	158	195
c/c	189	239

Some farmers are able to generate impressive corn yields with modest nitrogen applications. One is Mitch Hora who farms south of here in Washington County. You can check out his blog[4] and read how he grows 196 bushel per acre corn (about the statewide average) with 140 pounds per acre of nitrogen.

With examples like Mr. Hora scattered here and there, Average Joe and Mary can reasonably ask why we use more nitrogen than needed. The calculus on this is very simple: while the farmer absorbs the consequences of too little nitrogen, the public must absorb the consequences of too much, with these latter consequences being degraded water.

In fact, the calculus is SO simple and SO easy to understand that the industry has been compelled to construct a rhetorical brick firewall to hide it, one where the bricks are stamped with "spooning it on" and "we all want clean water." Another good one is that "nitrogen is expensive" which is spectacularly untrue considering that we still waste about 25% of it (or more) in some years and after 180 years of Iowa agriculture, the first case of nitrogen-loss-caused farmer bankruptcy has yet to be recorded, at least to my knowledge. Maybe there's one out there, I don't know.

This is all so comprehendible that I think a malaise about nitrogen rates has permeated much of the scientific community. A sort of a "who cares, it's boring" attitude. Indeed, scientists have been writing about the disconnect between fertilizer (manure and commercial) inputs and crop needs for decades, and there is disagreement about how important it is in the grand scheme of things. The Iowa Nutrient Reduction Strategy science assessment assigned a potential benefit to our streams from better fertilizer management of 10%.

Now it should be said that eight years after the Nutrient Strategy became policy, a 10% improvement would sound like sensational progress, considering that we can't even manage to get on the good side of zero improvement. Stream nitrate levels continue to get worse, a lot worse. More manure generated by more and more animals is not affecting sales of commercial fertilizer, at least not much, and thousands of miles of new drain tile are installed every year that help move the wasted nitrogen to our streams.

Am I crazy to suggest that agriculture get fertilizer inputs under control before asking the public for more money?

Continuing to talk about this at times feels purposeless. It seems to me that many of us scientists have turned our back on the flames and find peace of mind by studying the details. We've handed over the fire-fighting to the engineers, hoping they can stop the spreading blaze by building expensive solutions that only the aggregated wealth of the public can afford. Quite the convenient arrangement for the industry, I must say. Keep over-selling the pollutant, and let the public deal with the consequences. Ring me up about a bridge I've got for sale if you think anything short of a law will end that arrangement.

But yes, I do think somebody needs to continue to talk about this. Iowa is poised to raise its sales tax $0.01, in large part to fund water quality projects. My unscientific impression is that most people agree with this in principle. Is this public cooperation sustainable when the industry has an unregulated license to do as they please with fertilizer inputs? Is it sustainable when the trade group representing the retailers selling fertilizer has funding from the Iowa legislature to be the "official" measurer of water quality progress in Iowa? Is it sustainable when the degradation of our water continues unabated?

Does anybody care if it's sustainable, or is this just one more can-kicking down the road to nowhere?

Some people ask me why I write these essays and honestly, I ask myself that pretty often. I don't believe in having heroes, but I like Orwell's writing a lot. He said there are four reasons to write: ego, aestheticism, to record history, and a desire to push society in a certain direction. I'm not sure any of those work for me; the last one comes closest, but I have resigned myself to the futility of this. I suppose what works for me best are the words of another English writer, Ted Hughes: It's about trying to take fuller possession of the reality of your life.

THE ETHICS OF A PIG

Smith Fellow Dr. Bonnie McGill worked with me and others here at the University of Iowa for a short time in 2019-2020. Conversations with her inspired this essay, which focuses on globalization and the resulting pollution that is generated in Iowa and elsewhere. I often use a literary figure or work to leverage what I am trying to say. Here, it was the great short story writer O. Henry.

Writing with a great *nom de plume*, O. Henry[1] (William S. Porter) may have been the G.O.A.T. (Greatest Of All Time) short story writer and his best one was the ironic comedy, "The Gift of the Magi." O. Henry also wrote one titled "The Ethics of Pig," a double-crossed grifter's story of trying to work a swindle for a pricey porcine. Ok, there's my segue to Iowa hog production. More on O. Henry later.

O. Henry. By W.M. Vanderweyde, New York—NYPL Digital Gallery, Public Domain, https://commons.wikimedia.org/w/index.php?curid=9810360.

It's no secret that the production of Iowa hogs is nothing like it was 40 years ago. In 1980, 65,000 Iowa farmers raised a total of 13 million hogs (about 200 hogs per farmer); by 2002 the number of hogs had increased to 14 million but the farmers raising them had dwindled to 10,000.[2] At any one time, today's Iowa has about 25 million hogs raised by ~6,000 farmers.[3] A market weight hog is 6 months old and thus the annual total brought to market by Iowa farmers is about double the inventory.

Many of today's hogs are never owned by the Iowa farmer; rather they are raised on contract for large meat processing companies like Tyson, Smithfield Foods, and JBS. You may hear otherwise, but from what I've read, many farmers prefer these types of arrangements and I'm not questioning them.

These big companies are "vertically integrated," meaning their business strategy ties together two or more functions within one entity—in other words, they try to cut out some of the middlemen to create efficiencies that ultimately benefit them and perhaps lower the retail price the consumer pays for the product. This did in fact happen for pork, especially in the early stages of consolidation when prices dropped $29/year for the average U.S. customer.[4]

The number of Iowa live hogs owned by food and processing companies (versus farmer-owned) is not an easy figure to obtain. But it hardly matters. They own them all once they're in a box. The JBS processing facility in Ottumwa produces 1 billion pounds of pork per year—almost 3 million pounds per day. This much pork would require more than 7 million hogs to be processed per year. That's 800 per hour, assuming three shifts per day. Marshalltown and Council Bluffs are also home to JBS hog processing facilities. JBS profits in 2018 totaled more than $7 billion.[5] JBS is a Brazilian company that entered the U.S. market in 2007 with the purchase of Swift Packing Company.[6]

Smithfield Foods is the largest pork producer in the world[7] with a presence in the U.S., Mexico, Poland, Romania, Germany, and the U.K. They own facilities in Mason City, Carroll, Denison, Orange City, Sioux Center, Sioux Falls, and Omaha. Smithfield was once an American company but is now owned by the Chinese conglomerate

WH Group. The company has ~50,000 employees that generate $15 billion in annual revenues.[8]

Now it's undeniable that many Iowa residents—thousands in fact—earn their bacon working for these foreign-held companies. Hog production and processing here also puts bacon on the plates and in the pockets of lots of people in some other countries.

In an interview for a Reuters article, one Smithfield worker put it simply: "They got an order to fill: China."[9]

So back to O. Henry. Curiously enough, he coined the phrase Banana Republic in his 1904 story "The Admiral" to describe the mythical country of Anchuria, which is thought to represent Honduras where O. Henry was living at the time. The phrase soon gained popular use to describe the Central American countries ruthlessly compromised and exploited by the United Fruit Company and other American corporations for the purposes of supplying cheap bananas to the U.S. After a few decades of being casually used by parrotheads (i.e. Jimmy Buffett fans) and folks shopping for spring break clothes, the phrase's more sinister overtones have resurfaced of late thanks to economists using it to describe a plutocracy, i.e. government by the wealthy.

Now when I started writing this, my objective was to hammer on the point that hog production pollutes Iowa's water so that Chinese people can eat more pork chops and foreign billionaires can eat more caviar and then as they pick the fish eggs out of their teeth, they at least indirectly affect policy decisions that keep our water polluted. Iowa as a Banana Republic. Indeed, The Swine Republic. I sorta doubt that you'll hear Jimmy Buffett croon those words, or for that matter see it embroidered on the back pocket of a pair of cargo shorts.

But two things happened that made me rethink my original objective. One, I realized that I had already burned the obvious title for this one (Swine Republic) several months ago and I'm a better titler (long "i" sound) than I am a writer and I have expectations for myself. So, I added a letter to O. Henry's title.

Second, I started to think about all the human and environmental wreckage our own country has wrought elsewhere so we can have cheap(er) iPhones, energy, clothes, and a whole bunch of other stuff we use, wear, eat, and drink. Outsourcing pollution, it's been a thing[10] for a while now. I interrupted writing this to look at my own clothes. Shirt: Sri Lanka. Pants: Vietnam. Shoes: China. I'm all about south Asia until I put my jacket on: Portugal, although the brand is Norwegian. How much pollution my own clothes generated in these other countries: don't know. Shipping them to the U.S. certainly created some. Anyway, I thought I better not get too self-righteous here. What goes around comes around, as they say.

But still, have these foreign meat conglomerates brought general prosperity to rural Iowa? There's very little evidence that they have. Sure, thousands of people work in the slaughterhouses. The JBS Ottumwa facility employs 2,200 people and is the largest employer in Wapello County. And yet, the county's population has dropped 25% since 1950 and 11.5% since 1980.[11] And about those jobs. The average wage earned by a meat packing worker was 14-18% greater than the rest of U.S. manufacturing up until the 1970s. Now: 32% lower.[12]

So, I know, globalization blah blah blah, what can I add to the discussion. Well, this: it's polluting your water. And this: as we stand at the brink of taxing ourselves to help clean up this pollution, our state asks nothing of the people who benefit most from the arrangement.

Why?

I'M NOT A SCIENTIST

This was written at the start of the COVID pandemic, which further exposed the ongoing attempts to discredit science and scientists for political gain. Climate change is another topic where science has taken a beating. In my opinion, the scientific community has not responded forcefully enough to these attacks, mainly because we often rely on public funding and political goodwill to conduct our work. This essay explores this dynamic.

You may have noticed that we have few trained scientists occupying elected positions in the United States. In the 115th Congress, members include one chemist, one physicist and one microbiologist, all in the house. By comparison there are 218 attorneys (including 47 former prosecutors and 15 judges), 101 teachers, 26 farmers, 8 ordained ministers, 7 radio talk show hosts, 1 comedian and 1 rodeo announcer. There also are 14 physicians, 4 dentists and 3 veterinarians, all of whom would have had extensive scientific coursework, along with 8 engineers who were likely trained in the physical sciences.[1]

Thomas Jefferson was the closest thing we've had to a scientist president, although this was more a result of his Renaissance-Man-polymath persona, rather than any formal training. Jefferson helped develop modern agriculture and also devised a rudimentary smallpox vaccine. Herbert Hoover and Jimmy Carter were both trained engineers with extensive knowledge in geology (Hoover) and physics (Carter).

It's worth pointing out that Angela Merkel (Germany) holds a PhD in quantum chemistry, and that Margaret Thatcher (U.K.) was a research chemist for a time.

Reflecting back on the span of my life, it's hard for me to imagine a credible scientist tolerating American politics the past 40 years. I say this because so much of politics, and even our culture itself, has rejected empiricism to varying degrees, depending on the time, place and subject. An empirical world view within the context of science emphasizes evidence and holds that ideas must be tested against real-world observations (i.e., experiments). This is the foundation upon which the scientific method rests. Empiricism's competing world view is rationalism, which holds that intuition, rather than observation, is the foundation of certainty in knowledge.

It's been in vogue for a while now for politicians to say "I'm not a scientist" when confronted on some issue relating to the natural world, implying it takes some special insight to understand or believe in science (this is wrong). I think what these folks are really saying is "I'm not an empiricist," and by extension, "I'm not going to let evidence get in the way of decision-making."

This discussion was out in the open the past couple of days, way out in the open. NYU law professor Richard Epstein recently wrote and posted a two-part position paper of sorts concerning the COVID-19 pandemic. To make a long story short, he developed his own model of the disease based on what he knew of litigating court cases, advising medical professionals on their expert testimony, and some knowledge of the AIDS epidemic. He asserted that the spread and the threat of the Coronavirus had been exaggerated. His stature as one of the most-cited legal academics in America reportedly enticed many in our federal government to embrace his model, which was constructed without input from physicians or epidemiologists.

Isaac Chotineer, a journalist for *The New Yorker* magazine, questioned the legitimacy of Epstein's model and its conclusions in a contentious interview with him.[2] At one point Epstein said "look, I'm not an empiricist," apparently trying to separate himself from the vacuousness of the "I'm not a scientist" rhetoric. But in doing so, he admitted to something far worse, especially for an attorney: the evidence didn't matter. This is where we find ourselves, 500 years after empiricism began the struggle of carrying civilization into the sunshine.

Galileo Galilei, portrait by Justus Sustermans, Wikimedia commons.

The first great empiricist, Galileo, reflected his early optimism in writing, "I do not doubt that in the course of time this new science will be improved by further observations." But it has been a struggle ever since. Galileo was continuously harangued by the reigning political power of his time, the Vatican. Ever the rebel, he constantly tried to push the envelope to see what he could get away with. His great sin was writing directly for the com-

Isaac Newton, portrait by Godfrey Kneller, Wikimedia commons.

mon person, ignoring Latin and instead using a colloquial style and the languages of the masses. Stillman Drake, an interpreter of Galileo's writings, described his work thus: "The purely scientific material of his books was enlivened for the reader by the devastating sarcasm with which he was accustomed to puncture his pompous opponents." When faced with either renouncing his observations that the earth revolved around the sun, or torture, Galileo chose the former, while reportedly whispering under his breath at the end of his trial, "but it [the earth] moves." Curiously, and in what is perhaps the strangest of ironies, the head of today's Vatican, Pope Francis, holds a master's degree in chemistry, and has been predictably scorned by many of the reigning political powers of our day for some of his positions on science.

We'll never know if Isaac Newton learned from Galileo's experience, but working only 50 years later, it seems as if he did. Newton took his science into the shadows and was so averse to controversy that he didn't even respond to challenges of his conclusions.[3] Apparently, the work itself was the sole reward for Newton, and he wasn't going to do anything that would jeopardize his license to conduct it.

So, this is not to say that as empiricists, scientists are always right. You can't be great or even very good in science unless you do something new, and as Einstein said, a person who never made a mistake never tried anything new. There's a reason it's called trial and error. The greats were wrong all the time about a lot of stuff, Einstein, Darwin and yes, Galileo. Another example is Nobel-laureate Svante Arrhenius, the first notable scientist to predict that burning of fossil fuels would warm the earth. Arrhenius developed a series of calculations around 1896 that estimated a rise in global temperatures associated with increasing atmospheric CO_2 levels that were pretty much right, but he was also wildly wrong (unfortunately) by predicting it would take 3,000 years to double atmospheric CO_2 concentrations.[4] I doubt Arrhenius ever said, "the climate is always changing," but who knows.

Why have our politicians been so reluctant to embrace science, and more importantly, empiricism? Well, I think the answer is obvious.

To quote Ian Boyd, Professor of Biology at the University of St. Andrews in Scotland, "Vested interests do not want their political, social, and financial currency debased by being confronted by the real world."[5] I think we see this day after day after maddening day, at all levels of our government, and right here in Iowa. I mainly write about water quality, and I can tell you it is not hard to find elected and institutional leaders making claims about our water that are unanchored by empiricism.

Svante Arrhenius. Photo credit: Photogravure Meisenbach Riffarth & Co. Leipzig.-Zeitschrift fur Physikalische Chemie, Band 69, 1909.

It's fair to argue the costs, benefits and consequences of pursuing policy based on empirical observation. It's also courageous. What's not fair, and what's definitely not courageous, is to pretend to do so while doing otherwise. In fact, this is dangerous, and it has brought us to a point where we think if we repeat a falsehood enough, and hope with all our might that it is true, that "poof a miracle will happen" and it will be true. Science needs to respond to this not by whispering "but it moves," but rather by shouting it from the mountaintop.

Although exceptions are out there, it's my opinion that most professional scientists have not only shied away from Galileo's vision of speaking directly and candidly to the public in ways they can understand, we've all but repudiated it as an obligation to society. Newton, not Galileo, is our model; the work, and having a license to do it, is the reward. It's painfully obvious that this has helped our politicians retreat from empiricism. As large numbers of us are employed in the public sector, we've been compelled to make our deals with the devils, or else go find some other way to earn a living.

It should not and cannot be the job of science to call out every petty lie told by our politicians. As I understand it, that job belongs to the free press. What belongs to science, I believe, is the obligation to tenaciously defend the empirical foundation upon which modern society was constructed, because it's pretty clear that our body politic is not up to the job.

CONSERVATIONIST

A couple of Iowa politicians don't like me very well. One of them inspired this piece, which should be read as a sequel to "I'm Not a Scientist."

A few months ago, I wrote an essay that discussed the abandonment of empiricism and the contempt some of our elected leaders apparently have for science and scientists. A couple of recent items motivated me to write about this again.

The first was hearing one of the presidential candidates mocking his opponent with the line "he'll listen to the scientists." Ok, scientists don't know everything, and they make a lot of mistakes and most of us aren't nearly as smart as some would believe. And we're at least as vulnerable to temptation as the non-scientist. But, as we are hired by public, private and non-profit institutions to provide a service to society, a reasonable person might wonder, why have us around if you're not going to listen to us.

The second thing driving me to the keyboard was a candidate survey conducted by the organization Science Iowa, formerly March for Science. As coincidence would have it, the group invited me to present an overview of my work more than a year ago.

This question was on Science Iowa's candidate survey: What policies do you propose or support to reduce agricultural chemicals and animal waste in Iowa groundwater and streams?

One farmer-candidate responded with this: First of all, Iowa farmers are managing fertilizer and animal manure applications better than ever before. "Scientists" saying that animal waste is in groundwater and streams doesn't advance the conversation to finding solutions to reduce nitrate, phosphorus and bacteria. Iowa's Nutrient Reduction Strategy is working and I would be supportive of policy to continue the delivery of programs that are focused on this strategy.

Ok. The quotation marks around "scientists" were included in the candidate's answer. In my own abandonment of empiricism, a little non-scientist in my head whispered to me what name(s) this person might've had in mind when they added the "quote marks."

As far as the assertion that Iowa farmers are managing fertilizer and manure applications better than ever, well, maybe. If management includes reducing the amount applied based on Iowa State University recommendations, then this statement is laughably false. Some farmers are doing intuitive things they didn't do a generation ago, such as splitting the total amount applied into multiple applications or co-applying inhibitors which help stabilize nitrogen fertilizer. But where is the evidence that any of these things are improving water quality, especially when it comes nitrogen pollution? Our streams and lakes are worse than ever by that measure. We still can't come to grips with the fact that the system has a mass balance problem: inputs > outputs = polluted water. And we're still in denial that our quest to drain every last square inch of Iowa degrades our streams.

And as far as finding solutions, did this supposed fan of the nutrient strategy not review its science assessment? A menu of solutions produced by the strategy's science (not "science") team has been lying on the restaurant table for eight years now, while the industry waits outside for a "Free Lunch" sign to be posted.

As I've said before, I doubt anybody has ever met any farmers who didn't consider themselves conservationists. But for much of the year, our streams are still brown and foamy and our lakes still green and slimy. Are we conservationists, or are we "conservationists"? What do we even mean by the word?

Discrediting the messenger because you don't like the message is not a new tactic, but it seems to me this virus has become a little more sinister in recent years and threatens the role of science as an arbiter for the truths of the natural world and a tool for enhancing the greater good. I get it that some in agriculture want me to bite my tongue about the condition of our water. But permit me to state the obvious: if your goal is to do nothing, or generously, delay meaningful action for generations, you sure don't want somebody talking about the sorry state of the current condition.

More than a few people have told me to just ignore this sort of "thing." That's probably not bad advice, considered within the context of my own self-preservation. But I tend to believe the great Neils Bohr's famous words: "We [scientists] are actors as well as observers in the drama."

In his book *Serving the Reich, the Struggle for the Soul of Physics Under Hitler*, Philip Ball describes how the Nazis forsook the truth and divided physics into "Jewish" physics and "Aryan" physics. We know how that worked out: the Jewish scientists escaped with their lives, Heisenberg and Hitler failed to split the atom, and the Allies defeated Fascism. Prior to Einstein's escape (not really an escape per se, but a refusal to return), many of his non-Jewish colleagues resented his perceived activism, to which he said, "I do not share the view that the scientist should observe silence in political matters, therefore human affairs in the broader sense. Does not such restraint signify a lack of responsibility?" As Ball said in his book, the important point here is that Einstein equated "political" with "human affairs in the broader sense"; i.e., questions of right and wrong, and fair or unjust.

Truth be told, I'm probably an average scientist at best, and it goes without saying that nobody will confuse me with Bohr or Einstein. But I'm not going to let that stop me from saying this: the ongoing pollution of Iowa's water is a moral wrong, and it's unjust.

RIPE AS A ROADKILL RACCOON

A lot was going on when I wrote this: rampant COVID, economic upheaval, the George Floyd murder, and nationwide protests. The entire country's dirty laundry of division was being aired in the summer sun. Nowhere is the so-called urban-rural divide more visible than the Raccoon River Watershed: 11 rural counties that drain to two urban ones and the Des Moines metropolitan area, which uses the river as a source of municipal drinking water supply. The river has been and continues to be a third rail of Iowa politics mostly because the drinking water consumed by 25% of the state's population is impaired from the best crop land on earth farmed by some of the state's most prosperous farmers who are customers of powerful agribusiness interests. Hostility to change that would produce better water quality is the theme here.

Hydrologists classify watersheds using a hierarchical system that "nests" watersheds within one another, an idea that resembles a broad oak tree with the trunk being a large river such as the Mississippi and the countless branches its numerous tributaries. Each watershed or branch is given a number—a Hydrologic Unit Code (HUC) with the larger branches having the smaller numbers.

The continental U.S. is divided into 18 hydrologic regions, 6 of which drain through the outlets of the Mississippi River and its distributary, the Atchafalaya River, into the Gulf of Mexico. One of these six is the Upper Mississippi River, which is designated HUC 07, and thus all tributary sub watersheds draining to Upper Mississippi have a HUC number beginning with "07."

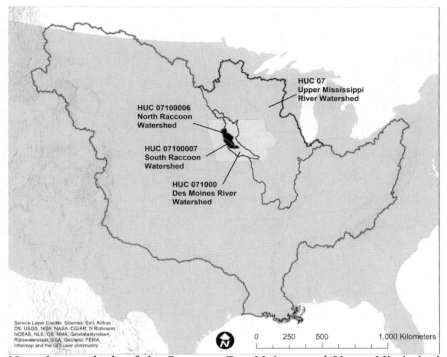

HUC 07
Upper Mississippi
River Watershed

HUC 07100006
North Raccoon
Watershed

HUC 07100007
South Raccoon
Watershed

HUC 071000
Des Moines River
Watershed

0   250   500   1,000 Kilometers

Nested watersheds of the Raccoon, Des Moines, and Upper Mississippi
River Basins. Map credit: Dan Gilles.

Scientists and conservationists commonly work at the HUC-12
(i.e., the HUC number has 12 digits) and HUC-8 (8 digits) scales
when conducting watershed research. HUC 12 watersheds drain from
10,000 to 40,000 acres and in Iowa there are 1,660 of them. Iowa
HUC-8s (56 of them) cover about 1,000 square miles on average.

The Raccoon River watershed is divided into two HUC-8s designated as the North and South Raccoon river. The Raccoon is actually fed by flows from three main branches: the South, Middle, and
North, with the North being the main branch. The South and Middle combine in western Dallas County and this combined flow joins
the North Raccoon a couple of miles downstream near the town
of Van Meter. The South Raccoon HUC-8 (07100007) includes the
area draining to the combined flows of the South and Middle Rac-

coon rivers; the North Raccoon HUC-8 includes the area draining to the North Raccoon main branch, but not including South/Middle Raccoon areas, to its confluence with the Des Moines River in downtown Des Moines. At the Raccoon outlet, about 70% of the water is sourced to the North Raccoon (07100006) while the other 30% is sourced to the South and Middle Raccoon (07100007).

Despite what some would have you believe,[1] people do drink water from the Raccoon River—20% of Iowa's population in fact, but probably closer to 100% when you include Iowans attending the state fair, sporting events, concerts, and the Des Moines farmers' market. Because of its importance as a drinking water supply and because it may contain more nitrate than any similarly sized stream in North America, there have been countless efforts spanning decades to engage landowners, agencies, utilities, NGOs, anglers, paddlers, local governments and the horses they all rode in on, in an effort to try to affect change. Frustration with the lack of change came to a head in 2015 when the Des Moines Water Works filed a complaint in US District Court against 13 drainage districts in 3 counties of the North Raccoon Watershed, a suit that was ultimately dismissed. At least a few reputations and careers have been muddied by the waters of the Raccoon River.

One effort at Raccoon River Watershed improvement was the formation of Watershed Management Authorities (WMAs). Iowa lawmakers passed legislation authorizing the creation of WMAs in 2010. WMAs provide a framework for stakeholders, Soil and Water Conservation Districts and local and county governments "to cooperatively engage in watershed planning and management." There are now 26 WMAs in Iowa and one in both of the Raccoon HUC-8s. There also is a WMA for the Walnut Creek Watershed which enters the Raccoon River in Des Moines Water Works Park. According to Iowa DNR,[2] "The WMA is formed by a Chapter 28E Agreement by two or more eligible political subdivisions within a specific eight-digit hydrologic unit code watershed."

So here is where the fun part begins.

The North Raccoon WMA has been in the news of late for a couple of reasons. It was awarded $2.5 million through a grant from the Housing and Urban Development (HUD) to implement "flood first" practices as part of the Iowa Watershed Approach (IWA) project.[3] The North Raccoon HUC 8 was one of nine Iowa watersheds where flood disaster declarations and other considerations created eligibility for the funds.

Water quality improvements were also expected to result from the implementation of wetlands, restored oxbows, and other structural practices in the IWA watersheds, but the pollution reduction component was by design not the primary consideration so as not to offend the sensibilities of landowners.

As of this writing, the North Raccoon WMA expects to spend about $545,000 on a nutrient reduction wetland, two stream restorations and a grade stabilization structure on Outlet Creek which drains Storm Lake (city and lake). The balance will go unspent, untapped by the farmers in what is likely the Corn Belt's most high-profile watershed. Watershed coordinator Marius Agua said "Only four of the dozens of landowners authority staff approached signed onto new conservation practices. In many cases, the landowners weren't agreeable to what we proposed. Most wanted their land still in production."[4]

In a second development,[5] perhaps in response to the nonspending problem, some of the northern counties have apparently decided that the (urban) Dallas and Polk county portions of the WMA are no longer welcome at the table, and that the WMA's watershed plan is unworkable. "There are serious fundamental differences between the developed Raccoon River area needs and the rural North Raccoon River area needs," according to Palo Alto County representative and tile drainage engineer Don Etler. "I seriously believe that forming two WMAs would be a major step in the right direction."[5] To that end, the Pocahontas Board of Supervisors passed a resolution that states:

> Polk and Dallas counties are not in the North Raccoon Watershed, and maps that show this (like the one shown above) have been produced erroneously by Iowa DNR;

> They (the supervisors) will not support any watershed management plan that the North Raccoon River Watershed Management Coalition may produce, which includes the Raccoon River, and any direct tributary land downstream from the mouth of the North Raccoon River.

Pocahontas County supervisor Clarence Siepker perhaps was the honest (if not noble) voice in this mess: "This just doesn't make sense to me. We want to make a watershed plan so we can get more grants, but we can't find a way to spend grant money on projects this cycle. What's the point?" And four other northern counties agreed. Using an argument riper than a roadkill raccoon on a July day, they asserted the plan should have focused more on water quality instead of flooding.

I've only written one piece for this space since March 4, compared to 2-3 per month over the previous year. One reason for this has been the pandemic; there has been so much news that I figured I might have a hard time competing for your reading time. Then, I had this one mostly written about 10 days ago, and all hell breaks loose [nationwide protests over the George Floyd murder]. But another reason I haven't written much lately relates to a harsh review of my essays by someone who gets paid to know the difference between good and bad writing.

One comment I received was that "we're not all as angry as he is" and that, to paraphrase, I should plot more of a middle-of-road strategy that lets the facts speak for themselves. Well, you know what, the facts have been speaking pretty dispassionately for a half a century and here we are, still arguing whether or not certain counties lie within well-established watershed boundaries, because those counties might actually want some accountability when it comes to their drinking water. If this doesn't make a person angry or frustrated, then I may not be their read du jour.

The multi-generational slog to improve Iowa water quality and especially that of the Raccoon River has often been portrayed as a struggle between city slickers and the hardscrabble rural Iowa underdog. Former Governor Branstad even said the Des Moines Water Works declared war on rural Iowa. My take on it is a little bit different.

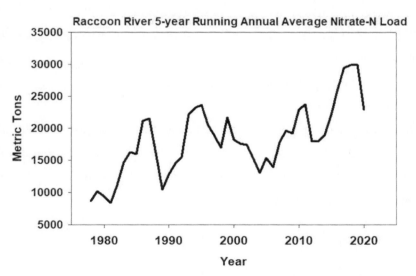

5-year running annual average Nitrate-N load for the Raccoon River at Des Moines. Since 1974, about 1.8 billion pounds of nitrogen have exited the Raccoon River at its confluence with the Des Moines River in downtown Des Moines.

At its core, the issue of Raccoon River water quality is this: a few holding as hostage the water belonging the masses. The real underdogs have always had to wallow in the downstream mud. How else do you explain a half century of bad water? I'll just say it: this is about a recalcitrant minority's license to impair the water and ensure that license lasts for as long as possible. How does a watershed's landowners leave $2 million in public funds lying on the table while more than 500,000 people are left to cope with the impairment? And how are we to embrace and invest in voluntary strategies when there are no volunteers?

In a 2018 letter to the *Des Moines Register*,[1] then-Des Moines Water Works General Manager Bill Stowe illustrated the contrast between the Iowa Great Lakes and the Raccoon River. Governor Reynolds had just signed a bill restricting pesticide applications near West Okoboji and other Iowa glacial lakes, upon whose shores lie some of Iowa's most expensive real estate. Stowe quoted Iowa legislators that were fearful that West Okoboji would become "another Flint, Michigan," and he lamented that the Raccoon River and Des Moines water customers didn't merit this sort of consideration. It's apparent where our body politic deems water quality regulation appropriate, and where it doesn't.

But I'm not hopeless and I'm certainly not always angry. I detect a different kind of vibe in this rotten raccoon story. Desperation. When you're redrawing maps to prevent the tide from eroding your petrified position, the gig is about up.

WHEN THE SHIP COMES IN

Presidential election campaigning, COVID pandemic, George Floyd murder, and Black Lives Matter protests were all happening in the summer of 2020 when I wrote this essay. A lot of the discussion around both COVID and BLM focused on rights and privileges and the difference between the two. I felt then and still do that this discussion is relevant within the context of Iowa's water quality, and what we value and don't value. Likely our most-valued natural resource for recreation is the Iowa Great Lakes region of Dickinson County. If Iowa has a playground for the rich and famous, this is it. It's not a coincidence that our lawmakers look at the water here differently than they do our polluted lakes and streams across the rest of the state.

The photo above (credit David Thoreson) was taken at Iowa's West Lake Okoboji this past 4th of July weekend. Ignoring for a while what it may show about the effectiveness of volunteerism in suppressing the coronavirus, I'd like to point out that this is one area of Iowa where our legislature has chosen to pursue a regulatory framework to protect water quality, ostensibly to protect West Okoboji as a source of drinking water. Speaking of drinking water, some of those boats do look nice enough to have a head but.....on second thought I won't take that sentence any further.

Dickinson County, home to West Okoboji and the other Iowa Great Lakes (Big Spirit, East Okoboji, and some smaller nearby lakes), has worked hard to protect their water resources, which they see as an economic engine for the region. Numerous watershed, wetland construction, monitoring, and urban stormwater projects help characterize the stressors and stem the flow of pollution into this interconnected lake system, and help make it a vacation destination.

The lakes still suffer from inputs of nutrients and other pollutants and the water quality on Big Spirit and East Okoboji is far from pristine. Nuisance algae blooms are fairly common and there are some other problems. But West Lake's depth (at 136 feet the deepest lake in Iowa) essentially entombs the incoming pollution, allowing the epilimnion (upper layer of the lake) to remain relatively unscathed. As a result, West Lake is very clear and hosts a great recreational fishery, of which I can attest.

I don't recommend fishing on July 4.

The unique (for Iowa) clarity of West Lake has helped make its shoreline the priciest real estate in Iowa. The state's most expensive single family dwelling is there, and a quick look at Zillow shows 20 lakeside residences currently for sale with an asking price greater than $1 million ($1.1 to 5 million). Zillow values almost every residence with frontage on West Okoboji, which is almost completely developed, at greater than $1 million. Nearby Big Spirit lake, also a good recreational fishery, is shallow and thus more vulnerable to nutrient pollution, and shorefront property there goes for much less than West Okoboji. Green water tends to suck the green out of nearby real estate.

As I said, Dickinson County and a long list of individuals and organizations have worked tirelessly to slow water quality degradation of the lakes. The county has been especially hostile to the livestock industry[1] and has long argued that the existing Master Matrix framework for livestock facility siting is a failure. In a 2015 letter to Iowa DNR,[1] the county supervisors said "Dickinson County relies on a combina-

West Lake Okoboji bass.

tion of industry, tourism and farming to advance our overall economic well-being. For more than a century, these economic forces have worked in concert such that today Dickinson County is one of the most economically stable and fastest growing counties in Iowa." Out of Iowa's 99 counties, Dickinson County is #2 in per capita income[2], beating out the city slickers in Polk (3rd), Linn (5th), Johnson (7th) and Scott (9th) counties.

Now there are some who say that manure actually protects water quality[3] and plays no role in the Gulf of Mexico Dead Zone,[4] and so some others might wonder why Dickinson County doesn't open the barn door to new CAFO construction. What is sort of curious is how the county has managed to be as successful as it has been in getting legislators, agencies and others to help them manage for a diverse economy that values their natural resources.

As you read what follows, rest assured that I think the lakes and especially West Okoboji merit special consideration and protective measures because of the unique ecological and geological features they provide to Iowans. But I have to say that we have many other natural gems that do not merit such attention. Clayton County's Bloody Run Creek, for example. This small, short and cold river supports an excellent trout fishery and has long been one of Iowa's most undisturbed streams. But time after time, the locals (Clayton and Allamakee counties, 74th and 84th in per capita income) are forced to defend the stream from stressors like highway construction (mid 1980s) and a 10,000 head cattle feedlot (2017), losing in both cases. The feedlot has twice been fined $10,000 for polluting the stream[5], which, at $2/cow doesn't seem like much when Iowa DNR values the economic value of a trout around $15.[6] Go figure, literally and figuratively.

Feel free to disagree, but I think I'm standing on a pretty sturdy limb when I say that the 4th of July photo shown above, the property values on West Lake Okoboji, our legislature's willingness to protect the lake with special laws, and the county supervisors' zeal in preserving its clarity, are all related. If you like fishing or swimming or sailing in Lake Darling or Backbone Lake or Bloody Run Creek and are bothered by their condition, well, you better learn to just deal with it.

When I first saw that Independence Day Okoboji photo, I couldn't help but think about it against the backdrop of everything else going on in our country right now, which to me circles around the words "privilege" and "right," and how we comingle them. The privilege/right to work from home, out of harm's way. The privilege/right to not wear a mask, to go to a bar, to be treated fairly and humanely by our police and our government. The right (privilege some would say) to protest injustice.

How does this all relate to our water here in Iowa? Clearly some have the privilege to impair our water, and many of those would say they have a right to do just that. And some of us have more of a privilege than others to use the cleanest of our lakes (and yes, I know there is public access to West Okoboji). I'd even count myself as among this last group, although I don't own any property there and don't know anybody that does.

If you have children coming of age, then I think you know that big change is at our doorstep. Some privileges may endure, but the privileged will have to fight dirty to keep them. Maybe I'm wrong, but I don't think I am. And I don't think I'm being political when I say that.

I've always been sort of fascinated by Bob Dylan, and when faced with questions about the (supposed) political nature of his early work, he said this: "To be on the side of people who are struggling for something doesn't necessarily mean you're being political." I think this is good and correct, and it's tragic that the privileged of our country have comingled "struggle" with "political" in a way that is not unlike the comingling of "privilege" and "right."

You might recognize the title of this essay as the same as the 1963 Bob Dylan song. The entire poem is like an Orwell prophesy. Here's the end:

Dylan. Photo credit: VF News and Columbia Records.

Oh, the foes will rise
With the sleep still in their eyes
And they'll jerk from their beds and think they're dreamin'
But they'll pinch themselves and squeal

And know that it's for real
The hour when the ship comes in
Then they'll raise their hands
Sayin' we'll meet all your demands
But we'll shout from the bow your days are numbered
And like Pharaoh's tribe
They'll be drownded in the tide
And like Goliath, they'll be conquered

EVERYONE IS RESPONSIBLE SO NO ONE IS RESPONSIBLE

About everybody has heard of the herbicide Roundup, which, along with ge-
netically modified (GMO) crops, revolutionized weed control in Corn Belt
agriculture. But as they say, nature bats last; in their haste to replace the
rapidly diminishing effectiveness of Roundup, farmers are looking to the past,
not the future.

Roundup is the Monsanto trade name for the isopropylamine salt of glyphosate, and it is also known to chemists as N-(phosphonomethyl)glycine. As organic compounds go, it is not a complex molecule.

Chemical structure of glyphosate (Roundup).

The chemical is a broad-spectrum herbicide, meaning it can kill a lot of plant species. It's been especially effective on annual grasses and broadleaf weeds that have been the bane of farmers since the dawn of agriculture. It was first synthesized by the Monsanto chemist John Franz and his team in 1970, and he received a $5 bonus for obtaining a patent for the chemical. Franz was a very distinguished scientist, and as far as I know, is still alive.

Glyphosate became one of the most important chemicals in human history when other Monsanto scientists were able to genetically modify annual crops in ways that left them invulnerable to the herbicide. It quickly became the dream chemical for agriculture, annihilating everything in its path that didn't have the DNA antidote that was inserted into canola, alfalfa, cotton, sorghum, wheat, sugar beets, and most importantly for Iowa, corn and soybeans. Roundup "ready" soybeans were developed in 1996, and farmers loved this weed control formula so much that by 2005, an astounding 87% of all U.S. soy contained the magic genes. In fact, farmers were so head-over-heels for Roundup, they loved it to death, as we shall see.

Now let me say at this point that I'm not, nor have I ever been, a Roundup hater. Firstly, the stuff was safer and easier to use, and seemed to be less toxic to humans and animals, than many of the older herbicides it displaced. Secondly, it very likely did have some peripheral environmental benefits because it reduced the need for weed control tillage, which reduced erosion. On the other hand, it was also so effective that it possibly contributed to the decline of milkweed which of course is necessary for the life cycle of the monarch butterfly. But on the whole, my view on Roundup/glyphosate has always been that if you're going to insist on having border-to-border corn and soy carpeting, you might as well Scotchgard it with Roundup.

But alas, it was inevitable that the law was going to catch up to Glyphosate and throw it in the hoosegow. The law of natural selection, that is.

It turns out that in nature, it's damn hard to kill every single individual of a species unless you eradicate its habitat. Any one or pair of individuals that survives an attempted murder by poisoning is going to pass on that skill to its offspring. And in the case of problem weeds, there are A LOT of offspring. One pigweed plant (Palmer Amaranth) can produce a million seeds. If only 0.01% of the seeds have Roundup resistant DNA, that leaves 100 potential plants producing 1 million seeds each the following year.

Soybean field filled with Roundup-resistant pigweed. Image credit: No-till Farmer.com.

Weed resistance was hastened by starry-eyed farmers whose over-reliance on glyphosate was, in the words of USDA researchers, "the primary factor underlying the evolution of GR (glyphosate resistant) weeds."[1] The fate of GMO soybeans was and is more closely tied to glyphosate than is corn; corn develops an early canopy and thus does a better job of depriving sunlight to growing weeds.

Enter Dicamba

Dicamba (3,6-dichloro-2-methoxybenzoic acid) has been around longer than glyphosate (depending on the source, it was discovered sometime between 1942 and 1958) and registered as an herbicide in the U.S. in 1962.[2] If like me you remember seeing Banvel commercials during halftime of the girls' state basketball tournament TV broadcast, well, that was dicamba. Until recently, dicamba was used mainly to kill broadleaf weeds in corn, and it's always been known

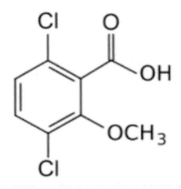
Chemical structure of Dicamba.

that it was a no-no around soybean, which of course is a broadleaf. But with Roundup facing a life sentence in Evolution Prison, the cowboys and cowgirls at Monsanto developed a soybean variety genetically modified to resist dicamba's killing action. EPA approved the technology in 2016, and thus began a rodeo that continues to this day.

The problem with dicamba is that it likes to ride the range, especially on hot and windy days. Roundup is like a plow horse compared to this wild mustang. And ride the range it did. Almost immediately, dicamba users started killing or damaging their neighbors' Roundup-ready and organic soybeans, peaches, grapes, tomatoes and who knows what all. Missouri and Arkansas banned dicamba in 2017 and lawsuits began to fly. Farmers elsewhere felt compelled to adopt the technology just so their crop wouldn't be at the mercy of their neighbors' dicamba. An attempt at herd immunity of sorts. If you can't count on your neighbor to stop community spread, then I guess you have to resort to drastic measures.

Which brings us to 2020. On June 3, EPA cancelled the registration for three dicamba formulations because those ponies wouldn't stay in the corral. Pretty much everybody had growing soybeans in the field by then and a lot of farmers were ready to spray dicamba onto them as a post-emergent herbicide. Having 10s or 100s of thousands of dollars of seeds in the ground, with potentially no ability to spray weed killer on the crop, put a lot of shorts in a bunch. Even though most states said they wouldn't enforce the ban, farmers all over Iowa went rogue and started applying the stuff in hot and windy conditions. I think you can probably guess what happened, but if you want the details, go to note 3 ("What went wrong in Iowa," Dicamba).[3]

Two things especially bothered me about this whole mess. The first was the kneejerk reaction to assign the calamity to the weather, and not to farmer decisions or production system vulnerabilities or an economic framework that compels individuals to put their own self-interest ahead of their neighbors' and the environment. Where have I heard that before? Time after time after maddening time, we hear our water quality problems are not because of our farming system, its practitioners, and its enablers, but rather the weather. Now this.

One commodity organization went so far as to say that the dicamba situation was the result of a "perfect storm" of weather conditions.[3] "There were poor weather conditions during application and then hot, dry conditions. It's tough to pinpoint the real culprit." Seriously? Is personal responsibility not part of the equation here? Here's the rub: everyone's responsible so no one is responsible. This is the same exact rationalization that drives water pollution in our state.

Am I crazy to ask this question: When will farmers and the industry in general ever take responsibility for the negative consequences that happen beyond the field? It's pretty clear the "feed the world" virtue signaling is designed, at least in part, to excuse the environmental wreckage produced by the system.

The second thing that motivated me to write this was a new term (for me) I read about: atmospheric loading. Loading is a term we frequently use in hydrology to describe the mass of a pollutant being transported by a stream. Here is what it means in the context of dicamba drift: "Atmospheric loading refers to so much dicamba moving into the atmosphere that it is difficult, if not impossible, to identify the specific application that resulted in injury to a field. This is what appears to have occurred across much of Iowa in 2020."[4]

Like Roundup, dicamba is not particularly toxic to human beings. That does not mean there is zero risk connected to exposures. With the smelly chemicals in manure regularly riding the wind into the center of Iowa's biggest cities, do we not have to consider the idea that just about every Iowan could have been breathing in some measurable amount of dicamba this summer? I challenge you to find any discussion about this from any of the Ag advocacy organizations, or from our agencies charged with serving all Iowans, and not just the 2% of us that farm.

So how to finish. Can we rely on producers to voluntarily fix our water quality problems, when they clearly have a brazen disregard for their own farmer neighbors? Count me as skeptical. From where I sit, this seems to be an industry that is drunk on propaganda, public subsidies, and political power, and that has a contempt for the environmental objectives of its neighbors and customers.

This is not sustainable.

LAND OF MILK AND MONEY

Hy-Vee, whose slogan is a "helpful smile in every aisle," is a big grocery store chain in Iowa and a few other states, and almost every living Iowan has been inside one of their stores. It's one of the largest privately held companies in the U.S. One of their Ankeny (Des Moines suburb) employees dumped warm milk down a storm drain in the wake of the 2020 derecho windstorm that left much of Iowa without electricity for days. The resulting fish kill in Fourmile Creek spawned social media outrage that also lasted for days and inspired this essay. Professors Silvia Secchi and Dave Cwiertny provided some information and inspiration for this one.

In the electricity-free aftermath of the derecho, somebody at the Ankeny Hy-Vee grocery store dumped 800 gallons of milk down the storm sewer. No number of helpful smiles were able to keep this milk from entering Fourmile Creek, which runs along the north and east sides of my hometown.

Ah yes, Fourmile. Way back before Gerald Ford was president, and long before today's suburban Little League infields looked like Wrigley on a Memorial Day afternoon, Ankeny boys like me played Little League baseball on dirt fields in the Fourmile floodplain east of town. There was none of today's pretentious sports complex naming associated with those four diamonds, as the only thing that was complex was the strange goo that coated the outfield after the crick's frequent wildcat floods. The place was not entirely without charm; I do recall a concession stand with Orange Crush and snow cones and such, which were your reward for a victory. Losers got cold rice topped with milk and cinnamon after they got back home. At least that's what you got at my house.

So enough of that reminiscing.

Storm sewers are meant (usually) to convey storm and snowmelt water directly to a receiving stream. But as you probably know, storm water can carry a lot of other junk into the sewer including dirt, trash, pet waste and who knows what else.

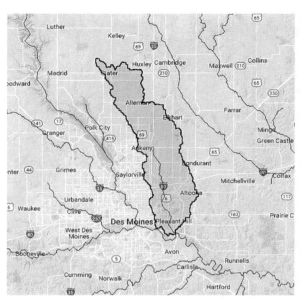

The Fourmile Creek watershed covers 93 square miles. The stream is about 40, not 4, miles long.

And doofuses do deliberately dump stuff into storm sewers despite (or maybe in spite of?) our efforts to label them with stenciled images of dead fish, ducks, and frogs.

The day after the Ankeny storm sewer became Milky Way, a bunch of Fourmile fish died because, as bacteria break down milk, they consume dissolved oxygen, and the fish suffocate. Milk has what we call in the biz a high Biochemical Oxygen Demand (BOD), which is a quantifiable water quality parameter and a mainstay of wastewater treatment plant operation, monitoring and regulation. The grocery store gaffe was intensified by the drought-driven low flow in Fourmile. To Hy-Vee's credit, they didn't blame the weather for their water pollution, like some others I could name.

As any kid knows, spilt 2% is hard to hide and our government agency charged with regulating and punishing such behavior (DNR) was on it like stink on sour milk. If you don't know, a regulatory

Milky Fourmile Creek. Photo credit: Iowa DNR.

agency looks at events such as this much like Mickey Mantle looked at hanging curve balls. Let's just say this one had "upper deck" written all over it from the start.

Mantle watching one fly into the upper deck. Photo credit: SI Vault.

And the outrage directed toward Hy-Vee on social media. Oh, the outrage. It made me wonder how our water got so degraded in the first place, and if any of these people had actually seen or smelled Fourmile Creek even once in the last 50 years.

Now, don't get me wrong here. Hy-Vee needs to be creamed by the DNR, but part of me has to wonder, why are we Iowans so callous about our water resources, and why would one of us thoughtlessly dump 800 gallons of anything down a storm sewer? It's not like we don't enjoy, or don't want to enjoy, recreating in our lakes and streams. Heck, I was at Saylorville

Reservoir outside of Des Moines last weekend, and the boats were too numerous to count. Folks were even awake for wake-boarding at 6:30 Sunday morning, but apparently not woke to the hazards of body contact with toxic algae in the green soup.

As it turns out, there is research that has examined this callous mentality. The economist Elinor Ostrom (1933-2012) was awarded the Nobel Prize in economics for her work analyzing economic governance of the commons. In this context, the commons is/are the cultural and natural resources accessible to all members of a society, including things like lakes and streams that are not owned privately and (presumably) managed for both individual and collective benefit.

In her 1999 paper "Revisiting the Commons: Local Lessons, Global Challenges,"[1] Ostrom stated that "For users [of the resource] to see major benefits, resource conditions must not have deteriorated to such an extent that the resource is useless, nor can the resource be so little used that few advantages result from organizing."

Fourmile Creek does have potential as a recreational water body for paddlers, anglers and wildlife observers. It's part of the Polk County Water Trails project, which aims to enhance water recreation opportunities in the

Elinor Ostrom. Photo credit: Holger Motzkau, Wikimedia Commons.

Des Moines metropolitan area. People have invested, both with their time and their money, in improving its condition.

But Fourmile has never really been more than a conduit for agricultural and urban runoff from northern and eastern Polk County, and northeast Des Moines proper has suffered devastating floods because of its altered hydrology. You can see small changes happening here and there with attempts at streambank restoration, but the water quality is not distinguishable from when I was getting eaten alive by mosquitos while playing right field in its floodplain.

Water quality in our big rivers like the Iowa, Cedar, Raccoon, and Des Moines (which receives water from Fourmile) will never get better until we fix the Fourmiles. How do we do it? Ostrom said that "in all cases, individuals must overcome their tendency to evaluate their own benefits and costs more intensely than the total benefits and costs for a group."

In other words, we need to quit thinking selfishly about the almighty dollar and give some thought to what is best for the common good.

ON BROTHELS AND CATHEDRALS

Although declining, Northeast Iowa's Bloody Run Creek has the best water quality of any stream in the state, mainly because not much of the watershed area is suitable for crop production. The watershed lies in Iowa's portion of the Driftless area, a unique and nearly unglaciated portion of the Corn Belt, unique because it is home to some cold water streams that support trout and other species that don't thrive elsewhere in the region. The area has always had some agriculture—mainly diverse crop-livestock farms and some dairy. But the last 30 years or so has seen a gradual transition from that production system to one more typical of the rest of Iowa: corn-soybean cash crops every year, with livestock in confinements. This is a story about Bloody Run Creek that is still ongoing as of February 2022.

Clayton County's Bloody Run Creek is designated an "Outstanding Iowa Water" by the Iowa DNR because limestone geology and a modestly undisturbed watershed support a clear, cold stream that is home to trout and other pollution-intolerant species. In a state with 72,000 miles of streams and 120 or so lakes and reservoirs, Bloody Run is one of only 34 water bodies we can call outstanding.

In the last 10 years, DNR has stocked more than 113,000 trout in Bloody Run,[1] and brown trout are naturally reproducing in the stream. DNR figures the economic value of a trout to be about $15,[2] so if your brain is angling to total that up, the public has invested about $1.7 million just in fish for this stream.

All things considered, a person might expect that our government would tenaciously protect, and our industries would respect, Bloody Run Creek and the other 33 "outstanding" waters, since there is only one for every 320,000 Iowans. Yes, a reasonable person could expect that.

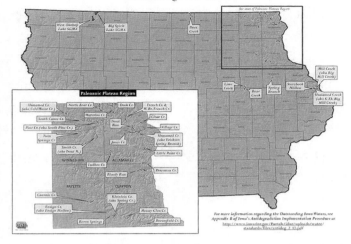

Outstanding Iowa Waters

Iowa Outstanding Waters. Image Credit: Iowa Department of Natural Resources.

In 2017, a company identified as Walz Energy began construction on a ~10,000 head cattle feedlot near Monona in the Bloody Run watershed. Cattle are big eating machines, and as such they produce a lot of waste, about 14 times as much as a human being when considering the nutrient and solids content of that waste. Even under the most ideal circumstances and weather conditions, it would be a colossal challenge to reconcile this operation with maintaining Bloody Run in its present condition. The creek's watershed is less than half the size of the city of Des Moines, where of course the human waste is processed and treated in a wastewater treatment plant.

In the case of Walz Energy, the original intention was to anaerobically digest the manure and then capture and sell the natural gas generated by the process. Now I will say that this is not a terrible idea if you're trying to manage a lot of manure, and as coincidence would have it, some years back I edited a textbook[3] on this subject.

Unfortunately, the Walz Energy operation was a Bloody mess from the beginning and a failure to control erosion during construction resulted in muddy runoff and two $10,000 fines from DNR. DNR staff requested the case be transferred to the Attorney General's office where fines can be much more punitive—up to $5,000 per day. But Walz made a pledge to the Jumbo Shrimp Commission in July 2018 to fix the problems,[4] and the commission declined to let the Attorney General take over. Wait a minute, what was I thinking, I meant the governor-appointed Environmental Protection Commission, which provides oversight for DNR's environmental protection efforts. Sorry for being such a (oxy)moron.

As it turns out, there were two parties in this deal. One side of beef was comprised of some energy guys and on the other side were some cattle guys, the Walzes. The energy guys apparently ran out of money before the $15 million digesters could get built.[5] Maybe they had some negative income (no more oxymorons, I promise). Or maybe those DNR fines were the straw that broke the camel's back, but 20 grand seems like chump change next to the $25 million that this idea was going to cost.

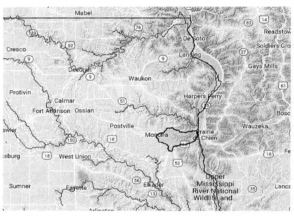

Bloody Run Creek Watershed of Northeast Iowa.

Anyway, the cattle guys saw red because supposedly they're out $10 million and so they filed a lawsuit late last year against the energy guys and blah blah blah rich guy problems. With cattlemen being what they are, however, they would still like to raise some cattle in the feedlots and accompanying six barns that have been built, and that brings us to the here and now.

Without a digester, that manure has to go somewhere nearby and that somewhere is crop ground. Remember that the Bloody Run watershed is less than half the size of the city of Des Moines. The operation, now called Supreme Beef, has submitted a proposed Nutrient Management Plan (NMP) to DNR for an 11,500-head cattle operation that will generate 30.5 million gallons of manure per year, and that manure will contain 1.2 million pounds of nitrogen (N) and 762,000 pounds of phosphorus (P).

To get rid of the manure, they will apply 269 lbs of N per acre of corn grown in consecutive years to land that they say will produce 224 bushels per acre of grain. I don't know if all the receiving fields are in Clayton County, but the average corn yield there the last five years has been 203 bu/ac, which would presumably require less N than 224 bu/ac corn. The bigger your expected yield, the more manure N you are allowed to apply.

Side Note: Almost every NMP I have ever seen, and I've seen a few, projects corn yields above the county average. Coincidence? To paraphrase Garrison Keillor, maybe Iowa is the place where all the farmers are good looking and all the corn yields are above average. Who knows.

Using Iowa State University's N rate calculator,[6] I get a recommended continuous corn application rate of 240 lbs/acre (29 lbs/ac less than the proposed) when I put in $3.25 per bushel for the current price of corn and $0 for the fertilizer cost, since they are getting free manure from their own cows.

On the phosphorus (P) side, many of the proposed fields have already tested in the Very High category, meaning that the crop would not need any added P. However, because you can't take P out of PooP, the fields are still going to get a heavy dose—41 pounds per acre, even though recommendations for continuous corn in this very high soil P condition would be zero pounds per acre.[7]

I might also say that this operation lies within the most environmentally sensitive part of Iowa, where the groundwater is already nitrate-contaminated[8] because many of the fields are like those in this NMP—20 to 30 inches of soil atop porous bedrock that it is a sieve for water-borne contaminants to travel through to aquifers and limestone streams like Bloody Run. Adding insult to insult, one of the fields is bordered by 11 mapped sinkholes which rapidly convey surface contaminants to aquifers.

If you're among the unwashed in such matters, what I just described may sound preposterous. Why would our laws and our government and one of our industries even consider something this atrocious? The truth is, what I just described repeats itself month after month, year after year, legally, all over Iowa, because of the way our laws governing livestock production are structured. This is one reason why our water, yours and mine, is polluted.

Are we not allowed to have even 34 "outstanding" waters? Apparently not. If agriculture is willing to take Bloody Run, rest assured they will take the other 33. And this should not surprise you, coming from an industry that is openly contemptuous of the state's largest city for wanting clean drinking water.

From where I sit, the industry doesn't even blush anymore when making a grab for our land and water. Where are the organizations (both on the Ag and environmental sides) that purport to be advocates of clean water? Are they ok with this? Where is the outrage? Or are they so concerned about self-preservation that they will sacrifice a Bloody Run? I think they are. I know they are. Our pollution problems have enabled more than a few to live a secure and comfortable life.

To be honest, and I mean this, I have to hand it to them on the Ag side—they have done a fantastic job of guarding their brothels. But who is guarding the public's cathedrals?

DREAM ON

Many of our lakes and streams are impaired by E. coli *bacteria. There has been a lot of discussion regarding this, and how much of a threat these organisms pose for people wanting to swim, paddle and fish in Iowa waters is questioned by some. My take on this is that our futility in trying to solve the problem has led some to think we should probably just live with it.*

E. coli *(Escherichia coli)* belong to a group of bacteria sourced to the intestinal tract of vertebrates, including human beings. Much of the mass contained within a stool is the living and dead bodies of these bacteria, and billions upon billions of them are necessary to orchestrate one movement.

There are many strains of E. coli and most do not cause disease. At least six strains, however, are known to be pathogenic (i.e. disease-causing) with the most common of these producing a toxin called "Shiga" which can damage your intestinal lining and cause diarrhea. This strain is commonly known as E. coli 0157:H7, and has also caused kidney failure and death in people who ingest it.

Chlorine easily kills E. coli and thus illness resulting from its presence in treated drinking water is rare. Public (municipal) water supplies regularly monitor for it, precisely because it is so abundant in fecal matter. It's a good indicator that a drinking water system may have been compromised by an intrusion of untreated sewage, usually in the piping that distributes water throughout a community.

Because the number of species of microorganisms present in a lake or river is vast, it's impossible to test for them all and so we also use E. coli as an indicator for safe water recreation. While E. coli themselves may not be pathogenic (although indeed they may be), their presence indicates the possible co-presence of other fecal organisms that are likely to be pathogens for most people. These include things like *Camphylobacter*, *Cryptosporidium*, and *Salmonella*, all of which can be found in animal and human waste. These organisms cause more than 3 million annual illnesses in the U.S.

Determining a "safe" or "protective" level of *E. coli* bacteria in a lake or river is complicated and not without controversy. EPA has settled on a value of 235 colony forming units (CFU) of *E. coli* per 100 ml of water. *E. coli* levels can vary dramatically over short periods of time, and so regulatory agencies can evaluate the geometric mean of multiple samples taken over 30 days; when the geo mean is used, the protective threshold for recreation is 126 CFU/100 ml.

What does EPA mean by "protective of human health" when considering *E. coli* and contact recreation in a lake or stream, where immersion and ingestion of the water is likely? In this case, a threshold of 235 CFU/100ml (or a geometric mean of 126) would be expected to produce illness in no more than 36 people in 1,000 (i.e. 3.6%). So, meeting the standard does not equate to zero risk.

Many Iowa lakes and streams harbor unacceptable levels of *E. coli*. Our state has 813 impairments of water quality on 622 lakes, stream stretches, and wetlands (some water bodies have more than one impairment). Of the 813 impairments, about half are caused by elevated *E. coli* levels, implying those waters are not suitable for body contact recreation sometime during the year. Other types of impairments include fish kills, low dissolved oxygen, and toxic chemicals.

Recently, I took a look at some *E. coli* data for the two major streams that meet in downtown Des Moines, the Raccoon and Des Moines rivers. Water skiing is popular on the Des Moines River above the Center Street dam; the Scott Street bridge and dam just below the confluence of the two rivers is the most fished place in Iowa; and the Raccoon River flows through Des Moines Water Works Park (largest municipal park in the U.S.) as well as Gray's Lake Park, Raccoon River Park, Walnut Woods State Park, and Browns Woods County Park, the last three situated in West Des Moines. You would be hard-pressed to find any city in the U.S. with a greater potential for river recreation than Des Moines and surrounding area.

But the water.

Using samples collected at the Des Moines Water Works intakes from 2010 up until the present day, I determined that the Raccoon River consistently meets the 235 CFU/100 ml threshold only during the cold weather months of November through March, when water recreation (at least for me) is limited to pulling fish up through holes in the ice. In the recreational season of April-October, more than half the days (50.2%) see *E. coli* levels exceed the protective threshold for safe recreation in the Raccoon River.

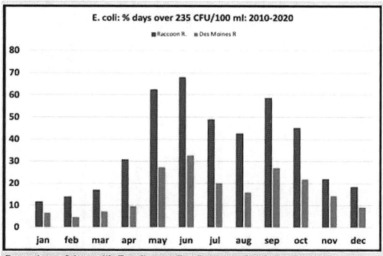

Percentage of days with *E. coli* exceeding the recreational standard (235 CFU/100ml) on the Des Moines and Raccoon Rivers.

The situation is modestly better for the Des Moines River, with 22% of the days in the recreational season (Apr-Oct) exceeding the protective threshold. It's not a mystery why *E. coli* levels are lower in the Des Moines River—detention of water 6 miles upstream in Saylorville Reservoir exposes the bacteria to sunlight and other stressors, causing them to perish before they exit the reservoir.

It's no secret that we have a lot of livestock in Iowa and clearly some of these bacteria come from animal manure and the soils it is applied to. But *E. coli* do live in the gut of humans, pets and wildlife, so we can't exclude the possibility these other sources are impairing the metro rivers. To try to get a handle on this, I compared the Raccoon and Des Moines river data with what I thought might be a similar situation—the Mississippi River in downtown Minneapolis. It's bigger than both the Raccoon and Des Moines, but not by a lot; Minneapolis Miss is about 1.4 times larger than the combined flow of the Raccoon and Des Moines rivers below Scott Street. It's reasonable to assume that the human, pet, and wildlife contributions in Minneapolis are no greater than they are in Des Moines.

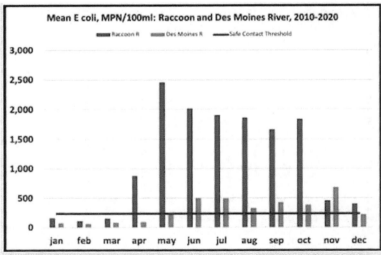

Mean (average) *E. coli* values on the Des Moines and Raccoon Rivers, with the safe contact threshold shown in the red line.

Using data from the Minnesota Pollution Control Agency, I found that the Mississippi is far cleaner, at least when it comes to fecal matter, than the Raccoon and Des Moines rivers. Looking at the

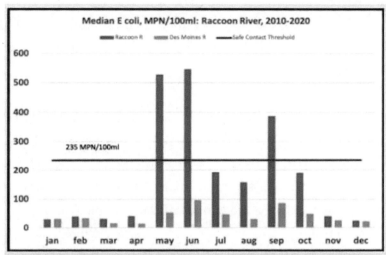

Median *E. coli* levels on the Des Moines and Raccoon Rivers, with the safe contact threshold shown by the red line. The median is the statistical value where half the samples are below, and half above, and some prefer this metric (over the mean) for bacteria levels.

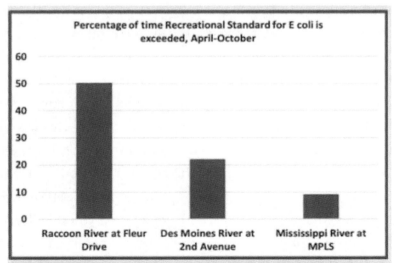

Percentage of time *E. coli* standard for safe recreation is exceeded, April-October.

April-October recreational period (no winter data was available), the Mississippi exceeds the recreational threshold only 9.2% of the time in downtown Minneapolis, compared to 22% of the time for the Des Moines River and 50.2% for the Raccoon River (2010-2019). What is especially striking are the "worst" or highest samples: 130,000 CFU/100 ml (Raccoon), 17,200 (Des Moines), but only 2,420 for the Mississippi.

There is some controversy in Iowa about whether or not *E. coli* is the best indicator for recreational suitability, and some would like to change the standard or the indicator or both. The impaired waters list is a lingering fart in the room that to some smells worse than liquid hog manure on a November night. My guess is that if we picked something other than *E. coli* to measure, these folks would stop grunting, at least for a while, because they think water quality would improve magically overnight—on paper. But the motives behind this idea are as transparent as gas station toilet tissue, in my estimation. Besides, if you start looking at other indicators, chances are you're going to find them unless they're unique to camels or elephants or some other exotic creature. This is definitely a "be careful what you wish for" scenario.

It's been more than a year ago now that I wrote "Iowa's Real Population," which featured the map on the right. Considering all our livestock animals and the waste they excrete, we effectively generate the fecal waste equivalent of Chicago, Tokyo, Rome, Paris, Oklahoma, and Alabama upstream of the city of Des Moines. Frankly, it would be a surprise if *E. coli* weren't lousy in the water flowing through Des Moines. And believe me when I tell you this: I'm not the first person doing science or policy to have thought this through.

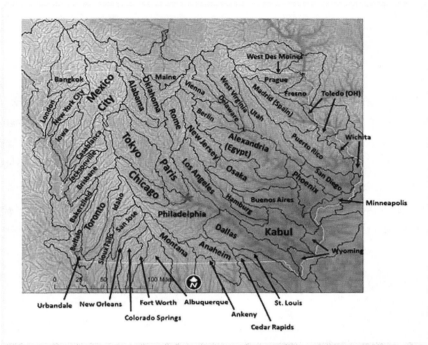

This map shows the human waste equivalent of the hogs, laying chickens, turkeys, and dairy and beef cattle in Iowa watersheds, based on literature values for nitrogen, phosphorus, and total solids content of the waste. The star represents the location of the city of Des Moines.

NO COUNTRY FOR OLD MEN

Trying to avoid contracting COVID over the 2020 Thanksgiving holiday, I drove my camper down to Arkansas, where the state park campgrounds were still open. I picked a park almost at random, jumped in the pickup and headed down there. It turned out to be a very enjoyable trip with a few nights spent at a beautiful location. This trip provided a contrast with our own sad situation in Iowa when it comes to the paucity of parks and other public lands where people can enjoy nature, and that inspired this essay.

I packed up my 20-year-old pickup and 35-year-old camper last week and took a Coronavirus-inspired trip to Arkansas. Iowa campgrounds have been closed for some time now, and those in Missouri closed October 31. Looking further south, I found that Arkansas state park campgrounds are open year-round, and I picked Crowley's Ridge State Park because of its proximity to Iowa (far NE Arkansas) and because there was a lake to fish.

Crowley's Ridge is one of the state's six landforms, a giant alluvial deposit formed near the prehistoric confluence of the Mississippi and Ohio Rivers. The 200-mile-long sandbar has been amended and elevated with an eon's worth of wind-blown loess, such that the feature bulges like an arthritic spine 200 feet above the surrounding alluvial plane.

Like Western Iowa's own Loess Hills, the soil on Crowley's Ridge is thick and fertile, and the first settlers to the area (Crowley was the first) farmed the ridge because the surrounding bottomlands were unmanageably wet. Also like our own Loess Hills, the soil was highly vulnerable to erosion because of slope and texture. But in contrast to Iowa, where 22% of the Loess Hills is still cropped with corn and soybean,[1] Arkansans had the good sense to surrender these hills to nature in the 1930s, and the ridge was re-forested to the original pine, oak and hickory, more characteristic of the Appalachians far to the east than the nearby Ozark Plateau to the west.

Arkansas landforms. Image credit: Arkansas Natural Heritage Commission.

The huge wetland complex that surrounded the ridge has been transformed to productive farm ground—soybeans and rice on the Mississippi side (east) and mainly rice on the Black River side (west). To and from the park, I drove along the west side and the views reminded me a lot of what I saw in Hubei Province, China. Table-top flat, a diesel pump, and an above ground fuel storage tank adorning the edge of every field, with dikes and water detention basins common. Much like Iowa, there was very little landscape diversity beyond rice production with exceptions being one field each of unharvested corn and sorghum. The Black River and its tributary, the Cache R., flow through this area and both looked as bad as anything you will see in Iowa. I did not see livestock other than an occasional goat and donkey, and the area did not look prosperous.

Although certainly no Iowa, agriculture is big in Arkansas with $8.5 billion in receipts, 15th-highest of the 50 states (Iowa is 2nd to California with $27.5 billion).[2] Like Iowa, Arkansas has also suffered from some high-profile water quality problems linked to agriculture. The state of Oklahoma sued 13 poultry producers in 2005 because phosphorus pollution from operators in both states was destroying the Illinois River and Ten Killer Lake.[3] Water quality improved over the last decade after the two states agreed on a stream standard for phosphorus of 0.037 ppm. Water quality standards for nutrients (nitrogen and phosphorus) have been strongly opposed by agricultural interests for Iowa lakes and streams.

Arkansas does clearly recognize that its natural areas have value. Somehow this state, with 30% less GDP, 10% fewer people and 15% less area, is able to afford 10 times more public land than Iowa. To be sure, our land is more valuable and more farmable. But if you've been to an Iowa park any time during

Civilian Conservation Corp Pavilion, Crowley's Ridge State Park.

the pandemic, you've seen the situation here in Iowa is disgraceful. All summer long, campgrounds, boat launches, the picnic areas and trails were busier than ever. Getting a weekend campsite was nearly impossible at times.

How does Arkansas do it? Arkansans voted in 1996 for a conservation sales tax that designates 1/8th of 1% percent of the state's general sales tax for their Game and Fish Commission (45% percent), State Parks (45%), Heritage Commission (9%) and Keep Arkansas Beautiful Commission (1%). Sound familiar?

It should sound familiar, because 63% of Iowa voters passed something similar in 2010, the Iowa Water and Land Legacy Act (IWILL), that created the Natural Resources and Outdoor Recreation Trust Fund. This would have designated a portion of new sales tax revenues to similar programs here in Iowa. But in Iowa, 63% isn't enough to overcome the entrenched power structure and the legislature thus far has refused to fund it.

You might recall that last year, Iowa legislators finally seemed like a decade was long enough to let the big hitters in agriculture get accustomed to ideas like the crazy liberals in Arkansas  have embraced: wildlife, nicer parks and better trails. But our guys warned us there was going to be a ransom: a reformulation of the funding scheme so more of the money would be funneled to farmers (i.e. on private land) because presumably they can't afford to stop polluting without public help.

So, speaking of money, it's interesting to take a look at farm incomes these past few years. USDA's Economic Research Service is forecasting net farm income to increase 43% in 2020, the fourth consecutive year of increase, bringing this metric to its highest level since 2013 and 32% higher than the 20-year average.[2] Although prices for corn, soybeans and some other commodities are a little higher than they have been in recent years, the main reason for robust farm profits is government money. Market Facilitation Payments (MFP) related to tariff relief and Coronavirus Food Assistance Program (CFAP) payments to farmers have ballooned the government portion of farm income to levels not seen in many years.

But still, it's a near certainty that if we want even a small taste of what Arkansas has, we will have to deal with extortion.

I know there are many people in Iowa's environmental community that are willing to capitulate and pay the ransom in a desperate attempt to claim one small victory for Iowa's natural resources. I have my own thoughts on this, and if you can't guess what they are by now, then I'm a really bad writer. Once again, I have to hand it to agriculture: they gambled 10 years ago that stalling would not be punished and the 63% would eventually become distracted. They knew their obfuscation would be rewarded.

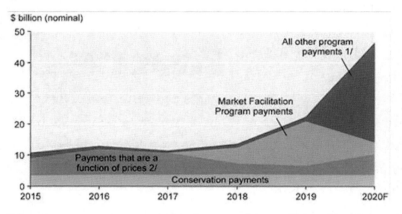

Direct government payments to farm producers, 2015-20F. Source: Economic Research Service, USDA, Farm Income and Wealth Statistics.

They were right.

Someone who is definitely not a bad writer is Cormac McCarthy. Toward the end of *No Country for Old Men*, a morose Sheriff Ed Tom Bell visits his hermit uncle Ellis, who is holed up with 12 cats in the ramshackle remains of an old ranch house in the West Texas desert. Ed Tom is despondent because he failed to capture the diabolical murderer, Anton Chigurh, before Chigurh killed several people and made off with $2.4 million in drug money. Ellis is trying to cheer up

Ed Tom the best he can when he tells him, "All the time you spend tryin' to get back what's been took from you, there's more going out the door. After a while you just try to get a tourniquet on it."

Is this where Iowans are, with our water, with our prairie streams and our great border rivers, the wetlands, and the rest of nature that was "took," first from the native people and then from us all? Sometimes I think it is.

DEFENDING PARIS

I once owned a 462 square foot house in Iowa City that was sold while I was assembling materials for this book. I used the utility charges on this tiny house to illustrate how city dwellers are required to mitigate stormwater pollution from their property compared to farmers.

The humble Iowa City Goosetown neighborhood is the location of my even humbler house, a three-room castle (three rooms, not three bedrooms) that can be seen in the background of the 1941 Grant Wood painting, *Spring in Town*. Wood taught painting at the University of Iowa from 1934-1941 before dying young in Iowa City of pancreatic cancer in 1942. *Spring in Town* was one of his last three works.

Grant Wood's *Spring in Town*, 1941. My house is in the upper right-hand corner.

The abstract for my house shows 1900 as the year of construction, 1900 being a euphemism the city uses for "unknown," which means it was built long before that. It's a cabin, basically. I'm not sure what the city does for houses actually built in 1900. There are several pre-Civil War houses in Iowa City.

The 462ft² house sits on a 6,750ft² lot; for the purposes of what I am writing here, I'm going to add 400ft² for my side of the street that runs in front of the house, so 7,150ft^2, or about 1/6th of an acre (0.16 ac).

The property taxes on this palace are $2,434 per year, which give-or-take is about what the property taxes are on 80 acres of earth's best farmland here in Iowa, an amount of land that can be worth more than $1,000,000 in some Iowa counties.

My house receives treated drinking water from the Iowa City water utility, my sanitary sewer waste is treated at the city's wastewater treatment plant, and of course there are monthly charges for both these things above and beyond the property tax bill.

I also pay $5 per month for a monthly stormwater utility charge. This is because Iowa City is an MS4 community,[1] meaning it has a Municipal Separated Storm Sewer System, 'separated' because it uses a different conveyance system than the sanitary sewer. Not all communities have separated sewers, but many larger cities do. Milwaukee is one exception that comes to mind; Des Moines has been in the process of separating its stormwater from its sanitary sewer for a while now.

As an MS4 community, Iowa City is required by EPA and Iowa DNR to conduct certain activities that (a) reduce pollution in stormwater runoff, (b) protect water quality and (c) satisfy water quality requirements of the Clean Water Act, and all this is governed by a National Pollution Discharge Elimination System (NPDES) permit. Thus, the stormwater running off heaven's (and my) half of a third of an acre is regulated. My lot is part of the 4% of the USA covered by the stormwater regulation, an area that is home to 80% of the country's population. Iowa City and other similarly-sized communities have been regulated under Phase II of the stormwater regulation since 1999.

Since 1995, $35 billion taxpayer dollars have supported Iowa's agricultural production system, about $1,200 in total for every acre of farm ground in the state.[2] This includes public subsidies for crop insurance, disaster payments, commodity programs, and conservation programs. Conservation payments, much of which is focused on improving water quality, exceed $6 billion during that time, or about $210/acre.

UTILITY BILL
PAY ONLINE:

BILL DATE	ZONE	ACCOUNT # - CID #
12/02/2020	A	1047705 - 406084

SERVICE ADDRESS

SERVICE FROM	SERVICE TO
10/26/2020	11/23/2020

JONES, CHRISTOPHER S

IOWA CITY, IA 52245-6027

PAST DUE AMOUNT	CURRENT BILL AMOUNT
$0.00	$55.14

DATE CURRENT BILL DUE	TOTAL BALANCE DUE
12/17/2020	$55.14

CONSUMPTION INFORMATION

Page 1 of 1

Meter Number	Present Reading	Previous Reading	Cubic Feet Used	Read Code
080670590	37375	37100	275	ACTUAL READ

USAGE INFORMATION

	Cubic Feet	Gallons
Present Usage:	275	2,057
Average Monthly Usage:	326	2,440
Usage One Year Ago:	525	3,927

SUMMARY OF CURRENT CHARGES

WATER	14.16
SEWER	15.13
REFUSE	12.00
RECYCLING	6.00
ORGANICS (YARD WASTE & COMPOST)	2.00
STORMWATER RESIDENTIAL	5.00
WATER EXCISE TAX	0.85
TOTAL CURRENT CHARGES	55.14
CURRENT DUE AFTER 12/24/2020 (includes 5% late fee)	$57.86

Utility bill for my house. Stormwater utility charge outlined in red. Check your own water or utility bill to see what your charges might be.

Contrast that to my place. I pay $375 per acre every year to mitigate the stormwater coming off my property ($5 per month multiplied by 12 months divided by 0.16 acres) for water that is far less polluted than water draining off most farm ground.

Yes, I do know that farmers spend their own money on conservation practices, but as I have stated before, these are very often targeted to things like terraces and grass waterways that are primarily designed to conserve the productive capacity of the farm, and not to deliver environmental outcomes beneficial to public. In the case of terraces, they can actually degrade stream water quality. But Iowa farmers (and their landlords, since more than 50% of Iowa land is rented) would have to spend nearly $11 billion per year in total on stormwater mitigation to equal the amount I pay on a per acre basis.

In the 2018 Iowa State University Rural Life Survey,[3] 41% of farm landlords stated THEY HAD SPENT NOTHING ON CONSERVATION over the PAST 10 YEARS COMBINED, and 78% of these folks had spent less than $5,000. And this is not per acre, it's TOTAL. And folks, these are not poor people polluting our water.

Why does this perversion exist? Mainly because the Clean Water Act, passed by congress over Nixon's veto in an era (1972) when cities were seriously degrading water resources, let agriculture off the hook. The cities were forced to man-up and clean-up, which they largely did, first with wastewater treatment and now stormwater. Water quality in places like Iowa, where unregulated agriculture dominates land use, lags far behind other (regulated) places in the U.S.

National Map of Regulated MS4s

Regulated MS4 area represents 4% of the U.S. land area and > 80% of the population

Phase I
Phase II

Map created 2009

But this perversion exists for another reason: as citizens, we permit it to exist. We give license to agriculture to pollute and we pay for their half-hearted attempts to mitigate it. Some might say this is a provocative or inflammatory statement, but it is the stone-cold truth. We have 71,000 miles of streams and a couple of hundred lakes, and the latest Iowa DNR impaired waters list shows only 16 waterbody segments meet the standards for all of their designated uses.[4]

Disgraceful.

If you're eager to hear about clean beaches and clear streams, well, you better just learn to make do with the success stories that the Ag Family of advocacy organizations lathers on like a teenage boy with a bottle of Axe cologne before a date with the homecoming queen. These stories often feature some publicly supported built project on private land that include catch phrases like "stewardship", "one size doesn't fit all", and "we all want clean water", and they are very infrequently supported by any sort of water monitoring. Ag communication shops also like to pump out stories that imply some sort of false equivalence between urban and agricultural water pollution. A recent one inspired this piece. These fairytales usually talk about how the cities need to partner up with somebody, because finger pointing, unlike somebody polluting your water, is impolite. I can tell you where there is equivalence: partnering = get out your checkbook, at least if you live in town.

To be fair, our agencies and environmental organizations that purport to protect our water also like success stories, and their yarns bear an eerie resemblance to those written by the Ag industry. They have their own set of catchwords: soil health, resilience, sustainability. But these folks are like the nerdy science kid—no amount of Axe is ever going to help them get lucky. They get snubbed year after year, hoping in vain for a blown kiss from the Ag cheerleaders or their booster club in the capital. Take it from me, about all they get from the bullies and the cool kids is snickering. Want proof? Look at or smell your water.

Iowa's water quality situation frequently reminds me of that old joke about France.

Q: How many Frenchmen does it take to defend Paris?

A: Nobody knows, because it's never been tried before. Honestly, at this point I can only applaud the industry: they had the will to triumph, and triumph they have. Your water and your pocketbook are the collateral damage.

THIS MIGHT HURT SOME FEELINGS

I wrote this one not long after the 2020 election. Some folks in conservation and academia naturally felt that a transition from Trump to Biden could generate momentum that would help transform Iowa's corn-soybean-CAFO production system into something more environmentally sustainable. This "something" was being branded as Regenerative Agriculture, a concept I can support, but also something I feel strongly should not be sold as a solution to Iowa's water quality problems. I also worry that regenerative agriculture programs could devour a lot of public money without producing measurable environmental outcomes and further discredit the roles of academia, NGOs, and government in helping fix the water quality problem. In this and several other of my essays, I try to leverage the ideas of historian Howard Zinn to make the point that Iowa's water will only improve if everyday Iowans hold the industry and legislature accountable for its condition.

"To be radical is to simply grasp the root of the problem. And the root is us."
—Howard Zinn, 1999.

There's a page on my website where I post the PowerPoint slides from presentations I conduct. I took a look at that page this morning, and over the last five years, I have conducted 69 programs for various groups, or about one a month on average. I reckon that at about half of these I get the question, "what

Howard Zinn in 2009. Image from Wikimedia commons.

can be done," this in regard to Iowa water quality and pollution generated by the corn-soybean-CAFO production model.

People have been thinking about "what can be done" for a long time. Because of industry and farmer recalcitrance and hostility toward regulation, various ideas for improving water quality have focused on either (a) enticing farmers to voluntarily adopt practices that reduce erosion and nutrient loss without major modifications to the production system or (b), promotion of concepts like increased crop diversity and improved soil health that do require substantial management changes. I suppose you could also throw land retirement in there, but this has not been tried on any significant scale in Iowa since the 1980s.

The public has long been expected to be a financial participant in category (a) solutions, and Iowa's nutrient reduction strategy is aligned with this cost-share concept. It's also been apparent for a while now that momentum is building to ask the public to financially support category (b) solutions, and in fact this has already happened with public dollars used for cover crops, which are unharvested plants that help retain water and nutrients and enhance desirable soil qualities, thereby reducing water pollution.

This momentum seems to have gained steam since the 2020 election with the category (b) concept being repackaged (yet again) as regenerative agriculture. Regenerative agriculture focuses on building (or rebuilding) soil organic matter to improve water and nutrient cycling, reduce erosion, increase biodiversity, and sequester greenhouse gases. You can think of soil organic matter as the waste of live stuff and the remains of dead stuff, along with some fungi and other microscopic beasties that live in the soil. Various modern farming practices, including chemical use and aggressive tillage, tend to reduce organic matter and degrade that which remains.

The idea of regenerative agriculture in its several nomenclatures has been floated many times over the past 80-90 years or so, and has been embraced with varying degrees of seriousness. But the concept has never had widespread buoyancy in Corn Belt agriculture beyond a modest turn to port on tillage, that is, less mold-board plow (overturning the soil on top of itself) and more "conservation" tillage (disking and chiseling, primarily), something that was tugged along by conservation compliance in the 1985 Farm Bill. Conservation compliance required farmers that were cropping highly erodible land to adopt various soil conservation practices or face the dire consequence of being ineligible for federal farm subsidies. In Iowa, about 21% of the crop land is still in conventional tillage, 34% no-till, and 42% in reduced or "conservation" tillage.[1] Tillage is seen by many farmers as more necessary for corn than soybean. Cover crops are used on about 4% of Iowa's cropland, according to the 2018-2019 Iowa Nutrient Strategy progress report.[2]

With the incoming Biden administration apparently serious about climate change, many in the NGO, foundation and academic world are excited about the prospect of the federal treasury's barn door being flung open to help proselytize for regenerative agriculture. Born-again farmers would be paid to implement regenerative agriculture practices that will lay carbon to rest in their soils, instead of having it marauding around the atmosphere, melting polar ice caps and energizing super storms. And presumably this will improve water quality for the reasons stated earlier. This all is what we call "monetizing ecosystem services" in the biz, because apparently the intrinsic value of healthy soil, reduced erosion, and cleaner water is so low to the farmer that they won't do it unless we pay them to do it.

Now permit me to say that I am all for regenerative agriculture and I have stated so previously, albeit without using the specific term.

But there is a whiff of something moldy hovering over this. Even the optimists know these types of approaches will likely take generations to deliver the water quality we want. But there is a feeling of futility about Iowa water quality common among many—4% of the land in cover crops after eight years of the Iowa Nutrient Reduction Strategy is a kick in the crotch, let's just be honest. So we're going to give mouth-to-mouth to the constipated soil health movement of the last decade and rebrand the resulting Lazarus as regenerative agriculture. It'll probably be worth at least another 4-8 years of relevance for a lot of folks, relevance being the real long-term goal here and one of the reasons our water still stinks.

Again, to emphasize—I'm down with regenerative agriculture or whatever fancy ornamental names you want to hang on this tree. But for crying out loud, shouldn't we be asking agriculture to perform at some baseline level of environmental performance before brainstorming yet another unaccountable way to funnel your money to them for uncertain outcomes? These are folks that brag about the size of their bulging federal largesse while the rest of the country tries to recover from the worst crisis in a century. The public has been asked to invest over and over and over again in this production system; isn't it about time we had a say in how it is operated?

There are things we can do now that would improve water quality now. But many of us need to quit worrying about our relevance for five minutes and have the courage to state the obvious. What follows is the answer I give when asked "what can be done." At least three of the five points I make are universally acknowledged throughout the industry to be bad practices. All five of them are things that allow the existing production system to remain largely intact, with or without soil health, regenerative agriculture, or whatever you want to call it. The reason we don't do these things isn't because they won't work, it's because there are a lot of cowards when it comes to Iowa water quality.

1. Ban row crop agriculture in the 2-year flood plain. We plant 400,000 acres where inputs like fertilizer and pesticides are washed away into the stream network and the Gulf of Mexico every other year.[3] This is an area of land that exceeds the combined area of all our state parks. This is perverse. Why are we doing this?

2. Ban fall tillage. Universally recognized as a practice with disproportionately bad environmental effects, people at Iowa State University have been discouraging it for decades. It's especially bad following a soybean crop. Increases soil erosion (keep your eye open for "snirt" this winter), increases nutrient loss, increases greenhouse gas losses from farmed fields. I get that if a farmer likes tillage and wants to farm a lot of acres, he/she might feel pressed for time in the spring to get it all plowed. And if you spend your winters in Ft. Myers or Scottsdale, it might be nice to have the plowing done so you have time to get the RV cleaned up for Northern Minnesota in July. Not my problem. It's polluting our water, it's not necessary for growing corn and soybeans in Iowa and it's ridiculous that we still allow this. Side story: Several years ago, I was talking about this in a meeting and farmer angrily pounded his fist on the table and said: "You know why we do fall tillage? Because we have to!" Ok. I would have liked to have said, "You know why I tolerate bad water? Because I have to!"

3. Ban manure on snow and frozen ground. Again, pretty much universally acknowledged as a sub-optimal practice, if not downright stupid. And in the case of manure on snow, clearly destructive of water quality. Yes, we already have some rules about this in Iowa, but they are so riddled with loopholes that they are practically meaningless. Example: if there is snow on the ground on February 28,

come the next day it will be pretty easy to find some with manure on it. Great for smelly snowball fights, really bad for our rivers. I get that the manure pit may fill up faster than expected; again, not my problem. Build a bigger pit!

4. Make farmers adhere to Iowa State University fertilization guidelines. What's the point of Iowa State University having nitrogen fertilizer recommendations if nobody is going to follow them? Despite what you might hear from the Ag advocacy organizations, farmers do over apply fertilizer. It's endemic to Iowa's production system. Also, newsflash: nitrogen IS cheap; in fact, it's hardly ever been cheaper than it is now. If I've said it once I will say it a thousand times: how do we give farmers license to do whatever they want with inputs and then ask the taxpayer to mitigate the pollution? It's insanity.

5. Reformulate CAFO regulations. Let's face it, Iowa's Master Matrix regulatory framework for livestock operations is like a zip tie handcuff on King Kong. It enables farmers to apply manure nutrients beyond crop needs, and it provides for no management of nutrient inputs at the watershed scale, sentencing many rivers to a polluted oblivion. We cannot continue to wantonly cram hogs into Iowa and meet the objectives of the nutrient strategy, at least not without effectively regulating nutrient inputs. And believe me, I am far from the only person that knows this. The fact that this continues to go unacknowledged by our politicians, the industry, and many of the state's institutions is nothing short of sinister.

Well, there you have it. Nothing on that list should cost you, the taxpayer, a dime. But I will tell you, if you want clean water, you will have to demand it.

If you don't know, Howard Zinn (quote at the beginning) managed to write at once what might be the most admired and the most hated book about America (the latter almost certainly is true): *A People's History of the United States.*[4] If Zinn was right, true change in America comes from below and progress only happens when people resist and organize. If you're waiting for the water quality elites here in Iowa (and you can put me in that group if you want to) to solve the water quality problem, you're going to wait a while. Sorry. The industry will pollute your water for as long and to the degree that you let it.

BIG POLLUTION

A lot of people are earning decent livings because Iowa has a pollution problem. I am one of them. The public holds many of us in high regard because presumably we are devoted not to money or career or stature, but to making Iowa's water cleaner. But are we?

It's always been in the best interests of the Ag industry to make nutrient pollution seem mysteriously complex. After all, complex problems rarely lend themselves well to simple solutions. Complex problems require lots and lots of time and money to solve, and the bigger the problem, the more likely the taxpayer is going to be asked to solve it with contributions from the public coffers. And the folks who own all this expensive farmland (worth well more than $200 billion in Iowa) surely can't be expected to own the pollution too! And remember, lest you get impatient, your tax dollar contributions are not so you can enjoy clean water, but so maybe your children and hopefully their children might someday look at the Floyd, Iowa, or Raccoon River and think, boy, I wish Granddad was still alive so he could see those old tires beneath this clear water he paid for.

The folks at the NGOs and foundations also don't mind themselves a little complexity, thank you, because big donors like to think big and the public dollars can and do find their way into the cash-strapped budgets of Nonprofitlandia. If you want to work on solving nutrient pollution, you'll probably meet this country's leaders at their capital, Starbucks City, to talk about grand visions and shared values over a cup of their national drink, French press coffee.

And you may or may not know that the universities have always wanted nutrient pollution to be seen as a labyrinth of weather, climate, soil, microbiology, hydrology, chemistry, agronomy, economics and sociology, a labyrinth that so completely confounds the scientists that they might have to (gulp) call in the engineers to help disentangle the mess. And let me tell you, them boys is nothin' if not expensive. No engineer would even so much as pick up a pencil for a "simple" problem. Complexity makes for some good grant proposals that include hip words like nexus and interdisciplinary and benchmark and resilience. And, perhaps stating the obvious, people don't spend years getting PhDs to work on simple problems.

You've probably heard of Big Oil, Big Ag (and its subsidiaries, Big Meat, Big Dairy and Big Organic), Big Government, Big Pharma, Big Tobacco and some other Bigs. Now I'm going to tell you I think we have another one here in Iowa: Big Pollution. We have a whole bunch of people whose livelihoods and relevance link back to water pollution, and especially nutrient pollution. I admit to being a card-carrying member.

But I am not one of the Brotherhood (or Sisterhood) of Big Pollution currently clamoring to monetize the latest craze: soil health practices. Like the poor water quality it purportedly will help improve, people want to tell you how complex this topic of soil health is, and how it requires experts from all branches of Big Pollution to help spend the taxpayer money currently on a barge traveling up the Mississippi River, destination Iowa and other Corn Belt states.

The absurdity of this was recently featured in a *Des Moines Register* editorial[1] written by an Iowa farmer. He described how reduced tillage and continuous cover (i.e. using cover crops) improved his bottom line $138 per acre while reducing nitrate loss from the farm. He goes on to speculate why more farmers don't do this: IT'S SCARY.

Bear in mind this is a group that seemingly will buy skunk piss from a certified crop advisor if that person promises the infamous "two-to-five-bushel yield bump." OK, I'm kidding on the skunk piss, but listen closely to the radio or tv when a commercial comes on for any Ag product; it's ALWAYS 2-5 bushels. But I digress.

Back to the *Register* editorial. The farmer writes that "it's time for our elected leaders in Des Moines and Washington D.C. to help us with research, technical support and incentives." If you haven't noticed, Big Pollution just loves MOAR research (unis), MOAR technical support (NGOs, and the agencies, to be fair), and MOAR incentives (Ag industry). He goes on to say that "State legislators can take a step in the right direction by supporting House File 646 this session, a bill that would lay the groundwork for helping farmers adopt the practices."

MOAR (urban dictionary): Combination of "more" and "roar" meaning an insatiable demand for more.

Well, it goes without saying that the Nonprofitlandians are gleeful about HF 646, hoping, as they are, that the Road to Ag Damascus will be an 8-lane highway that takes decades to pave, and that will run right through the middle of their country. Hopefully no coffee shops will be in the path. Several politicians on the left are equally giddy, cosplaying environmentalism and celebrating the bill as a potential milestone, with Big Ag finally coming around to the century-old idea that slash and burn farming maybe is sub-optimal in the long haul.

If at this point you think I'm just an angry old cynic, shaking his fist at the sky, well, so be it. But this writing comes on the heels of yet another person "on the inside" telling me late last week about the copious amounts of nitrogen fertilizer used by the typical Iowa farmer. And phosphorus is an even worse horror story. Piling manure phosphorus onto soils categorized as already "very high" for this nutrient is de rigueur and always will be until a majority in the legislature can summon the courage to protect your water and say enough is enough. So, if you ask why, oh why do we continue to concoct schemes to pay farmers to try to restrain the excess nutrients we allow them to buy and apply? Two words: Big Pollution.

I will finish this with a story from about two years ago. I'd be hesitant to recount this here were it not for the fact that there were a couple of hundred witnesses to the event. At the SOIL 2019 meeting in Des Moines, a "conservation" farmer and one-time candidate for secretary of agriculture said if the public wanted the nitrogen problem solved, they needed to "show me the money!" My opinion: paying farmers for soil health without first addressing the nutrient imbalance on our landscape is the biggest can kick in conservation history, at least in the context of water quality.

But, as always, Big Pollution thanks you for your contribution.

ENVIRONMENTAL INJUSTICE

The year of 2021 saw the emergence of Critical Race Theory as a big discussion topic, and racism, or the purported absence of racism, was a hot topic in that year's Iowa legislature, as was free speech on Iowa's state university campuses. By this time, it was well known that my essays were provocative and upset some people. Iowa state legislator, Chuck Isenhart, warned me that Environmental Justice was a topic that might provoke some of his colleagues. So that's what inspired me to write this one.

Using 2017 data,[1] USDA has identified 86,104 people as the "primary producer" (e.g., farmer) on Iowa farms. Of these folks, 378 (0.4%) identified as of Hispanic origin, 45 (<0.1%) as Native American, 64 (<0.1%) as Asian, 40 (<0.1%) as African American, 6 (<0.1%) as Pacific Islander, and 85,827 (99.7%) as white. Of these white folks, 80% are male and the average age is almost as old as I am: 58.9 years. Incredibly, only 15,430 (18%) of these farmers are under the age of 45. I bet you can't name another profession where 75% of their members are AARP-eligible. I can't, unless there are some buggy whip makers or blacksmiths still around. Long and short, Iowa farming is whiter and older and manlier than the Caddyshack country club.

Without attempting continuity (at least for now), let's look at the city of Ottumwa. This is the childhood home of my grandfather, Roscoe Wagner, and the place his dad (John) landed after he gave up on farming. John Wagner's grandfather, William Wagner, left what is now Germany in 1846 to settle and farm in the southeastern part of the new state of Iowa. Ottumwa has about 24,400 people, down from its peak of 33,900 in 1960, the year my great grandfather died. It's now the 20th largest city in Iowa, and one of the state's more diverse communities, with about 20% of the population identifying as Hispanic or non-white, similar to Des Moines and Sioux City, but far more diverse than Cedar Rapids and slightly more than Davenport. The median age in Ottumwa is 33 and 65% of the population is under the age of

Observe 50th Anniversary

Stella and John Wagner.

45. Ottumwa is also one of the poorest cities in Iowa. Depending on the data source, it ranks in the mid-700s out of about 900 Iowa communities in median household income, which is remarkable considering its relatively large size (for Iowa). The city lies in Wapello County, which is 94th out of 99 Iowa counties in median household income in 2019.[2]

What links paragraphs 1 and 2 is water, specifically the Des Moines River. From its source in southwest Minnesota, Iowa's largest inland stream travels through north central and southeast Iowa (and Ottumwa) to its confluence with the Mississippi at Keokuk. The river and its tributaries drain more than 14,000 square miles and some of the most-coveted farmland on earth, which lies especially in the areas upstream of Des Moines. This ground is underlain with an intricate cobweb of drainage pipes (tiles) that all but extirpated an entire wetland ecosystem while leaking enough fertilizer and manure nitrogen to kill an estuary 1500 miles away. As Todd Dorman of the *Cedar Rapids Gazette* has said, The Dead Zone Starts Here. That nitrogen reaches the stream network as nitrate, which is a regulated drinking water contaminant and the Gordian knot of Iowa agriculture.

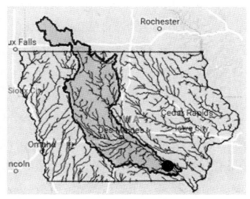

Des Moines River watershed with black dot showing location of Ottumwa.

Without a license to pollute the public's waters with this contaminant, the corn/soybean/CAFO system can't exist in its current configuration. I can confidently say that most people in the public don't realize this, but astute people in agriculture certainly do. That's why the industry tenaciously fought the failed Des Moines Water Works lawsuit of a few years ago that sought redress for the contamination of the drinking water consumed by 20% of Iowa's population. Something you don't hear a lot about is that contamination makes its way down to Ottumwa, which like Des Moines, also uses the Des Moines River as a drinking water source. In the last 5 years, Des Moines River nitrate has exceeded 10 mg/L (the drinking water standard) just downstream from Ottumwa at Keosauqua on at least 76 days and exceeded 8 mg/L (a level where your shorts get in a bunch if you're a water treatment plant operator) on another 106 days.

You could easily say the nitrate threat is greater in Ottumwa than it is in Des Moines because Ottumwa lacks the diversity of water sources and treatment plants that Des Moines has. Ottumwa's aging (I've been in it twice) drinking water treatment plant does not have nitrate removal capacity like Des Moines and the utility relies on water from a former quarry to dilute the Des Moines River nitrate as it is pumped into the treatment plant. And that's always a crapshoot because these quarries can be cauldrons for nuisance and harmful algae that are a threat in and of themselves.

While you can argue "fairness" all day long, the truth is the Des Moines area has the resources to cope with this problem. You can't very confidently say the same thing about Ottumwa. And to circle back to my first paragraph, Iowa's landed gentry, mainly white, many wealthy, some especially wealthy, are polluting the water of a community where many are poor, and many are people of color. And in a bit of an irony, many of the Ottumwa folks earn their living by slaughtering the hogs that help pollute the water and are produced by the landed gentry. The JBS hog processing facility in Ottumwa processes a staggering 7 million hogs per year and 1 million pounds of pork per day.[3]

Wagner house on N. Ward Street in Ottumwa.

Do the workers care that their drinking water is affected? Or that there is increasing evidence that nitrate in drinking water is a carcinogen? I don't know. Iowa's politicians certainly don't seem to care. Try to find one, just one, from either party that has talked about Ottumwa's drinking water. These politicians do, however, like to spend time trying to put money into the pockets of the landed gentry. We're told just this month that they need "resources and regulatory relief" to reduce nutrient runoff. Did I miss something? Are regulations causing this problem? Or is regulatory relief the "Ransom" that I wrote about two years ago? Hmm. A person could reasonably ask just what about agricultural water quality do we seriously regulate.

I don't know of anything. But if they do come up with something, Ottumwa, hear this: your water is being held hostage.

I'm writing this one today against the backdrop of a political climate that is suggesting that we in the public sector not talk about certain subjects. Of course, one of these is racism and another is environmental justice, and I guess the thinking is that if we don't talk about them, they won't exist. Ironically, the same people pushing this are the same ones saying Orwell this, Orwell that, and it's pretty clear none of them have read many of George's books. I kind of wonder if most of them don't think that *Animal Farm* was published by ISU Extension. But I digress.

It's also clear that environmental justice does not exist in Iowa, and I sure don't want to be the guy blamed for its emergence. What does exist in spades is environmental injustice, and since nobody has explicitly said that topic is taboo, well, essay. Ottumwa is an example. I don't see any elected person out there in either political party that gives a rat's behind about it. Of course, the industry rationalizes this injustice by telling us that we should turn a blind eye to the pollution that their practitioners, all (white) paragons of virtue of course, need to generate because they are feeding the world. You can't make an omelet, after all, without breaking a few eggs. And some of those eggs, maybe more than the average hen is going to lay, are going to be brown.

Ottumwans: suck it up and be thankful you have those hogs to butcher.

DR. JEKYLL AND MR. HYDE

Soil erosion has been a problem here in Iowa since the first plow broke the prairie, but we've never been unwilling to talk about it. Des Moines Register *editorial cartoonist Ding Darling (after whom the state park was named) was commenting about it in that and 150 other newspapers in the 1920s. More attention to soil conservation is still urgently needed, and discussion of this topic has always been fair game when agriculture, conservation and politics bellied up to the bar. Not so with nutrient pollution. It's always taken more courage to talk about loss of nutrients, and especially nitrogen. The conventional wisdom is that "bad" farmers let their soil wash away. On the other hand, nitrogen pollution is the cost of doing business in the Corn Belt, and even "good" farmers lose some, and so talking about it is tantamount to airing dirty laundry that is best kept in the cellar.*

Recently someone in my peer group publicly stated, "I counsel students if they conduct research for an academic institution (to) avoid advocacy related to their professional focus. Your research will become biased or perceived as such and you lose credibility." Now this statement, mind you, comes from a person who some might say has strenuously advocated for the prevention of soil erosion throughout their career. As a long-term observer of this advocacy, I will say it did nothing to hurt this person's credibility, and in fact enhanced it. Thus, I am a little perplexed by the statement and can only conclude that the students felt like advocating for the wrong thing. Clearly it could not have been the prevention of soil erosion.

Who determines what is acceptable advocacy? Important people, I guess. I have some ideas on that.

Ruminating on this a little bit, I thought that it might be an opportunity to illustrate the contrasting mindsets we have here in Iowa for soil erosion and water pollution, especially nutrient pollution. It is surely true that soil erosion degrades water quality and rivals hydrological modification and nutrification

Fredric March portrayed both Dr. Jekyll and Mr. Hyde in the 1931 film of that name. Image credit: Paramount 1932.

for the amount of damage it has done to our waterways. While any drive across the countryside shows there is a wide range of tolerance amongst farmers for erosion, most recognize it as a threat to their bottom line, the long-term productive capacity of the farm, and the value of their land. I suppose they might exist, but I know of no person anywhere that has been criticized for zealously advocating against soil erosion. Nutrient loss and the related water pollution—not so much. This is not a new phenomenon (it goes back decades) and it should be curious to us. Why do Dr. Jekylls advocate against soil erosion while Mr. Hydes snort anhydrous ammonia?

There are probably a range of answers for the dichotomy that exists vis a vis erosion versus nutrient loss, and I speculate on some here:

1. Fertilizer sales data, estimates from the federal government, and farmer surveys all illustrate that on average, Iowa farmers disagree with Iowa State University recommendations on fertilizer amounts. That is, farmers think they need more.

2. A lot of money is being made in the industry overselling nitrogen fertilizer, and there are no negative consequences to doing so.

And if they get a squeamish farmer who wants to apply recommended amounts (or less), you can always try to sell inhibitor products that purport to keep the nitrogen on the field. And what business doesn't want to sell more stuff? Nobody wants to sell less stuff.

3. Soil erosion is highly visible to both the farmer and his/her neighbors. It's a stigma. By contrast, nitrogen pollution doesn't show up to the human eye until it has traveled downstream where a few algae cells stumble onto it like teenagers finding keg of Busch Lite and before you know it, the entire senior class is having a pool party and breaking the furniture. Or something like that.

4. Wasting nitrogen does little or no long-term damage to the farm compared to soil erosion.

5. Erosion is regulated—nitrogen pollution isn't, and powerful people want to keep it that way. You may not know it, but we have had federal rules in place since 1985 to reduce erosion. That year's farm bill created Conservation Compliance, which requires farmers cropping highly erodible land (HEL) to operate in certain ways if they want to participate in federal farm programs. We have no such framework for nutrients, although we sorely need it.

6. Excess nutrification is intimately connected to the livestock industry. Over-fertilization with manure is embedded into and endorsed by the manure management plans required by our current CAFO regulations, which even allow 100 pounds per acre of nitrogen application to soybeans. Industry people love this like the senior class loves Busch Lite.

7. Max Bushels. I've written in the past about our Max Acres culture, but we could also depict it as a Max Bushels culture as well. Eking out that last bushel may require an economically unwise amount of fertilizer, but who cares! More bushels mean more money is juicing the system at both the front end (seeds, insurance, fertilizer) and

the back end (drying, shipping, storing, checkoff dollars for commodity organizations). Erosion means the opposite.

Well, there you have it. If there are any students reading this, I hope you fight like hell for what you believe in, because Iowa is not going to get any better unless you do.

IFYOUCANTBEATEMJOINEMITIS

In this essay I highlight how those on the supposed good side of the clean water issue can be complicit and help maintain the impairment of Iowa water, year after year, decade after decade. I also discuss the 4D strategy of deny, distract, deflect and delay that agriculture and other industries have used to resist and obstruct change on environmental issues.

"The dramatic threat of ecological breakdown is teaching us the extent to which greed and selfishness, both individual and collective, are contrary to the order of creation."—Pope John Paul II.

Polk County is one out of 99 in Iowa, but one in six Iowans live there, and about one in four are there on any given day. The biggest city, Des Moines, has had a high-profile nitrate impairment of its drinking water since Watergate (the real Watergate) and the agriculture establishment would've liked to have impeached Des Moines Water Works' CEO Bill Stowe for leading a failed lawsuit that sought remedy for it.

The *Des Moines Register* recently ran a lengthy article[1] about the implementation of farm conservation in Polk County. Much of the article focused on what we call Edge of Field (EOF) practices designed to capture nitrate from underground drainage pipes (tiles) that lower the water table in perhaps half of farmed Iowa and all of northern Polk County. These tile systems are the main pathway for nitrate to enter the stream network. There is no longer any doubt that these EOF practices, namely, woodchip bioreactors, constructed wetlands, and saturated (wet) buffers, work.

One of two bioreactors being installed by the city of Des Moines on the Bogard Family Farm in Polk County, Iowa a mile south of Easter Lake. The next step is to place wood chips in the pit. Photo credit: SWCS/IDALS Photo by Lynn Betts.

At their core, they all function in the same way, namely, by detaining water just long enough in a carbon-rich environment for non-crop organisms to consume the lost and wasted nitrogen. The reason they exist is because the Ag industry has been mostly unable and unwilling to control nitrogen in the field and so they've asked the public to help them pay to capture it at the edge of the field. The Polk County plan would ultimately install 200 of these practices at a cost well north of $1 million in one of Iowa's least-farmed counties. Polk County Soil and Water Commissioner John Norwood stated in the *Register* article that "we need to be building 100 (of these practices) at a time, not one or two."

The *Register* rhetorically asked if this aggressive plan would work for all of Iowa. But that isn't really the right question here. These practices will work about anywhere there's adequate space to situate them and a tile effluent that can be captured. But the expense of construction and need for land (for wetlands especially) prevent this from being a landscape scale solution, at least as long as we still want stuff like public schools, roads, libraries and such. It's like this:

you can treat a stain on your shirt with Shout, but it's impractical to do the whole load of laundry with it.

Studying and implementing EOF practices have been important components of many careers over the last 20 years, including mine. I authored a journal paper on woodchip bioreactors and was co-author on a couple of wetland papers. And we are currently monitoring a saturated buffer site in southwest Iowa. But in recent years I have become increasingly cynical about this sort of thing, and I'm going to tell you why.

EOF practices fit nicely into a 4D strategy the Ag industry has been implementing for 50 years now on water quality: deny, distract, deflect and finally delay. First, deny there is a problem at all. We started moving past that in the late 80s with the groundwater pesticide scare best illustrated by water quality monitoring data from the Karst areas of northeast Iowa, including the Big Spring fish hatchery in Elkader. At that time Ag drainage wells, which captured tile water and sent it down to the aquifer, dotted the landscape across northern Iowa, and people realized that we were poisoning our own rural drinking water. We started (and still are) closing them, rerouting the water to the stream network and letting rich downstream city folks deal with removing the chemicals from their drinking water.

Next, distract. The opening of the world's largest nitrate removal plant in Des Moines in 1992 was a stain that couldn't be Shouted out, but the nitrate problem could still be cynically blamed on wastewater treatment plants, combined sewer overflows, septic tanks, lawns, golf courses, rotting leaves, geese, deer, raccoons and Uncle Bob pissing off his deck after a night of beer drinking. Any time spent thinking about these phony distractions would cause a reasonable person to chuckle, and so on to the next level—deflect.

"Feeding the World" is the best example, and it goes like this: pollution, no matter how severe, is better than millions of people starving to death. Two problems with this: 60% of our corn is used to make ethanol, and most of our meat is eaten by wealthy people, wealthy at least relative to the world as a whole. Not many Africans have ever sat down to a meal of Iowa chops.

So now we're on to the delay portion of this scheme, which by that I mean delay implementation of structural change that needs to occur at the landscape scale, structural change that will end or at least substantially reduce the water pollution coming from the corn-soybean-CAFO model of production agriculture. Good first steps would be policy changes ending or altering practices and subsidies that keep fertilizer prices low, stimulate overapplication of nutrients, and promote high stakes farming on marginal land. Build in accountability for taxpayer money spent on conservation. Ban or restrict environmentally destructive practices. Manage livestock populations and nutrient inputs at the watershed scale. This approach is not anti-corn/soybean, pro-organic, anti-GMO, or anti-CAFO. It's pro-society and pro-Iowa and pro-America. And pro-environment.

Unfortunately, Iowa's political and economic establishment is pro status quo and would prefer you focus on things like a bioreactor treating 40 acres, rather than the structural change we need. These projects help maintain the status quo. If they happen to improve water quality, well that's ok, but that's not the objective. The farmer or landowner objective may indeed be to improve water quality, but the establishment's real interest in these projects is that they support their objective to forestall regulation and structural change. And these folks can be surprisingly candid about this at times. They're "not opposed to clean water" as a certain legislator has stated,[2] it's just that it's no big deal to them beyond the threat of regulation that dirty water presents.

The Ag advocacy organizations form a wagon circle around the idea that the industry needs a license to pollute. There are so many of these groups that they form coalitions of groups just to keep it all straight. It's not all one big happy Family (I capitalize family here intentionally because they call themselves The Family) but they are laser-focused on keeping Iowa farming unregulated. It's the sine qua non of Iowa Ag and politics. Making the public think the industry is dedicated to an Iowa with clean water is integral to maintaining an unregulated countryside.

If you observe this stuff as I do, you can see that on the environmental side, there is no cohesive message and no unifying objective. The environmental groups are the F Troop compared to Ag's Prussian soldiers. Like the F Troop, the enviros are stationed at Fort Courage where they are busy adopting their adversary's tactic of promoting soil health for carbon sequestration and improved water quality. We had a soil health bill in the legislature this last session, and USDA secretary Tom Vilsack is promoting this concept as a water quality and climate change solution, and many of the environmental groups are all in with this stuff.

One minor problem here: POOR SOIL HEALTH IS NOT WHY WE HAVE BAD WATER QUALITY IN IOWA. But sure, create another publicly funded revenue stream for farmers because that has worked so well to improve water quality.

Just to be clear: I'm for soil health. And I'm for a bioreactor or a saturated buffer or a wetland if the farmer wants to do that. And I will give some qualified support for using public money for these sorts of things. But these approaches will never meaningfully improve our water quality unless they are accompanied by the needed structural changes in our production system:

> We can't achieve our water quality objectives by grossly overapplying nutrients to crops.

> We can't achieve our water quality objectives with state-endorsed overapplication of manure to fields.

> We can't achieve our water quality objectives by mindlessly cramming livestock into the state.

> We can't achieve our water quality objectives by mindlessly farming floodplains and sensitive lands like northeast Iowa.

> We can't achieve our water quality objectives by giving farmers license do whatever they want on the field and then asking the taxpayer to pay for the collateral damage.

But alas, it seems everybody in this game cares about being relevant and I guess you can't be relevant if you lose all the time. People crave victories, even the Pyrrhic kind, apparently, if it means staying relevant. So, what we have here is a contagion burning through the Iowa Water Quality Community. The resulting disease: Ifyoucantbeatemjoinemitis. Symptoms: malaise, anxiety, feelings of hopelessness. The cure: the Matrix's blue pill, the one that allows the swallower to remain in a fabricated reality.

Now you might say, what's the harm. A little bridge building, that sort of the thing. Here's the harm: you enable the delay tactic, in spades. However long it will take to clean up our water, add 25 years to that (at least) if you're going to hang your hat on soil health to deliver. After a half a century of 4D and bad water, we deserve better than this! We deserve courage.

Some might ask, where do I get off, pontificating from a university? What has academia done to solve these problems? You would be right to ask that. The currency here in academia is grant money, and PhD graduates, and publications. And relevancy. Oh my yes, relevancy. There ain't nothin' more pathetic than academics who've lost their relevance. (And believe me when I tell you that The Family is keenly aware of this.) And when relevance sneaks out the back door, that other stuff marches out the front. Only the crazy throw caution to the wind on relevancy. Joan of Arc is not exactly our role model. The Ivory Tower has no more courage than the F Troop's Fort Courage when it comes to water quality. But if you'd like to get a PhD while learning about bad water, we're here for you. We're also ready to pour soil health gravy all over the existing research programs that have been so successful at cleaning up your water.

It's apparent that to solve this thing, it will take courage from the highest levels. And we just don't have that kind of courage right now in Iowa, or nationally for that matter. It's so painfully obvious. You have a hard time finding issues that have bipartisan support these days, but dirty water is one of them. To paraphrase Republican political guru Kevin Phillips—the Democratic Party is history's second-most enthusiastic dirty water party. Addressing the structural framework that produces the polluted water that we have is the third rail of Iowa politics. To end this, I guess I would invite you to examine for yourself why.

TAKE THIS STREAM AND SHOVE IT

I've published several scientific papers that focused on the Raccoon River of central Iowa, and I looked at it nearly every day during the eight years that I worked at Des Moines Water Works. The stream is a drinking water source for the Des Moines metropolitan area, and I can't think of a large city anywhere in the U.S. where the municipal source supply is in worse condition. The Raccoon very likely has the highest nitrate levels of any stream of its size in North America. There have been two failed lawsuits seeking redress from agriculture for its condition; this essay was written after the Iowa Supreme Court dismissed the second.

You may have heard that another lawsuit concerning the Raccoon River was dismissed by the Iowa Supreme Court.[1] This latest one, pink-slipped in a 4-3 decision, was filed by Iowa Citizens for Community Improvement and Food and Water Watch. They asserted that the State of Iowa had violated the public trust doctrine, meaning the citizens of Iowa conveyed stewardship of our shared natural resources to the state and the state failed to fulfill that obligation with regard to the Raccoon River. The groups asked that the state create a mandatory remedial plan that would reduce nutrient pollution and ban new concentrated animal feeding operations (CAFOs) in the watershed until the plan was implemented.

I'm not an attorney and I write this not to comment on the legal merits of the decision. Rather, I thought some dot connecting might be helpful and so that is my objective here.

The watershed drains 2.3 million acres of land (approximately 6% of Iowa) lying northwest of Des Moines. More than 75% of the area is cropped and there is intense livestock production in the upper reaches of the basin. Much of the western and southern extent of the watershed traces the edge of the Wisconsin glacier, and melting ice created lakes along this edge, most notably Storm and Blackhawk Lakes, 10,000 years ago.

The southern edge of the advancing glacier bulldozed grape-fruit-sized rubble to the present-day Raccoon River valley in Polk and Dallas Counties. Torrents of glacial meltwater covered the rubble with sand, creating a one-in-a-million, Goldilocks (just right) alluvial aquifer where sand-filtered river water was easily extractable from the buried rubble. Engineers constructed a clever groundwater collection system that provided Des Moines perhaps the safest pre-World War II drinking water of any big city in the United States. While thousands died of cholera contracted from drinking bad water at the turn of the last century, Des Moines was left unscathed thanks to rocks and ice.

Yield (volume) of water from the groundwater collection system couldn't keep up with post-war population growth, and the Des Moines water utility started drawing water directly from the river in the late 1940s. Not long after that, cropping systems all over the Corn Belt underwent a transformation which saw the adoption of the current all-cash-crop-all-of-the-time scheme which reduced plant diversity in the Raccoon watershed and increased the use of chemical fertilizers. This resulted in regular contamination of the river and the alluvial aquifer with nitrate. Awareness of the problem increased in the 1970s, concurrent with enactment of the Safe Drinking Water Act (1974). The utility began removing nitrate from the treated water in 1992, and a few years later received a grant from EPA to conduct monitoring and public engagement activities to raise awareness of the need for better water quality.

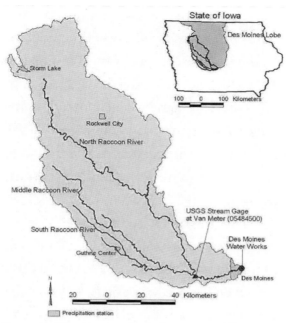

Raccoon River watershed; Iowa map illustrates the position of Wisconsin glacier 10,000 years ago.

There's been plenty of posturing and grandstanding over Raccoon River water quality since then, but at times there seemed to be reason for optimism. There did appear to be some pause in the increase of nitrate levels in the 2000-2010 period, but the pollution came roaring back after the 2012 drought and the worst nitrate years have occurred since then. This ominous cloud is one of the few clouds hanging over Iowa during this current drought year, and there likely will be very bad news when the rains return. But despite the occasional ray of hope that happens to appear every few years or so, looking back, I have to say the watershed has probably been a lost cause for quite a while now.

In 2010, Iowa DNR received funds from the American Recovery and Reinvestment Act to develop a water quality master plan for the watershed. Stakeholder organizations sent representatives on a week-long retreat to help provide information and expertise to develop the plan. I was one of those people. A plan was created and posted for public comment. Iowa Farm Bureau Federation commented thus: "IFBF asks the final master plan focus on implementation options that recognize (the) right of watersheds to develop a voluntary plan of action to address the agricultural nonpoint source issues, that support ongoing water monitoring and science development, and avoids numeric targets for nitrogen, phosphorus and sediment or regulatory actions affecting fertilizer applications or other farmer management decisions."

Consider that comment "Mission Accomplished."

Paraphrasing Matt Damon in *The Martian*, the scientists are going to science the shit out of this baby (currently about 2,000 scientific journal articles at least mention the watershed). The human genome may have been mapped in 13 years, but evidently that is child's play compared to sourcing Raccoon River pollution to its origin. Various groups are going to continue monitoring the river and its tributaries, and Iowa DNR and the governor-appointed Environmental Protection Commission (EPC) will continue ignoring the data so they can cowardly avoid establishing numeric water quality targets. Farmers continue to have license to apply as much fertilizer as they wish and in the manner that suits them, and people in the upstream watershed WILL recognize their right to develop (or not develop, as the case may be) voluntary plans of action.

I know some will hate this paragraph, but I think it needs to be said. Over the past 20 years, agribusiness and the watershed's farmers have made a mockery of efforts to improve the drinking water source serving 1/6th of Iowa's people, and Iowa's appointed and elected leaders, including supreme court justices, have for the most part endorsed this. Supported by Iowa's economic and political establishment, the larger body of the watershed's farmers have no intention of trying to reduce nutrient pollution, and this has always been so. I've seen firsthand on many occasions the hostility to change, and this was before both lawsuits. I'm not stating this as a casual observer.

I do see an upside to it all and that is that agriculture has, whether they like it or not, claimed the stream for their own. The people who say they hate finger-pointing have shown us their middle finger, and in doing so have told the world who's to blame for the water in the Raccoon River.

It's all yours, boys.

THE SWINE AND THE SWILL

There are many similarities in how agriculture responds to the issues of climate change and water quality. In fact, agriculture seems to be using the same water quality playbook as climate change mitigation becomes front and center: ok maybe there's a problem, it's not really our fault, but if you want us to help solve it, please send us money and we'll think about it.

The physicist Edward Teller emigrated to the United States from Hungary in the 1930s and played an integral role in the Manhattan Project. He later derived the principles behind the hydrogen bombs that make up much of our present nuclear arsenal. Teller was also known for his irascible personality and political conservatism, and his testimony was a major factor in J. Robert Oppenheimer's (the leader of the Manhattan project) fall from grace within the U.S. government. For these reasons, he was hated and ostracized by many in science and politics.

Oppenheimer (L) and Teller (R). Image credit: University of British Columbia, Wikipedia commons.

I recently came across a three-year-old article[1] about Teller and global warming. In 1959, he was the guest of honor at the Energy and Man symposium that celebrated the 100th anniversary of the oil industry. He surprised the audience of oil industry executives and other VIPs with these words: Whenever you burn conventional fuel, you create carbon dioxide. [....] The carbon dioxide is invisible, it is transparent, you can't smell it, it is not dangerous to health, so why should one worry about it? Carbon dioxide has a strange property. It transmits visible light but it absorbs the infrared radiation which is emitted from the earth. Its presence in the atmosphere causes a greenhouse effect.

Proceeding on, Teller said, "At present the carbon dioxide in the atmosphere has risen by 2 per cent over normal. By 1970, it will be perhaps 4 per cent, by 1980, 8 per cent, by 1990, 16 per cent, if we keep on with our exponential rise in the use of purely conventional fuels. By that time, there will be a serious additional impediment for the radiation leaving the earth. Our planet will get a little warmer. It is hard to say whether it will be 2 degrees Fahrenheit or only one or 5. But when the temperature does rise by a few degrees over the whole globe, there is a possibility that the icecaps will start melting and the level of the oceans will begin to rise."

I know that right now, your inner Paul Harvey is telling you that you know the rest of the story: the oil industry went on their merry way making bank, and now it's 108 in Seattle and 114 in Portland as I write this. Even with the fate of civilization hanging in the balance, the industry acted in its own self-interest, and, wait for it.....FAILED TO REGULATE ITSELF.

Perhaps stating the obvious, the thing to like about physicists is that they look at life from the perspective of physics. Do you like people who respect "THE LAW"? Hey, then a physicist is your person. They love laws. Teller looked at the carbon-oxygen double bond of CO_2 and was like, dudes, shit's gonna get real in a few decades. This was not a complicated problem to him. Teller was just stating the obvious, as anyone that paid attention in Physics 101 knows.

The oil industry execs didn't care.

As you know, I do water quality and about the only law we have in this gig is, don't upset agriculture's fragile psyche. They're sensitive, and might lash out. The original environmentalists, as characterized by Ag giant Syngenta,[2] don't like us to talk about our water here in Iowa. Being the habitual offender that I am, however, I can't help myself sometimes. As Edward Teller's good friend Ronald Reagan would say, here I go again.

I probably shouldn't beat a dead carp since I wrote about it once already (essay "Hello Darling"), but for crying out loud, Lake Darling. Last week, the Washington County Lake had the ignominy of being the only place in Iowa with both *E. coli* and microcystin (toxins from blue green algae, otherwise known as cyanobacteria) advisories. In 2014, the state spent $16 million to restore the lake, named after what some others (probably not Syngenta though) would say was Iowa's first environmentalist, Ding Darling. And Lake Darling isn't the county's only offender. Crooked Creek, which flows through the northern part of the county, is one of the highest nitrate streams in Iowa.

This story might be curious to some since Washington County, home to the Darling nutrient cauldron, is the undisputed soil health and cover crop champion of Iowa. Here, celebrity farmers can be routinely heard belting songs from the soil health hymnal, which of course they know by heart. And cover crop coverage may be as high as 15% of the crop acres, about three times higher than the

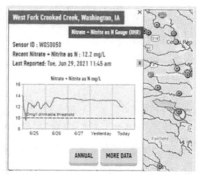

Current nitrate levels in West Fork Crooked Creek, Washington County.

state average.[3] These practices are supposed to improve water quality. Curious, indeed.

What gives? After all, we're being force-fed the message that we need to invest in a new holy grail, this one filled with the soil health elixir that will solve both climate change[4] and water quality.[5] Let me guess, works on stains too, I'll bet.

This is where I queue my inner Edward Teller and say, hey, did you guys notice those hogs? According to USDA data for 2017 (latest available), the county of Washington has more hogs than any other in Iowa, 1.3 million.[6] It comprises 1% of Iowa land but is home to 6% of the state's oinkers. Call me crazy, but it seems like there might be a connection between the swine and the swill that is Lake Darling.

Yes, I know we're hoping the industry will regulate itself and do the right thing by us, and in the by and by, we'll all sing Beautiful River together, in communion with our wormy soils, winter rye and triticale cover crops. But seriously folks, we have a problem of scale here that no amount of cover crop preaching and soil health proselyting, however well-intentioned, is going to overcome. If Washington County is our model, holy moly. And like those oil executives back in 1959, the industry is going to keep on keepin' on, at least until somebody comes along with the courage to talk about scale. At least somebody more important than me.

MAMAS, DON'T LET YOUR BABIES GROW UP TO BE FARMERS

I stumbled across the narrative Goodbye to a River *in a stack of used books knowing nothing about the author, John Graves. The poignant title containing the word "river" inspired me to take a chance on it and the book is a gem. Oftentimes I try to weave my past reading into my current writing which results in some disparate (and maybe desperate) dot connecting that may seem absurd to some but serves as a method for me to generate ideas. The title and content of* Goodbye *seemed like it would fit perfectly into this approach, but I just couldn't figure out how to make it work. So, I ordered a couple of other Graves titles, one being* A John Graves Reader. *These pieces of fiction and non-fiction were selected by Graves as his favorites. One of the essays fit the bill for me:* Cowboys, A Few Thoughts from the Sidelines, *and it meanders in and out of the piece that follows. At the time of writing, I felt this piece was my best work (and still do), but my book manuscript had already been accepted for publication. Just prior to the printing of this book, I got wind that some important folks considered this one my absolute worst. Figuring that hate readers are still readers, after all, the presses were stopped at the last minute to slip this one in.*

Texan John Graves (1920-2013) might be the best writer you've never heard of (unless you have) and I can tell you in his hands the English language was like a basketball in Michael Jordan's. Not only did he make it do stuff that you didn't know was possible, his words make you feel things you didn't know you could feel. If *Goodbye to a River* isn't the best book of its kind ever written, I'll drink a straight up gallon of any Iowa river after a springtime gully washer.

It wasn't *Goodbye* that inspired this essay, but rather his essay "Cowboys: A Few Thoughts from the Sidelines." Graves grew up when the legendary Texas cowboy of old was still a thing, riding the range, ropin', fencin' and castratin' for months at a time without a day off. Sleeping under the stars and wolfing down food as it became available, earning meager wages that were squandered getting drunk on whiskey and a hooker really frisky.

A myth developed around these hard fellows that the country and even the world fondly embraced, a myth that still persists today, even though the real McCoy cowboys haven't existed since the years immediately after World War II, when barbed wire and the economic realities of feedlot beef conspired to cancel the occupation. Certainly many of the real cowboys were an embodiment of courage and hard work, virtues this country, rightly or wrongly, considers supremely American. And as such, many in the public emulate the cowboy wardrobe and other aspects of their appearance and demeanor, something Graves tells us was uncommon during the real cowboy era.

But Graves also tells us that myth and truth entangle in ways that confound our thinking and cause us to misjudge the cowboys' motives and conduct, despite the lofty ideals that many of them had toward hard work, determination and loyalty. And as the title here gives away, this got me to thinking about the myth of the Iowa farmer and how it affects our thinking about the occupation today.

The 40,000 full time and similar number of part time Iowa farmers are outnumbered by several professions, including frequently vilified teachers, but yet we've made farmers the soul of the state. We're asked to thank them at every turn and we groom our school children to hold them in the highest regard.[1] We bestow favorable tax policy upon them along with public money to bolster and indemnify their operations. We bless the damage their overweight vehicles and equipment impart to our roads and bridges and most aggravating, turn a blind eye to their pollution.

Our politicians swoon like teen-age girls when these barnyard Beatles take the stage, and in unity with them don the phony pharmer chic of denim and flannel, pro-wrestling-sized belt buckles, and boots. Especially boots—not shiny new Tony Lamas, but scuffed square-toed shit kickers that track dust and manure crud and cred across every carpet they touch, just so you'll know their veins course with farmer blood and their feet are caked with dirt road mud. It's almost like John Travolta and Debra Winger were running our state. Years and beers may have made my memory a little hazy these days, but I sure don't remember Harold Hughes and Bob Ray (Iowa governors from Ida Grove and Des Moines in the 60s and 70s) acting like this, back when real farmers didn't ask the public to fawn over them, and we weren't required to put a salve on their festering insecurities with buffoonish "feed the world" and "god made a farmer" baloney.

(It did come to me that Hughes may have worn a bolo tie with a flannel shirt in public once in a while.)

It's interesting that the myth of the Iowa farmer has grown inversely with the level of their toil and travail but in lockstep with their wealth and the number of paid mythmakers that loiter around the industry like barking hyenas. Like Graves and his cowboys, I have some fond remembrances of Iowa and the Iowa farmer that existed in my childhood and before. But over the last 40 years, the myth has become ever less objectively based and the myth creation ever more sophisticated, which I suppose is necessary because it exists almost solely on nostalgia and the power of propaganda.

I hear people in agriculture decry the public's ignorance of the trade and the industry, but at the same time they project images of farming that only rarely still exist—agrarians hardened by weather and worry, managing diverse farms with modest outdoor animal populations. It's no wonder they need the mythmaker army when the truth is something so altogether different.

But perhaps I'm too harsh. Maybe I should let go, embrace all the myths about Iowa agriculture managing the impossibly complex task (for mortals, anyway) of being the world's first environmentalists while at the same time feeding, fueling, and fibering the entire world, and thus I feel, for only a moment, that I should join the masses in thanking Iowa agriculture and its farmers. So here goes.

Thank you, Iowa agriculture, for allowing us to have 1,576 square miles of public land, half of which is in road right-of-ways. Our percentage of public land (2.8%) is an enviable 48th-most of any state, a number that is sure to entice our young people to remain here and forgo miserable outposts like Minnesota, Colorado, and Oregon.

Thank you, Iowa agriculture, for leaving us 15 stretches in 70,000 miles of streams that meet their Clean Water Act designated uses. That's one good stretch of river for every 200,000 Iowans—not bad! Take that, Rhode Island!

Thank you, Iowa agriculture, for helping to eliminate only 720 million grassland birds (61% of them), just in the span of my life.[2] I used to see meadowlarks as commonly as robins in town when I was growing up and now through the good graces of Iowa agriculture I might see a couple or three on a two-hour drive across the Iowa countryside. And thank you,0 Iowa agriculture, for waiting until my quail-hunting granddad died before making the bobwhites scarcer than hens' teeth.

Thank you, Iowa agriculture, for showing us how foolhardy it was to construct several dozen lakes across the state, all at taxpayer expense. We should've known your sediment and nutrients would make these cauldrons of green stew, so please forgive our ignorance on that. We've learned our lesson and won't make the same mistake again in the future.

Thank you, Iowa and U.S. agriculture, for graciously accepting our $300 billion spent since 1936 (in adjusted 2009 dollars)[3] so you could try to stop losing your soil to erosion. Soil loss in Iowa averages 5.4 tons per year,[4] still above the USDA threshold for "sustainable," but, good try. We still have some checks in the checkbook.

The owners of 55,000 tested wells that have not been contaminated with nitrate to unsafe levels say, thank you, Iowa agriculture. The owners of 6,600 others that have been contaminated wish to say they fully understand and know that you would never, ever prioritize your crop yield over the safety of your neighbors' drinking water, and that the contaminated wells are just an unfortunate circumstance of a golf course being located in the next county.

Thank you, Iowa agriculture, for allowing us to keep 30,000 of the original 7,600,000 acres of wetlands (20% of Iowa) that were home to countless waterfowl and other birds, reptiles, amphibians, mammals, and insects. And we're eternally grateful for the 5,000 of the original 3,000,000 acres of prairie pothole wetlands that have been left to remain on Iowa's Des Moines Lobe. We know it's been a tough job laying drain tile on every last wet spot, but by god, you got the job done! If the remaining wetland birds could thank you also, I'm sure they would.

Thank you, Iowa agriculture, for letting us retain 0.1% of our native tallgrass prairie ecosystem. Sure, it helped that a lot of this was in pioneer cemeteries but let's just be honest, corn could grow there, and you guys were nice enough to leave our great-great-grandparents to rest in peace where postage stamp-sized prairies could survive.

Thank you, Iowa agriculture, for leaving at least some of our streams in eastern Iowa unstraightened, and thank you for polluting the straightened ones in western Iowa to such an extent that it's impossible for anyone alive to have any nostalgia about what they once were.

Thank you to all the aggressive tillers out there that are willing to accept our tax dollars for wind breaks to slow erosive winds. Yes, we know that laws banning mindless practices like fall tillage would be more effective and cost us nothing, but buying things like wind breaks helps us feel like we are part of the action, and helps us understand the forces you deal with.

And thank you, Iowa agriculture, for graciously accepting our funds to create pollinator habitat for the monarch butterfly, driven to the brink of extinction at least in part by your farming practices. After all, who could've predicted that all those years of ditch mowing and herbicide drenching would have negative consequences.

I had hard time knowing how to finish this one, so I'll let Graves do it. He said that, like art, "Myth can influence the direction of human life, and may even influence its live subject matter if the timing is right. The popular cowboy myth was not shaped for cowboys, but a non-Western public who seized on it. But it reached real cowboys as well, and they seized on it too." Can it be possible that this hasn't happened here in Iowa? It surely has. The industry and its practitioners would have us believe that these heroes need our help, crave and deserve our admiration, and above all, need us to overlook the negative consequences of their actions. Of course without the myth and the mythmakers, we might be less inclined to do that last thing.

BREAKING WIND

I know from firsthand experience that many in Iowa agriculture are climate change denialists and this has been confirmed by the Iowa Farm and Rural Life Poll done at Iowa State University. This is curious when you consider this is perhaps an industry almost uniquely vulnerable to weather and climate disruptions. Curious, that is, until you realize that the taxpayer indemnifies the farmers against the risks.

The *Des Moines Register* published an opinion piece[1] on July 6th, this written by H. Sterling Burnett of the Heartland Institute think tank in Arlington Heights, IL. The column, titled "Iowa crop yields are setting records, not failing, amid modest warming," asserts that farmers are right to be global warming skeptics because they are dialed into the weather patterns and thus presumably know better than anybody if the climate is changing, or not. Increased crop yields associated with wetter weather and a longer growing season have been good for farmers, according to Burnett, and "Iowa farmers seem not to have been fooled by alarmists' claims that climate change threatens their futures." The *Register* went so far as to summarize the piece as such: "Modest climate change has improved conditions for farmers, so there's no need for concern about the future."

Although I hate the smell, I do really appreciate it when Ag defenders go around breaking wind with little posterior emissions such as this, because it gives me something to write about. Ideas don't grow on cornstalks, after all.

Firstly, it's interesting to hear someone assign these increased crop yield trends the industry brags about to something other than the ingenuity of the Iowa farmer and the wizardry of crop geneticists (the most arrogant scientists on earth, in my experience). By golly, it was just the weather. Whooda thunk it. But what struck me most about the article was this Alfred E. Neuman-like "what, me worry?" attitude when it comes to climate change, especially from an industry vulnerable to it like no other.

Alfred E. Neuman. Image credit: Imgflip, Vince Vance, and *Mad Magazine.*

But then some work done by my IIHR colleague, Antonio Arenas, was returned to what's left of my memory, and I started to think, this H. Sterling guy might have a point. Why should Iowa farmers worry? Like an ambulance-chasing law firm, the Iowa (and U.S.) taxpayer does the worrying for them!

Antonio analyzed crop insurance data for Iowa and a few other states for the period 1991-2018. Iowa's indemnity (payout): $9.6 billion. The amount sourced to the taxpayer through subsidized crop insurance: $6.3 billion. The amount sourced to the farmer through their portion of the insurance premiums: $3.4 billion. And a whopping 68% of that $9.6 billion was paid out in only four relatively recent years: 2008 (wet), 2012 (drought), 2013 (wet spring then drought), and 2014 (drought).

Crops in southern Iowa counties tend to be more vulnerable to weather calamity than other parts of the state, and this is true on both ends of the rain gauge, drought and excess moisture. Total crop insurance payouts in several Iowa counties exceed $1,000 per acre since 1991. So maybe it's understandable that the Iowa farmer feels like he/she can whistle by the global warming graveyard, as long as the taxpayers are paying for the ambulance. I for one think things might be a little different if we weren't.

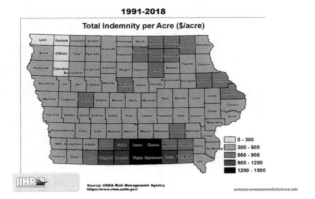

Iowa crop insurance payouts, 1991-2018.

CROPAGANDA

The Ag advocacy organizations are numerous in Iowa and nearly all of them have a communications department tasked with molding public opinion on Iowa Agriculture. I know because I worked at one of these organizations. Communicating with the public on environmental issues is, as you might imagine, a challenge for them, and I find some of the material they generate laughable and absurd. The title for this essay did not come from my head; I first heard it used by my colleague Silvia Secchi, who heard her daughter say it.

Ag media is like the sound of thunder at 3AM when I'm suffering from an inspiration drought. I can always count on them, especially the communication shops at the advocacy organizations, to provide a timely soaker just when I'm most parched.

The most recent gully-washer was a You Tube video[1] posted by our favorite insurance company (photo next page). Four middle-aged and snappily dressed Randys, looking as though they saw no need to change clothes after just filming a Cialis commercial, pose as Iowa farmers chugging coffee in a small-town café. Also making an easy transition from the Cialis set is the bragging about their performance, but in this skit the boasting relates to their success in reducing nutrient pollution. Astonished waitresses look on admiringly as these virile countryside titans extol the enormity of their prowess in satisfying Iowans' urges for cleaner water. The background narrator tells us that "Iowa farmers are celebrating the decline of nutrients in surface water" and, "their ongoing voluntary efforts like no-till, terracing and contour farming have made Iowa's waterways cleaner," and finishing with "Iowa farmers, doing their part to make a difference."

It's hard to know where exactly to begin farming this virgin soil, but let's start with the no-till. Only about 1/3 of our cropped acres are classified as no-till,[2] and that doesn't mean those acres never get tilled. A farmer might till a field for a corn crop but not the following soybean crop. Only about ¼ of our no-till area is planted to corn.[3]

Secondly, yes, we have a lot of terraces. I once heard a guy from the Agribusiness Association of Iowa boast that Iowa farmers have erected a length of terraces that exceeds the combined length of all our streams. I have no reason to doubt this claim, but it only takes one glance or sniff of our lakes and streams to know that terrace length doesn't mean everything. A mile of terrace does not give you a mile of good water. Taxpayer-funded terraces do a fine job of increasing the value of a farmer's land investment by enabling sloped land to be cropped in the first place. So yes, if you insist on cropping a steep hillside, you're going to need a terrace to reduce soil erosion. But downstream consequences are not always or even usually beneficial. Surface runoff water is captured by intake structures and routed directly to streams. This water is what we call "sediment hungry," meaning it is energized and capable of aggressively eroding stream banks and beds, increasing stream sediment transport in some circumstances. And terraces can increase stream nitrate through a couple of mechanisms—firstly, they bring uncropped and unfertilized land into production, and secondly, they increase infiltration in and around the terrace, providing a nitrate loss pathway to the stream.[4,5]

Lastly contour farming. Are we really still giving farmers the attaboy for contour farming? Congratulating farmers for contour farming is a bit like applauding Nurse Ratched for trying to improve her bedside manner. If you don't know, contour farming is when farm rows follow a constant elevation line around a hill, as opposed to cropping up and down the hill with rows of varying elevation, which is much more erosive. If you live in Iowa you know that a lot of it is hilly; without contour farming, we'd be comparing our crop outputs with Kentucky and not Illinois because most of our farms would be in the Gulf of Mexico. Contour farming has been used as an environmental virtue signal for decades and even as far back as 75 years ago, Aldo Leopold[6] called out the phonyism of this bragging: "If he [a farmer] plants his crops on contour, he is still entitled to all the privileges and emoluments of his Soil Conservation District." So please, just spare me on contouring.

To finish up with the assertion that nutrients have declined in surface water, well, I'm tempted to embed that Jennifer Lawrence mocking thumbs up gif.[7] In fact, that gif could serve as the entire blog post, and I could've saved you five minutes. Not an iota of actual water monitoring data could have went into that mendacious claim. Yes, some models do show phosphorus reductions based on practice adoption (like no-till and terraces), but this is not borne out by the water quality data for Iowa streams.[8] And literally no one is convinced that nitrogen levels are declining; in fact, there are strong upward trends statewide since 2003.[9]

So in conclusion, if you find yourself believing cropaganda for more than four hours, please call your doctor immediately.

GOD MADE ME DO IT

You can't write much if you don't read much. And you just never know when or how things you are reading will intersect. I wrote this while reading Howard Zinn's Declarations of Independence *and in fact that is where I first read the Carl Sandburg poem at the beginning of the essay. Around that same time, some promotional material from one of the numerous agricultural advocacy organizations landed in my inbox. The essay is a result of the confluence. Note: the late Bill Stowe, named in the essay, was former CEO/General Manager of Des Moines Water Works.*

From Carl Sandburg's book/poem, *The People, Yes* (1936):

"Get off this estate."
"What for?"
"Because it's mine."
"Where did you get it?"
"From my father."
"Where did he get it?"
"From his father."
"And where did he get it?"
"He fought for it."
"Well, I'll fight you for it."

Carl Sandburg in 1955. Photo Credit: Al Ravenna. New York World Telegram Collection. Library of Congress, Public domain.

The Ag communication shops are the answer to all my prayers when it comes to inspiration. I read something a month or so ago from one of them and I knew I had to write about it, but it took a while for an idea to tassel out. The piece profiles an Iowa farmer who apparently is on a mission from God to grow corn and soybeans. Most human beings, including the one writing these words here, try to derive some meaning from their existence and so I don't fault that if that is the angle. I did, however, find this quote revealing: "If you can raise more corn and beans on this acre of ground the good lord gave you, you darn well better be doing that."

As far as God giving "us" the land, there's a few descendants of a continental-scale genocide who would like a word regarding this farmer's god. But ignoring that for the moment, yes, it's true enough that you can raise a lot of corn and beans on Iowa land, and a lot of other stuff that we don't grow anymore: oats, apples, vegetables, oak trees, and so on. And rest assured if corporate CEOs wanted Iowa farmers to grow that other stuff instead of corn and soy, that is what they would be growing, and God could just go pound sand. You gotta know who's the boss, after all.

I do find it interesting that agriculture apparently is looking to God for endorsement of what we've done to this corner of His earth. If you've been part of a system that extirpated three ecosystems, straightened and ditched thousands of miles of streams, drained millions of acres of wetlands, felled the great pine, oak and walnut forest of the northeast corner and killed off part of an ocean 1,500 miles away, mainly so we could save a nickel on a gallon of automobile fuel and have corn syrup and bacon creatively jammed into every food dish imaginable, I guess God is your logical last refuge. Luckily, He's a forgiving god.

Thankfully, God has gone on the record on this subject. Paul said to the Romans (8:18-21) "For the creation waits with eager longing for the revealing of the children of God; for the creation was subjected to futility, not of its own will but by the will of the one who subjected it." And a thousand years before, Isaiah (24:4-6) told the

Hebrews that "The earth dries up and withers, the world languishes and withers; the heavens languish together with the earth. The earth lies polluted under its inhabitants; for they have transgressed laws, violated the statutes, broken the everlasting covenant." Other similar quotes abound, but curiously, He is silent about growing *Zea mays* (corn) and *Glycine max* (soybean).

Now I'm not here to proselytize or demonstrate expertise on the Christian or any other bible. I am here, today anyway, to say that it's way past time for Iowa agriculture to get down on its knees and show some humility and contrition for what has been done and continues to be done to the creation to serve the corporate masters.

In an interesting bit of cancel (agri)culture, the Des Moines Water Works announced a few months ago[1] that they were giving up hope for the Raccoon River after using it as a source supply for the city for the last 74 years. Alternative water sources are being explored. This story barely broke through the noise here in Iowa, even though several national outlets ran with it. The Iowa political and establishment elite were crickets, as they always are, when it comes to these sorts of things.

The plight of the Raccoon River is one of many examples of how the condition of our water is a moral failure of our government to safeguard the public's property, i.e., our lakes, streams and aquifers. I say to those that want better water and think we can vote our way to it: better say your prayers. The Iowa power structure that maintains the environmental status quo is bipartisan and always has been. Some have recognized this—Bill Stowe, to name one. He tried the courts, and failed, as about everybody knows.

But when you examine these sorts of struggles for justice, which is what this really is, the courts tend to follow, rather than lead, public sentiment. One only need look at the struggle for civil rights in the U.S. South. Court cases only started going the way of oppressed black Americans after protests began in the 1950s. Rosa Parks famously refused to relinquish her bus seat in Alabama in 1955, and the yearlong Montgomery bus boycott followed. Only then did a federal court, followed by the Supreme Court, find that the 180-year-old Constitution outlawed bus segregation.[2] Numerous other examples of this script played out in the 50s and 60s.

Rosa Parks. Photo credit: Wikipedia commons.

Our water here in Iowa is polluted just as legally as black people were segregated. The agricultural and political establishment have made sure of that. They're so confident in their power that they're not even shy about telling you that. But should that be the standard, legal, or not legal? For an industry and its practitioners who mostly claim to embrace conservative and traditional and moral values, should not the standard be what is just? Call me crazy, but if agriculture had the moral high ground here, they probably wouldn't need "communicators" to force feed us on how righteous they are.

I think sometimes we lean on Aldo Leopold more than we should; quoting him can become almost trite at times. But as I've read and re-read his words, it seems to me that Leopold transcends all other environmental writers in that he's an Orwell-like figure; by that I mean his 80-year-old observations seem like they were articulated only yesterday. It's interesting and probably not coincidental that his name rarely or never crosses the lips of people in establishment agri-

Aldo Leopold. Photo credit: University of Wisconsin.

culture. He saw early on that what was driving conservation decisions was profit, not environmental outcomes, and certainly not justice.[3] "The farmers, in short, have selected those remedial practices which were profitable anyhow, and ignored those which were profitable to the community, but clearly not profitable to themselves." This so very accurately crystallizes how our industry and elected leaders and agencies think about the environmental condition here in Iowa, i.e., if it doesn't make economic sense, forget it. This is an injustice to us as citizens that are at the mercy of the polluters.

To circle back to Carl Sandburg, I am convinced the only way we will get clean water here in Iowa is if we fight for it. Some might say it is a Utopian fantasy to think we can have clean water here, after a 180-year-long assault on our streams and lakes. But in my estimation, the idea of clean water has moral power.

And ideas with moral power don't die easily.[4]

RANCID TURKEY

Farmers buy a lot of stuff—seed, chemicals, fertilizer, equipment—and there are a lot of retailers scattered across Iowa to sell them that stuff, more than a thousand, in fact. These retailers have done some damage to Iowa lakes, streams and aquifers by spilling or improperly disposing of farm chemicals. One such incident happened in 2020 in Northeast Iowa's Turkey River watershed. What was maddening about this incident was the trivial size of the fine ($6,000) and comments made by Iowa DNR, which to my mind were meant to excuse the seriousness of the incident. Like in so many states, our agency assigned to protect our environment seems often to be very lenient with the polluters.

In recent news,[1] the Iowa DNR announced they were fining Three Rivers Coop of Elkader $6,000 for a release of anhydrous ammonia into Roberts Creek that flows into the Turkey River in Clayton County. Nitrogen fertilizer is commonly applied in Iowa in the ammonia form (NH_3) and in a process controlled by temperature and other factors, is converted to nitrate (NO_3) over time in the soil profile. When ammonia enters a stream or lake with warm water, as was the case in this incident (July 2020), this conversion is rapid. Immobile species are toasted in this process as they usually are, but in this case and many others, dissolved oxygen levels in the stream crashed so rapidly that the aquatic life that otherwise could flee the contamination also perished. It's really too bad that the release wasn't into a tributary of Roberts Creek, then we could call it Killed Three Rivers Coop instead of, you know, the much less colorful real name.

Although this isn't saying much, the Turkey River is one of our better streams. This is mainly because only about ½ of the land in the watershed is suitable for the stuff Three Rivers and the other area Ag retailers sell to farmers, compared to about 75% statewide. Alas, if only an acre of trees (of which there are quite a few up there) needed 200 pounds of nitrogen and all that other junk like fungicide, glyphosate, dicamba, super triple phosphate, diammonium phosphate, monoammonium phosphate, urea, urea ammonium nitrate, neonicotinoids, nitrogen stabilizers, insecticides and on and on, the Turkey watershed could perform up to the standards set by the rest of its Iowa brethren like the Boyer and Floyd and Soldier river watersheds, where nobody need care about fish kills because you can't kill what ain't there. Ammonia release into the Boyer River? Pfft. Fart in a hurricane.

In the Turkey River incident, an Iowa angler, all of whom should probably be deputized when they buy their fishing license, "noticed

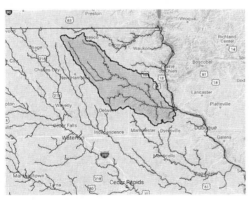

Turkey River watershed.

dead fish where the creek meets the river near Elkader on July 18, 2020." This was DNR's description[2] of the incident a year ago: "DNR field staff investigated the site on July 21, finding elevated ammonia levels in a drainage ditch below the Three Rivers FS, an agricultural cooperative. Coop staff indicated they emptied a secondary containment structure around a fertilizer tank on July 20. DNR field tests show water emptied from the structure had high levels of ammonia."

This is DNR's *Onion*-ized description of the incident now,[1] a year later: "An unknown quantity of the fertilizer — which is highly attracted to water — might have leaked from storage tanks there, possibly during transfer to other containers," said Jessica Ragsdale, an environmental specialist for the Iowa Department of Natural Resources. "The ammonia just finds water and goes into it," Ragsdale said. "They thought they were testing it properly and thought it was clean and good to go." Three Rivers employees routinely pumped rainwater and snow melt from the anhydrous storage area onto a gravel-covered area, according to a DNR administrative order dated Sept. 28. From there, the water flowed to a culvert, a drainage ditch, a creek and, finally, the river. The state stocks the Turkey River with trout.

I mean seriously, folks, ammonia just finds water and goes into it? It's like beer just finds my body and goes into it. It's not my fault that I'm overweight.

How can anybody take this stuff seriously?

Clearly, we must have communications people, all seemingly graduates of the Josef Goebbels School of Journalism, planted in damn near every one of the state's institutions and organizations where they are assigned to absolve those working in agriculture of any responsibility for the pollution we see and smell day after maddening day so they can make a buck or a million bucks or many millions of bucks without regard for the tiny slice of Iowa nature that they haven't already used for their toilet. And the fine, $6,000, I just don't know how to do anything other than assign the morbid humor to this process that it richly deserves. Six grand is just a sick joke. I'll have to check my latest data, but one of my daughters may have run up that much in traffic tickets. Speed just finds its way into her car. There's no figuring it out.

But wait, this story gets worse.

The Ag retailers want to sell more anhydrous ammonia and other nitrogen fertilizers.[3] Since, as they say, God isn't making any more

Iowa land, and since pretty much all of it that can grow corn, is growing corn, the only way for these outfits to sell more product is to sell more on the land that already receives it. To that end, it would sure help more cash find its way into the pockets of Iowa agribusiness if those agronomists at Iowa State University could discover the courage needed to tell farmers they should apply MORE NITROGEN. "What some of them want, especially those interested in selling fertilizer, is for recommended rates to be higher. If we recommend higher rates, some farmers may be happy, but they will get less profits and we'll contaminate the water even more."[3] Oh really. Knock me over with a feather.

And yet, it still gets worse.

The legislature has tasked the Iowa Agribusiness Association (yeah the guys that sell stuff to farmers) with helping us dumb scientists track progress toward Iowa Nutrient Reduction Strategy goals.[4]

That's it for now. Lunch just finds my stomach and goes into it around this time of day.

ON POPCORN FARTS AND PORCUPINE PISS

Wet years following drought produce some of Iowa's worst water quality. We've known this for a while but getting farmers to plan for this circumstance is Mission Impossible. So, I wrote this one as farce. The DNR quote at the end was a real thing but spoken not about porcupine pee but anhydrous ammonia.

There was a terrible drought in Iowa in 1976 and 1977 and the only time Raccoon River nitrate (at Fleur Drive in Des Moines) measured greater than 20 ppm followed. The only time, that is, until the Raccoon peaked out at 24.7 ppm nitrate in 2013, immediately following the 2012 drought.

Now you may know that much of Iowa has been moderately dry, to severely dry, to popcorn fart dry in 2021. As a result, faculty at Iowa State University and staff at Iowa Corn Growers' Association have been imploring farmers in the media[1-7] to be cognizant of nitrate left behind in their fields because of poor crop nitrogen uptake. Also, less has been lost to the stream network and aquifers so more will be vulnerable to loss when the rains return. It's like when you forget to put the trash out, then next week you have twice as much. Surplus nitrogen, like your trash, doesn't just disappear into the Milky Way. Ironically, there are a lot of reports of good crop yields this fall, so a reasonable person might ask why they applied so much in the first place. But hey, that's just me. What do I know?

Not that it matters at all, but I commend ISU for proactively warning farmers that business-as-usual decisions on fertilization will pollute our water later. In fact, I would say this is a landmark event for a couple reasons. First, we have establishment agriculture admitting in the *DES MOINES REGISTER* no less that farmer decisions end up polluting our water, and secondly, that actual purchased fertilizer is part of the problem. Much of this discussion, after all, has focused on the idea that the pollution isn't the farmers' fault, it comes FROM THE SOIL. Big hitters in the legislature say this all the time.

But I also decry the fact that, at this late date, we still need to tell farmers this. WE HAVE KNOWN THIS FOR 50 YEARS. I took about a 1-hour look at the scientific literature on this, and scientists and extension agents have been publishing stuff on this since at least 1983; I can find 45 published papers without even trying very hard. I even wrote one of them.

I was sitting in my boat recently and during an extended gap between caught fish, I thought about this and decided to have a little fun with it. Imagine, if you will, a scientist published a paper in 1983 that promised the magical 2-5 bushel yield bump (ever notice how it's always 2-5 in the tv commercials for Ag products?) if farmers added a little porcupine piss to their fertility regimen. Replicated strip trials at Nashua, Gilmore City, and Crawfordsville (now called Quillville by agronomy grad students) ISU research farms show a 50.1% chance of returns on a $10/acre investment in this new, mysterious nutrient. "I'm getting an extra 0.8 kernels per ear," reports Kossuth County farmer Harold Johnson, while holding up 4/5th of a kernel. He notes the effect may be less in southern Iowa counties. Farmers everywhere flood Iowa Ag retailers for requests to be first in line for the product, marketed by Agrichem Canada.

A cascade of events ensues. ISU Cyclone basketball meets the Kansas Jayhawks, not in Hilton Coliseum, but in the Porcupine Palace where Quill Magic pops the 2nd-ranked Jayhawks' hopes in the last second. On the gridiron, a little gold plate engraved with the word "Hawkeyes" is annually attached not to the Cy-Hawk Trophy, but the Porcupine Plaque. Iowa coach Kirk Ferentz gets another raise. Iowa State researchers plan proposal partnerships with Purdue University to investigate the synergies at the nexus of porcupine and pork, because USDA and NSF have millions to study the issue's effect on distressed rural communities left behind by consolidation in agriculture. UI flood researchers want in, because, you know, porcupines can't swim and they don't know how to climb a levee, either. Iowa's governor carves 10 days out of her busy schedule to hand out Porcupine-On-a-Stick, I mean On-a-Quill, at the Iowa State Fair. Porc is the new pork, according to the governor. The other-other white meat. Iowa billionaire schemes with has-been former governor to get taxpayers to pay for a Porcupine Pipeline ("it's a win-win," says ex-guv) that will pump the porcupine piss from the Boreal forests of northern Canada straight to Agribusiness Association of Iowa members, so their staff can promptly spray it onto the parking lot during a thunderstorm, where it runs off and kills some fish. "Porcupine piss just finds water and goes into it," reports Iowa DNR.[1]

The point here is that if something improves crop yields, well, there's not much need for ISU researchers to implore farmers and agribusiness to embrace it. When it comes to YOUR water, we have to beg farmers for a half century (or more) to do it. The basic fundamentals of what is driving erosion and nutrient loss have been known for decades. DECADES. GENERATIONS.

Ted Corrigan, now CEO at Des Moines Water Works and my direct supervisor when I worked there, was fond of telling me that the best predictor of future behavior was past behavior. Tell me again why we don't need regulation in agriculture.

CALL ME CRAZY

The price of Iowa farmland is insanely high and makes entry into the profession nearly impossible for anyone other than the descendants of farmers. This, along with the large percentage of land that is rented, is a big obstacle as we try to develop and implement water quality improvement strategies.

People tell me I too frequently use the word "insanity," but I reckon that is like telling a farmer he uses the word "money" too much. As the old saying goes, write what you know, and I think I know crazy when I see it. So I'm not inclined to change my schtick.

Speaking of money, some guy named Kevin Cone posted a video on his twitter feed last week that caught my eye. I don't know the fellow, but his twitter bio says he is an "Auctioneer-Iowa Auction Group, NW Iowa Farmer, Coach, Ordained Minister, Former World Champion Horseshoe Pitcher," or in other words, pretty much your average Twitter user. For the record, I like pitching leaners and ringers about as much as I like pitching sarcasm, but none of my relationship partners could warm up to the idea of a horseshoe pit in the back yard. So what are you going do. Choose your spouse wisely, I guess. At any rate, at least part of this guy's schtick is auctioning Iowa farmland.

The video in question features two long rows of rust-free pickups, most of Trump-Trade War-Relief-Payment vintage (in other words, brand new) sitting atop 127 pancake-flat acres of earth's best farmland on Iowa's Des Moines Lobe. The horseshoe stud tweeted that the land sold for $18,500/acre, or $2.35 million in total, coincidentally the approximate value of the 50 or so pickups sitting there. Karma, baby. Remember that, if you're planning to sell some land.

We hear often that a lot of young Iowans want to farm, but can't, and you can see why. They can't afford the land. Iowa farming these days is for rich people. According to ISU,[1] the average net farm income last year was $134,119. Total farm assets average $2.52 million and average farm net worth is $1.80 million. For reference, the average Iowan makes $49,280 per year.[2] Those rich city-slickers that Chuck Grassley likes to slime make an average of about $55,000/year in Iowa.

Establishment agriculture's response to the scarcity of land for aspiring farmers has been to make it more difficult for land to be donated for use by the public.[3] And our very own Department of Natural Resources rents 29,000 acres of your public land for farming. Iowa ranks 47th out of 50 states in percentage of land that is public, and a large proportion of ours, maybe about half, is in road easements[4]. We have less public land than New Hampshire, Hawai`i, and New Jersey combined.

When it comes to land prices, here is something that doesn't get talked about much: not holding agriculture accountable for their water pollution almost certainly inflates land values, which of course restricts opportunities for aspiring farmers. Let's say we did something completely insane and regulated pollution leaving the farm in ways that made farmers and/or agribusiness financially responsible for its mitigation, pretty much what we do for every other business in the U.S. It doesn't take a genius to figure out that the value of the factory, which in this case is the land, would take a hit.

Except we don't do that. We do quite the opposite. We ask the average Iowan, making 41% of the money made by the average farmer and with a fraction of the net worth, to pay farmers to stop polluting, and don't hold them accountable when the desired outcome goes unmet.

Insanity.

People in the conservation world wring their hands about rented farmland—i.e., how can we ask farmers to be accountable for the pollution leaving land they don't own? This indeed is a good and an important question. Most reports on this show more than half of Iowa land is farmed by someone other than the owner and many of these people (>34%) HAVE NEVER FARMED.[6] On average they rent out about 130 acres, which in Iowa means they are millionaires. The idle rich. The people at least partly responsible for polluting the public's water. At least some of them living it up at the one place in Iowa you *can* find clean water, West Lake Okoboji, during the summer.

So I get that Iowans don't want to put a regulatory burden on 75-year-old Uncle Harold, still farming the home section up in Calhoun County after all these years. Believe me, I get that. But for the love of God, why do we let these rich landlords off the hook? Why do our legislators condone this?

Here's an insane idea: require Iowa farm landlords to have cover crops on all their land. Limit fertilizer use to ISU recommendations. Ban new tile installation on the ground.

Novel idea, you say? Well, the Clean Water Act requires me (and probably you, if you own property in a city with a population greater than 10,000) to pay for stormwater mitigation related to your property. For me, it's $375 per acre per year.

And people say I'm the crazy one.

REMARKS TO THE SOILS MEETING

I almost always use PowerPoint slides when I'm invited to speak at meetings. This particular occasion, the SOILs meeting at Drake University, was an exception. Knowing who the audience would be, I knew what I wanted to do as soon as my friend Neil Hamilton, professor emeritus of law at the Drake Law school, invited me. The meeting was postponed a couple of times because of COVID and ultimately, I was lucky to be able to deliver these words in person. They did not sit well with some farmer-legislators in the audience, a couple of whom walked out in the middle.

Thank you for the invitation to speak here at SOILs. I'm honored to participate in this meeting, and I thank Neil Hamilton, who has done so much for Iowa by articulating the challenges we have.

I didn't bring slides today but have hundreds, maybe thousands of slides on my website and if you want to look at them, by all means, I encourage you to go there and take a look.

I didn't bring slides because I have come to realize these past few years that the presentation of graphs, and tables of data, and conceptual models about soil health and edge of field treatments and cover crops and so forth, won't affect change here in Iowa when it comes to water quality.

Here's an example of what I'm talking about, and I quote: "Take Weaver's discovery that the composition of the plant community determines the ability of soils to retain their granulation, and hence their stability. This new principle may necessitate the revision of our entire system of thought on flood control and erosion control." Aldo Leopold said that about cover crops in 1938. Before I was born, and even before my mother was born. And we have what, 5%, 7% of our land in cover crops.

The statewide stream load of nitrogen has approximately doubled since 2003. Phosphorus loading, while not increasing nearly as much as nitrogen, is indeed still increasing when we evaluate actual water quality data—27% when compared to a pre-1996 baseline. If you listen to the artfully named Iowa Nutrient Research and Education Council, housed within the Agribusiness Association of Iowa and funded by the Iowa legislature to track progress for the Iowa nutrient strategy, phosphorus loads are down 22% and they tell us, and I quote, "Iowa Agriculture has nearly met the 29% non-point source reduction goal." Not one shred of water quality data went into this mendacious claim. Not one shred. It's pretty clear that establishment agriculture is itching to hang the "Mission Accomplished" banner on the Wallace Building, regardless of what our water looks and smells like.

Something Mary Skopec [who was on the panel with me] knows about is the Iowa Water Quality Index—a single-metric indicator of the condition of Iowa streams—was dumped several years ago. That index credibly illustrated the sorry condition of the vast majority of Iowa streams. I was funded a while later to create a new index, which I did, which uses the Iowa DNR ambient water monitoring database of turbidity, nitrogen, phosphorus, E. coli, and dissolved oxygen to assign a single number to the water quality condition of Iowa streams. Evaluating data going back 22 years to the year 2000, I find that overall water quality has improved on only three out of 44 Iowa stream sites, is declining at 25, and constant at the other 16. Curiously, the watershed of our most improved stream, the North River at Norwalk, has undergone extensive urbanization during that time. Most alarmingly, our best streams, all of which are located in northeast Iowa, streams like the Upper Iowa, Turkey, and Yellow Rivers, have degraded more than the others.

You may have heard Bloody Run Creek in Clayton County described as "pristine" in the news media in recent months. Here's what qualifies as pristine in Iowa over the last five years: average *E. coli* levels of 1,400 colonies per 100 ml, 6 times the recreational standard, and average nitrate concentrations of 7 mg/L, higher than even the Raccoon River. Yet our friends in agriculture stand by silent as one of their own tries to squeeze 11,000 cattle into the headwaters of this 6-mile-long stream. Freedom to farm trumps your "privilege," they say, to have clean water.

We know beyond a shadow of a doubt that drainage tile is the nitrate delivery mechanism from farmed fields to the stream network. Yet our research at UI finds thousands of miles of new drainage tile being installed every year in Iowa. In only the middle Cedar Watershed, one of 56 watersheds of its size in Iowa, we estimate 1,200 miles of new tile are installed every year. Just to account for the new nitrogen load associated with new tile, we would need 136 new woodchip bioreactors, every year, year after year, just to maintain the water quality status quo in the middle Cedar. If you don't know, we have less than 100 woodchip bioreactors statewide.

We also know beyond a shadow of a doubt that, as a whole, Iowa farmers are overapplying nitrogen—by a lot. In some areas, inputs are twice that of ISU recommendations. Statewide, we are very likely applying 20-30% more nitrogen than what our crops need. Why? Because the taxpayer shoulders the burden for the environmental consequences caused by the excess. Yet we're forced to swallow the Ag rhetoric that no farmer wants to lose his nitrogen, all while 600 million pounds of it leaves Iowa in its rivers in an average year.

Iowa State faculty travel the countryside this fall imploring farmers to test their soil nitrogen and refrain from fall application in this post drought condition. Yet here's Iowa farmer Kelly Garrett in *Successful Farming* just this week, and I quote: "we need to push anhydrous applications harder than usual this fall, and we are pushing out plant food at a record rate."

Here's a quote from an Iowa State researcher in a paper published in the *Journal of Environmental Quality*: "The large leaching losses of nitrate measured from Iowa farm fields are of environmental, economic, and energy concern. The quality of tile drainage water is important because this water can be a significant portion of total stream flow."

The year that was published, Sandra Day O'Connor became the first female Supreme Court Justice, Muhammad Ali fought his last fight, Lech Walesa met with Pope John Paul II in the Vatican, and Bobby Knight and Isaiah Thomas led the Indiana Hoosiers to the NCAA basketball title. 1981.

We know beyond a shadow of a doubt we over apply phosphorus. We know that nearly every county in Iowa has excess soil phosphorus. We also know that availability of manure nutrients has little to no impact on commercial fertilizer sales. Farmers in livestock dense watersheds apply almost as much commercial fertilizer as those where livestock is sparse, and sometimes more. Why? Because farmer peace of mind is more important than our children having clean water.

We know that our manure management plans, governed by the master matrix laws, endorse an overapplication of manure nutrients based on a theory of fertilization discredited decades ago—the yield goal. Why? Well, because the industry and their advocates in the legislature know that if we made farmers adhere to crop needs, we would constrict the expansion of the livestock industry by increasing the amount of land area necessary to apply manure. Quite likely this artificially inflates land prices, favoring millionaire farmers and limiting opportunities for young people who would like to farm.

Why do we give farmers license to apply however much nutrient they want, and then expect the taxpayer to pay to capture the surplus with edge of field treatments and cover crops? The taxpayer has even helped pay for nitrogen inhibitors, products that have been shown to do little or nothing for water quality. But they do provide a few more bushels for farmers and a few more dollars for Dow Chemical, courtesy of the Iowa taxpayer.

We often hear that the way to cleaner water here in Iowa is "partnerships." We even have an organization called Iowa Partnership for Clean Water. Their home page says they "work to inform all stakeholders—both rural and urban—about the consequences of frivolous legal action against farmers and the agriculture industry." I don't think they've done much since the Des Moines Water Works lawsuit was dropped.

We also have alliances—Iowa Agricultural Water Alliance, Agriculture's Clean Water Alliance, the Dickinson County Clean Water Alliance, the Rathbun Land and Water Alliance, and so on and so on. Our quantity of partnerships and alliances has become one more output we measure as we search for success, like hands shaken and money spent. At any rate, partnerships are a key component of what science calls the Watershed Approach, something we've been closely involved with at the University of Iowa with the Iowa Watershed Approach Project—$94 million dollars from HUD to improve several Iowa watersheds, and now winding down.

We billed it as a "flood first" approach, at least in part so as not to offend the sensibility of farmers by talking about water quality. The Watershed Approach is a widely accepted, methodical strategy to achieve water quality objectives. But what happens when your partners aren't operating in good faith? What happens when they're not willing to sacrifice even one bushel for the common good? Are we to throw up our hands in exasperation? Where's the backstop when the public is dodging beanballs thrown by agriculture?

Let me read you five quotes from a publication I found in the Iowa State University Digital Repository:

1. Agricultural practices which contribute to nutrient-related water quality problems include excessive soil erosion; use of fertilizers in excess of crop needs; failure to account for nutrient contributions of legumes and animal manures; and failure to coordinate timing of fertilizer applications according to crop needs.

2. Will farmers, agribusiness, and other groups in the agricultural community support and work to implement these voluntary water protection initiatives? Past history suggests they may not.

3. Recent sociological research suggests that the voluntary approach may not be highly successful. A recent survey of Iowa farmers characterized Iowa agriculture as "highly dependent on external inputs, and one where strong motivations toward changes are not pre-existing."

4. While it is likely that the ongoing voluntary programs will be given a reasonable period to work before a more regulatory approach is adopted, this period will certainly be far shorter than the 50-year period given for voluntary soil conservation programs to work.

5. At this point, the challenge is clear. Will the agricultural community voluntarily take the actions necessary to protect and improve Iowa's water quality? There are many who say this will not happen.

Those lines are from a publication submitted and accepted to the Proceedings of the Crop Production and Protection Conference at Iowa State University in 1990, almost 32 years ago, by 3 staff members at, believe or not, Iowa DNR—Ubbo Agena, Bill Bryant and Tom Oswald. Try to imagine a DNR staff person saying such things today—you can't. Today DNR seems preoccupied with helping agriculture skirt what weak regulations we have. It's hard to make the case that the agency works for all Iowans, rather than just agriculture.

Agriculture has been telling us they would fix our water quality problems for the last 40 years, maybe more. Yet the most significant thing that has happened during that time was a regulation, Conservation Compliance, that was part of the 1985 Farm Bill. Conservation Compliance required farmers on Highly Erodible Ground to follow various soil conservation measures if they wanted to participate in federal farm programs. It worked. We saw almost instantaneous improvement in the clarity of Iowa streams, documented by researchers at both ISU and UI.

Yet agriculture gaslights us about how regulation won't work, it can't work. We're told 40,000 full time farmers, all growing the same two crops and a subset of them raising the same three animals, all within a mere 3 degrees of latitude and 6 degrees of longitude, are too diverse and too different for regulation to ever work. If you want better water, says establishment agriculture, you're just going to have to wait until we're good and ready to give it to you. In the meantime, keep sending us money and we'll keep giving lip service to water quality and crumbs to the Iowa taxpayer, if we feel like it.

If you read anything that I write, you may know that for me, this has become an issue of justice. How is it just that the Iowa taxpayer, with an average yearly income of about $49,000 per year, is told that he or she must pay the Iowa farmer, with an average yearly income of $134,000 per year and a net worth upwards of $2 million, if we are to have clean water? What reasonable person accepts this calculus? I for one do not. I was here a couple of years ago and heard an

Iowa farmer say that if we wanted less nitrogen pollution, we needed to "show him the money." And I'll be damned if he didn't say it again today! I can't go there anymore. I won't go there anymore. That approach is not morally defensible in my view and if your head is still in that place, I really don't know what to say to you. I'm tired of being played as a fool.

The public has invested heavily in this current production system—last year, nearly 40% of farm income came from the federal government, 40%. So, a reasonable person might say that the taxpayer has a stake in the system. I would. And as such, I say, we should have a say, in how the system is operated. So here are my five things I think the public should ask for before we hand over even one more dime of our money to millionaire farmers.

1. Ban fall tillage. Iowa State has been putting out guidance on this since the 1980s and it all says one thing: don't do it. Increases erosion, increases nutrient loss. Convenience is the only rational explanation for doing it, and I'm sorry, farmer convenience is not my or the public's problem.

2. Ban manure to snow and frozen ground. Yes, there are rules on this, but they are so weak and ineffectual that if there is snow on the ground on February 28, you will see manure on it on March 1. Again, farmer convenience trumps the common good.

3. Stop farming in the 2-year flood plain, and mandate buffers for the banks of perennial streams. We have 400,000 acres that are cropped in the two-year flood plain. Why? Why do we indemnify this activity? If we cannot shore up the riparian corridors, there truly is no hope for what is left of our streams.

4. Make farmers adhere to the ISU recommendations for nitrogen application. Virtually everybody in my world knows farmers look at nitrogen as cheap insurance. Why? Because the taxpayer is forced

to shoulder the burden for the environmental consequences. This is immoral in my view.

5. Rewrite the Master Matrix livestock rules such that the manure management plans are digitized for effective enforcement and require nutrient application at rates commensurate with crop needs.

People tell me these are just small things; they won't solve the problem. I say they are "just" things, as in justice. And I think you could get close to the nutrient strategy objective of 45% with "just" those five things.

When I first got hired at the Des Moines Water Works, my immediate supervisor was Ted Corrigan, who now of course is the General Manager. Ted was fond of telling me that the best indicator of future behavior is past behavior. Folks—the jury is in, and it has been for a while. Agriculture is not going to fix this, and I think it is foolhardy and irresponsible to cling to that fantasy. And yes, I know that making laws is probably impossible in the short term, and tortuous in the long term. But it is what the public deserves, and especially, it is what agriculture deserves.

C IS FOR CARBONALISM

I wrote this one as a comment on the proposed carbon-capture pipeline, an idea spearheaded by long-time Iowa mover and shaker Bruce Rastetter. Former Iowa governor Terry Branstad (R) is also on the payroll of this venture, as is the son of another former Iowa governor, USDA Secretary Tom Vilsack (D). Carbon dioxide (CO2) capture and entombment in the bedrock thousands of feet down is an idea that has been around for a long time, and one that is now getting some legs because there is money to be made on it. This is an example of how many in Iowa aren't eager to embrace environmental improvement unless there is money to be made doing it.

I sometimes worry that these essays are too similar to one another. But then I think about Sue Grafton, who became rich and famous by writing much the same book 25 times, and that makes me feel better. *F Is for Formulaic* was my personal favorite. She tragically died after *Y Is for Yesterday* which is maybe something to keep in mind.

Scientists can rival Grafton, Louis L'Amour and the old pulp fiction writers of yore when it comes to formulaic. I wrote about that once a couple of years ago with the essay "Déjà Vu All Over Again." Along those lines, I'm considering submitting a book proposal for the "Dummies" series to be titled *Creeping Incrementalism for Dummies* that features agriculture's environmental performance. You know the ending.

Writing papers for submission to a scientific journal requires a review of existing literature. When you do what I do, this can be downright depressing because so much of what we know about the causes and solutions for bad water and bad air has been known for a loooooong time. You can almost sense the researchers' frustration festering between statements of fact that are repeated year after year, paper after paper. I'm working on a soil carbon paper with some other people here, and I came across an example of this in a 2009 paper written by World Food Prize Laureate Rattan Lal: "Numerous and wide-ranging benefits of soil organic matter (SOM or organic carbon) for enhancing soil quality and influencing the underlying pedological processes were quantified by Jenny.[1] Some direct benefits of the SOM pool include improvement in soil structure, retention of water and plant nutrients, increase in soil biodiversity and decrease in risks of soil erosion and the related degradation." Jenny was esteemed soil scientist Hans Jenny, who had to write not one but two papers 20 years after the original as if to say, hey, dudes, did you not see this paper I wrote 20 years ago? And if alive, he would probably still be writing the same paper again and again because agriculture is a stubborn ass when it comes to change. Unless of course if it has anything to do with bushels. There are a lot of early adopters when it comes to anything bushel related. Weird how that works.

Hans Jenny. Photo credit: University of California, Berkeley.

Having failed to convince farmers over the last 80 years that sequestering carbon in their soil is a good thing, the Government-Academia-NGO-Ag Industrial complex is poised to capitalize, or carbonalize, I might say, on the public's climate change angst in ways that funnel money to farmers to do the right thing, even though the right thing is largely in the farmers' best interest. Of course, many in the complex are eager to skim a little of that money off the top, don't you know.

There's an important lesson here and that lesson is that improvements in Ag's environmental outcomes rarely happen unless they can be monetized. Doing it for the common or greater good? C'mon, that's for sissies and socialists, and not the kind of socialists who are on the receiving end of farm subsidies. The bad kind.

So, speaking of monetization, there are some rich guys that also want to monetize the carbon dioxide (CO_2) resulting from fuel ethanol production.[2,3] The idea is to capture this CO_2 and pipe it up to North Dakota because, well, climate change. Supposedly. And capitalism. A new breed of capitalism, carbonalism, that has one customer—the federal government. A system that millionaires can use to cynically exploit the damage already done to our atmosphere. I'd be shocked if these people are as worried about climate change as they are about the price of Johnny Walker. But hey, if there's a buck to be made from the suckers that worry about the earth our grandchildren will inherit, why not? In the name of capitalism, oops, I mean carbonalism, MONETIZE EVERYTHING.

If carbon capture from ethanol production is such a good idea, you might ask, why didn't they do it decades ago when the industry was developed and when scientists knew pretty much all of what we know now about greenhouse gases and climate? Answer (a): because the suckers weren't worried enough then. Answer (b): Enhanced Oil Recovery (EOR). Potential windfalls exist for the pipeliners if they can sell the CO_2 to North Dakota oil drillers to help scavenge recalcitrant petroleum from geological formations that are nearly exhausted—a tradeoff that hardly is much of a climate change benefit for the public. A win-lose, in other words.

So, buckle up for months of pipe-aganda about how journeyman and -woman pipefitters and earthmovers and surveyors and various other rugged workers will revitalize rural Iowa by occupying hotel rooms and washing down months' worth of pork tenderloin sandwiches with rivers of Busch Light at every Forgottenville, Iowa, tavern on the NW-SE axis. We'll probably hear soon that Casey's convenience store is reserving container ship space for all the extra breakfast pizza ingredients they will need to ship in to feed this starving mob of high paid workers. This will all somehow make up for the wreckage wrought on rural Iowa by the Ag Titans over the past 50 years through consolidation and creation of the three-headed corn-soy-CAFO Frankenstein monster. We're told this is the most sustainable model for Iowa, and indeed for a present-day farmer in present-day Iowa, it may be, at least at the farm scale. But this phony sustainability rests squarely upon the backs of the taxpayer and the public's tolerance of its externalities, namely, polluted water and air.

Also folks, be prepared for the Johnny Walker drinkers to advocate for higher nitrogen fertilizer application rates in the name of climate change. You heard it here first.

THE MAGINOT LINE

You can learn a lot about Iowa farming just by driving the countryside with your eyes wide-open. A four-hour drive on Christmas Eve, 2021, inspired this essay, along with our willingness to monetize, rather than solve, Iowa's poor water quality.

The Maginot Line was a continuous series of fortifications built along the French-German border by the war-weary French in the 1930s, with the hope it would deter the fascists from invading.

You know how that worked out.

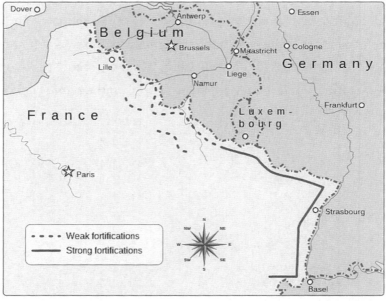

The Maginot Line. Image credit: Goran-teken, Wikimedia commons.

I traveled the 225 miles from Lansing (Iowa) to Ankeny on Christmas Eve, a drive through an Iowa landscape left snowless by an Arkansas December. Since the harvest is now long over, every square inch of land is left exposed, and lot of it is really, really exposed. My best estimate is that at least 50% and maybe as many as 70% of the fields were tilled. I don't have any data on this, but anecdotally fall tillage seems to be increasing, in my observation.

I can also say that I saw visible cover crops on only two fields, one near the town of Orchard and the other at mile marker 139 on Interstate 35.

I posted these observations on my twitter feed, and not surprisingly, that inspired some lively farmer responses that can be summed up mostly as such:

1. We want more time.
2. We want more money.

Now I'd like to reply with the old joke about people in hell wanting ice water, but in this case, Satan is a sympathizer, and these fellows are probably going to be provided with unlimited amounts of both.

I also got some replies that poor cover crop germination and growth this fall due to unfavorable weather has left more fields bare than what would otherwise be the case. Ok, I have no reason to dispute this, but if true, it casts serious doubt on the efficacy of cover crops to improve water quality and soil health since Iowa has some of the most dynamic weather on earth.

One of the latter responses was from a fellow who asked me to become a "certified investor" in his soil health consulting firm, so many of which seem to be sprouting like pigweed in a soybean field with a Roundup hangover. These outfits can smell taxpayer money like a hog smells a buried acorn. With U.S. Secretary of Agriculture Tom Vilsack mocking the European Union's "Farm to Fork" regulatory approach to improved environmental performance from agriculture,[1] soil health is being propped up as a Maginot Line of sorts that will defend Gaul from the Prussian Blitzkrieg of more hogs, more tile, more fertilizer, and more ethanol, even though there's abundant evidence we can't cope with the present levels.

The current conventional wisdom seems to be that if we're too cowardly to regulate Iowa's terrible water quality, then by god, let's monetize it! And that goes double for climate change, the change in this case being money from your pocket into the pocket of Agribusiness in the name of climate.

And paralleling the Maginot Line, we already have a Vichy government in-waiting comprised of the usual suspects in the agencies, academia, and non-profits. Back in March, coincidentally (?) about the same time word got out that the Iowa legislature was discussing Soil Heath legislation, The Nature Conservancy announced that they are "building a portfolio of agtech ventures to improve soil health," and that "The Nature Conservancy has formed a partnership with iSelect Fund, an impact venture firm that invests mainly in agriculture and healthcare [quite a pair, don't you think?], to source and invest in early-stage agtech ventures targeting soil health issues."[2]

Well, isn't that special. Instead of building pipelines for CO2, maybe we could just go ahead and build one that pumps money into humanitarian aid for Meeting Attenders that helps them quaff more Manhattans in the hotel bar after a hot, grueling day in the Marriott conference room. And to think Iowa farmers get mad at me. Go figure.

If farmers want to improve their soil "health," which basically means increasing organic matter, then hey, they should knock themselves out. Every conservationist ever has been saying that for decades. The benefits to the farmer are numerous and quantifiable, and these translate to more money and better land value.

But to ask the taxpayer to pay for this under the guise of improved water quality and climate change mitigation is a wagonload of horseshit that your children and grandchildren will be paying for, right along with the peel-and-eat shrimp that come with each Manhattan. How about we give these a try:

1. Make farmers apply ISU-recommended amounts of nitrogen.

2. Quit farming in the two-year floodplain, and buffer perennial streams.

3. Ban fall tillage.

4. Ban application of manure to snow and frozen ground.

5. Rework the master matrix livestock rules such that DNR can effectively enforce them and require N and P application at recommended rates commensurate with ISU guidelines in the N rate calculator.

Cost to the taxpayer: zero dollars.

IOWA 2021: THE YEAR IN REVIEW

I wrote this one sitting at the kitchen table on New Year's Day, 2022. It probably wouldn't exist had I not gotten rid of television; the temptation of watching football might have been too much. So much of the time, our efforts to improve water quality in Iowa seem farcical. They are farcical, in my opinion. This essay was meant to articulate that, without actually saying it. The context here may escape you, if you don't live in Iowa, or don't follow the debate around water quality and agriculture. The public and political figures mentioned here are indeed real people; the others, including the farmers, are not. DITCHs is a euphemism of sort for the ongoing STRIPs project run out of Iowa State.

Note: This is a work of fiction. Mostly.

After hastily changing their drawers following GM and Ford announcements that they would soon be all-electric, the Ethanolians redoubled their efforts to force corn ethanol down the vehicular gullets of America, and Iowa politicians from one end of the political spectrum to the other were eager to help. So, so eager to help. One politician was heard to remark that if clean water had lobbyists like corn ethanol, well, obviously we would have more of the former and less of the latter. Rebranding E10 as Octane 88 in cartoon videos featuring wealthy-looking, environmentally conscious millennials was one of the industry's more noticeable propaganda pieces. It fit nicely with their scheme to pipe ethanol-plant CO_2 to North Dakota and/or Illinois where it can be entombed or, in the case of North Dakota, force to the surface...yes, believe it or not...fossil fuel where it can be burned with ethanol to emit more CO_2. I'm ranking this as 2021's top story.

Other significant stories include:

Against his stomach's best wishes, Iowa agriculture secretary Mike Naig announced he was running for re-election. After his 638th lunch with Iowa farmers and agribusiness interests across the state over the past 5+ years, Naig was heard to say, "how much pork loin, green bean casserole, scalloped potatoes and apple crisp is a guy expected to eat in one term?" Naig remained silent when a reporter pointed out that Bill Northey and Sonny Perdue were champs when it came to this sort of thing. As to Naig's opposition, Democrats appeared poised to nominate a guy who seemed like he was practicing for a job interview with the Clinton Administration.

Speaking of politics, the Biden Administration announced the appointments of Matt (pray for clean water because nothing else has worked) Russell as Iowa Farm Services Agency director and Theresa (Octane 88) Greenfield as head of Iowa Rural Development, the top two USDA jobs in Iowa. USDA Secretary Tom Vilsack said both are well equipped to bring 20th century Ag policy to the Iowa landscape.

EPA Head Michael Regan visited Iowa in May and emphasized that he was committed to Iowa agriculture's voluntary approach to nutrient pollution. When asked by a reporter how he would rank the strategy's effectiveness, Regan responded with a brilliant assemblage of meaningless platitudes that included "You know, I haven't looked at it closely." (That is not fiction, by the way.) Regan said he might later go take a close look at the Raccoon River, but he wanted to have a couple of Manhattans in the hotel bar first.

In an amazing example of concurrent scientific discovery, NGOs and land grant universities across the country simultaneously announced that plowing the shit out of your soil and repeatedly sterilizing it with petrochemicals might be bad. This curiously coincided with Joe Biden and Tom Vilsack returning to the federal government. Asked by one grad student if this was a coincidence, a famous soil scientist remarked, "inspiration is where you find it." Conservationists everywhere are promising that this newfound emphasis on "Soil Health" will deliver cleaner water and a cooler climate by the year 2250, give or take a century.

Iowa State University announced a novel conservation strategy they have coined DITCHs: Demonstrable Idea That Could Happen. Groundbreaking research is showing that un-mowed ditches can provide bird habitat. Appanoose County farmer Harold Anderson participated in a pilot project and had this to say: "I saved a bunch of money on gas and wear and tear on my mower. Those ditches just filled up with pheasants. I told my brother-in-law Jerry that he could road hunt that section if he wanted to, but he had to give me half the birds. He wasn't too happy about that last part, or when his son shot out the windshield on his brand-new F150."

The North Raccoon Watershed Management Authority (WMA) announced that they are sick and tired of the Raccoon River flowing through Dallas and Polk County. With the help of engineer Ron Hetler, they have devised a scheme to reroute the river to the Missouri River basin. One Buena Vista County supervisor, who farms in the river's headwaters, said, "Look, that water needs to go where people won't be whining about it all the time. Those liberals down there in Des Moines show no appreciation for all the nutrients we are sending them. When was the last time you heard anybody complain about the (Missouri River tributary) Boyer River? Like, NEVER."

Iowa DNR unveiled their new smartphone app that sends an alert to individual livestock farmers anytime their manure management plan is pulled out of the DNR area field office filing cabinet. DNR vehicles have also been outfitted with transponders that send signals via the app so farmers can see where field office staff are located in real time. DNR Director Kayla Lyon said "We're not cops, we're facilitators. We want to work with farmers so their livestock operations kill fewer fish, in the areas where fish and other aquatic life may still exist." For the rare farmer that does end up with a fine, Iowa commodity groups have set up a "Go Fund Me" account that enables the public to pitch in with a tax-deductible contribution that helps pay the fine.

Iowa Farm Bureau Federation continued their crusade against EPA's inhumane Waters of the United States (WOTUS) rule. "This over-reach is an ongoing human tragedy for the Iowa family farm," outgoing IFBF president Craig Hill said of the rule, which thus far has claimed zero farms and produced fines totaling $00,000,000. U.S. Congresswomen Ashley Hinson and Marianette Miller-Meeks, along with U.S. Senator Joni Ernst, dramatically drenched themselves in red paint at the Shelby County Farm Bureau meeting to illustrate how much of Iowa the rule would regulate. Finally, two Linn County shopping mall developers implored the Professional Developers of Iowa to grant the association's 2021 "Carrying the Water" award to IFBF.

On December 30th, Des Moines Water Works CEO Ted Corrigan warned for the 78th time in 2021 that the drinking water supply for 1/5th of Iowa's residents was perilously close to a crisis situation. Iowa agribusiness and legislature response: meh.

The Iowa Drainage District Association announced a new program targeting elementary school students called "Just Say No To Wet Spots." Educational materials will be provided to rural school districts that emphasize the importance of tile drainage. Association president Walt Olson said that impressionable minds can't be led to believe that the pre-settlement wetland landscape was a good thing. "Once you get hooked on clean water and wildlife, there's no going back," said Olson.

Finally, Iowa's oldest corn-soybean farmer, 106-year-old Harold Johnson of Grundy County, decided to call it quits, handing over the farm to his 30-year-old great-grandson, Dusty. Harold's son, Harold Jr., and grandson, Harold III, both died in recent years, apparently out of frustration while awaiting their inheritance of the Johnson place. Dusty said he was thankful his great granddad had faith in him, and that his parents didn't name him Harold. Perhaps not co-incidentally, Harold Sr. was not only Iowa's oldest farmer, but he also held the lifetime record for most USDA subsidies. 98-year-old Larry Hanson is now Iowa's oldest farmer, and he also is out to break Harold's USDA subsidy record. "I figure that record is reachable," said Larry, "if my cousin Harold Hanson doesn't get there first." The other Harold (Hanson) is 96.

So those were the highlights, at least as I saw them. Feel free to send your suggestions for the next edition a year from now if I'm still employed.

CATCH-2022

I live in Iowa City but grew up in the Des Moines area. My mother is still living there in the suburb of Ankeny, and whenever an article about water appears in the Des Moines Register, *she takes a photo of it and texts it to me. One of these inspired this essay.*

If you keep it dirty
And I keep it clean
Then you don't know
What keepin' it dirty means
—Bill Hinkley and Judy Larson, recording of the song
Keep it Clean, Willie Watson, 1930.

This morning (1/9/22) the *Des Moines Register* ran an editorial[1] titled "Spend every spare dime on Iowa's water." The column made the case that as much as possible of Iowa's current $1.2 billion budget surplus be applied to improving the state's water quality. This of course is, or should be, music to the ears of Big Meat (Tyson, JBS, Cargill, and others), Big Seed (Bayer-ex Monsanto, DowDuPont-Pioneer), Big Fertilizer (Mosaic, Nutrien, Koch) and Big Chemical (Bayer, BASF, Corteva), who've never been asked to spare a single dime or even a nickel for Iowa water quality while they've made billions as our streams were wrecked.

Those lower on the Ag food chain, i.e., agribusiness that retails Big products, and those who buy and use Big products, should be similarly happy with that *Register* headline because it endorses the idea that our bad water is because of a lack of money, and not their actions or motives, which of course are as pure as the driven dough.

I've said many times that I can agree with public money being used to help farmers improve their environmental outcomes. But how do we continue this farce without asking agriculture to be accountable? How is this good government? This is an industry that en masse refuses to limit livestock expansion, refuses to limit tile drainage, refuses to adequately account for nutrient inputs, and refuses to buffer streams, among many other refusals. No most certainly means no when it comes to agriculture. The taxpayer is asked over and over and over again to mitigate the consequences of their actions as if we were the ones making the decisions that are polluting the water. It's like we collectively lay awake at night thinking, if only we had given the farmers more money, maybe our water would be better.

Joseph Heller, from *Joseph Heller, a Descriptive Bibliography*, by Matthew Bruccoli and Park Brucker.

The absurdity of it all reminds me of Joseph Heller's masterpiece, *Catch-22* (1961). The main character, John Yossarian, is a U.S. bombardier in WWII Europe who comes to see the enemy not only as German soldiers, but also anybody that is making decisions that might get him killed. This includes many dim-witted officers but especially the careerist and General wannabe Colonel Cathcart, who keeps increasing the number of bombing missions necessary to return home.

Heller basically tells some form of the same absurd joke page after page after page to make his points. For example: "He was polite to his elders, who disliked him." Far be it from me to know what makes a great novel, but Heller's method seems to succeed in creating an environment where nothing makes sense, and that's the way everybody likes it, except Yossarian.

Heller writes not only about the absurdity of war and military life, but the human condition in general, and sees people everywhere willing to turn a buck on tragedy. Farming does not escape his gaze as he describes the farmer father of Major Major, the latter being one of the book's main characters: "He was a long-limbed farmer, a God-fearing, freedom-loving, law-abiding rugged individualist who held that federal aid to anyone but farmers was creeping socialism... (he) was an outspoken champion of economy in government, provided it did not interfere with the sacred duty of government to pay farmers as much as they could get.... He was a proud and independent man who was opposed to unemployment insurance and never hesitated to whine, whimper, wheedle, and extort for as much as he could get from whomever he could." The farmer himself says that "the Lord gave us good farmers two strong hands so that we could take as much as we could grab with both of them."

If we are going drop serious money on Iowa water quality, I've got two words for you: Northeast Iowa. This is where our best streams are, but also where streams are degrading most rapidly. Agricultural production is least intense here—only about half the land in Iowa's Driftless Area is cropped. The streams still have some biological integrity and are mostly un-straightened. There are several good-to-excellent trout streams in the Driftless. Our best warm water streams are also in the Driftless or just off it—the Upper Wapsi, for example.

This may seem unfair to Iowans who are Driftless-distant; it's a six-hour drive from Hamburg to Decorah. But if we want to have rivers that look like actual rivers, we need to pull out all the stops to protect Northeast Iowa.

Tributaries of the Missouri River are wrecked and are not coming back. A famous hydrologist once told me that it will take another ice age to restore these streams. (A possible exception here is the upper reach of the Little Sioux.) These rivers have all been straightened to square up fields for farming and the cost to re-meander streams at the large scale is a non-starter. Not to mention that landowners would never agree to allow this to happen. This is not to say that these streams have zero value; we know that people will use even the worst streams. But my opinion is that money spent in these watersheds will produce relatively small benefits for Iowans.

In between the Hopeless Area and the Driftless Area are the North Raccoon, Boone, Upper Cedar and Shellrock, all of which are high nitrate streams but yet still have potential. They could be saved but in the case of the North Raccoon, money is no object. In other words, the farmers don't even want it. They are happy with the status quo.

Yossarian's Catch-22 went like this: Only crazy people agree to fly more missions, but only sane people ask to be grounded, and if you're sane, strap on the parachute, sucker. Here in Iowa, we might say Catch-2022 goes like this: only crazy people say we should regulate agriculture for better water quality, but only sane people say it will work.

Wrap your head around that one.

MALICE IN WONDERLAND

From time to time someone will tell me my essays are too angry. Admittedly, I'm not happy about the state of nature here in Iowa, and I make no apologies for articulating that, but I do think people sometimes mistake honest writing for angry writing. I do try to sprinkle some humor in my essays, what I call my funnies. I try to put a couple or three funnies in every essay to get some balance. This essay is indeed a bit of a rant; thus, I tried to throw some good funnies in there for balance.

A trio of events occurred this week that produced a visceral reaction in my viscera, which I now know must be in the middle of my brain because each event made my brain feel like a bulging aneurysm was about to burst forth with such magnitude that the blood would spray out each ear like an astronaut losing his pressurized helmet in some gory sci-fi movie taking place on the planet Ucornus.

Yes, I've been told to be less evocative.

Since my reaction after each event was WHAT THE HELL, I thought it best to wait a few days to write something, giving the pressurized aneurysm time to dissipate. Alas, I'm still wondering WHAT THE HELL, so here goes. I'm not putting these in the order of occurrence, I'm just letting that aneurytic pressure drain out through my fingertips organically.

FIELD OF SCHEMES

Governor Kim Reynolds announced that Iowa was going to use $38 million from the Water Infrastructure Fund to pay for three water quality and infrastructure projects across Iowa,[1] with $11 million going to the Dyersville East Road Utilities Project at the *Field of Dreams* movie site, for water distribution and wastewater collection infrastructure. "The project will serve 114,000 Iowans across two counties and create approximately 350 jobs." Indeed, the combined population of Dubuque and Delaware county is about 114,000, but Dubuque city (population 59,000) and most of the rest of the municipalities in the two counties already have water and wastewater treatment, not that some of them couldn't use some upgrades. I think the city of Dubuque is in pretty good shape.

Call me a cynic if you must, but I feel like the manager just called a squeeze play or a double steal or a pitchout or whatever baseball lingo works best here. A person can only imagine that the governor or some other titan of Iowa business or politics rang up Commissioner of Major League Baseball Rob Manfred last August after the wildly-popular Field of Dreams televised game between the Yankees and White Sox and said "Dude, we just looooved that 3-hour long corn commercial," and Manfred replying something to effect of "Well, [Yankees star] Giancarlo Stanton has a $135 million contract, and neither he nor [*Field of Dreams* movie star] Kevin Costner likes having to crap in a porta potty. Let's talk turkey."

Voilà, water infrastructure comes to a ball diamond carved out of a corn field. Interestingly, Dyersville is home to the National Farm Toy Museum, which is a nice segue to the next story.

TOY PLANTER

Polk County announced they are buying a $600,000 cover crop planter, because apparently the owners of the most valuable farmland on earth are unable to part with enough of the beer money they saved for the winter in Fort Myers to get pollution-reducing cover crop seed in the ground in the Raccoon and Des Moines River watersheds.[2] Some of the quotes on this story are just golden. "Our hope is for the machine to travel around and get some excitement." And, "We recognize the value this project can have in sharing some of the responsibility to protect our public waterways and watersheds."

Context people, context. They *hope* to plant cover crops on 10,000 acres using the machine. There about 6 million acres in the two watersheds, 75% of it cropped. The average nitrate-nitrogen load traveling through the city of Des Moines in the two rivers is 105,000,000 pounds, per year. Best case scenario is the planter will reduce that 0.1%, or about 80,000 pounds. Cost for farmers to buy that lost nitrogen in the first place: $67,000. Bear in mind you (and yes I mean you) still have to buy the seeds, and the thing needs to be carted around which surely cannot be cheap. I'm told that dispersing the cover crop seed into a standing corn crop with an airplane is just about as effective and costs $7/acre. But, this shiny contraption for sure will make a nice prop for public figures to stand next to at the State Fair and ride in Suburbanville's 2022 4th of July parade, peacocking their water quality cred. The most puzzling thing about this hog and pony show is the fact that Des Moines Water Works, who knows context better than anybody, has now apparently decided to be a contestant on "Who Wants to be a Millionaire's Patsy," Iowa's longest-running TV gameshow, by pitching in to help buy the thing. On what planet (other than Ucornus) does this make sense?

HOMEBUILDERS, UNITE!

Evidently the Homebuilders of Iowa have finally learned a thing or two from their countryside compatriots that have put up all these hog buildings the last 20 years. Of course, the livestock industry has their "Master Matrix" regulation, if you want to call it that (regulation, that is) that prevents the counties from regulating the livestock industry. (Just writing that sentence makes it feel like the aneurysm is pressurizing again.) The homebuilders are like "Dudes, sweet law!" So of course, we get legislation proposed in the Iowa legislature this session,[3] sponsored by Shannon Lundgren of Peosta, that prevents municipal governments from making their own stormwater mitigation rules. So who registers "for" this bill? But of course, the Iowa Association of Business and Industry, and them good ol' boys at the Homebuilders Association of Iowa. And the irony, after decades of having agriculture drag out the bogeyman of urban storm water runoff, rural legislators want to conspire with the homebuilders to keep the cities from doing anything about it.

Iowa. You couldn't make this stuff up if you tried.

To finish up with a bit on cover crops. Since 1995, Iowa farmers have received more than $10 billion dollars in taxpayer-funded indemnity payments, and the feds pay out $1.5 billion per year of your tax dollars to insurance companies to administer the crop insurance program. Cover crops are known to reduce weather and pest risks to crops. Why not require cover crops on a field if it is to receive taxpayer-funded crop insurance? On what planet (other than Ucornus) does this not make sense? But when I bring this up, some farmer inevitably counters with "well, they don't work in the northeast corner of the southwest section of Contrarian County where the old schoolhouse used to be, so we can't require them, or any other damn thing for that matter." At times I feel like Alice in wonderland at the mad tea party. The characters bombard Alice with farcical and nonsensical riddles until she finally gives up and tells them this is the stupidest goddamn tea party she's ever been to.

We literally let agriculture dictate to us how water quality is to be addressed in this state. Our water will be terrible until we summon the courage to change this dynamic.

IOWA IS ADDICTED TO CORNOGRAPHY

Growing corn is our birthright here in Iowa, and our devotion to the production of this crop is at the root of many of our environmental problems. At the time of this writing, about 60% of Iowa corn is being used to produce ethanol. The agricultural industry hails ethanol as a "green" fuel that is an important solution for climate change mitigation. But cracks in that narrative are developing. Some recent research is showing corn ethanol may increase greenhouse gas emissions relative to petroleum. At the same time, the solar power industry is maturing rapidly, and coupled with electric cars, poses a threat to the ethanol industry. These issues inspired this essay.

The *Oxford English Dictionary* defines a renewable source of energy as one not depleted when used. Wikipedia says that it is energy that is collected from resources that are naturally replenished on a human timescale. If you've been listening or watching Iowa news the past month or so, you've probably heard that ethanol made from corn grain is the renewablist source of energy available thanks to the Iowa farmer who returns like clockwork from Florida each spring to his or her photosynthesis mine where he or she helps untold billions of corn plants convert sunshine into starch and thence the two-carbon-, six-hydrogen-, one-oxygen clear, flammable liquid that has 3/5ths of the energy of the 1/10th of the gasoline that it displaces in our fuel tanks.

Growing corn requires a lot of fossil fuel energy. The vast majority (probably 80% or more) of this energy links to nitrogen fertilizer, which is made using natural gas. I heard someone say once that at its essence, corn production is converting natural gas to starch, and I think that is a clean way of stating it.

I get a lot of comments that the fossil fuel energy required to produce corn and corn ethanol exceeds the energy content of the ethanol itself. Based on everything I know about the subject, I do not believe that to be true. There are about 75,000 BTU in a gallon of ethanol; it takes about 35,000 BTU to grow the corn and produce the ethanol; you can get about 500 gallons of ethanol from an acre of corn; and thus the net energy gain is about 20 million BTU per acre.

But it's just beyond argument that this 20 million BTU comes at a high environmental cost: soil erosion, nutrient pollution, degraded streams, lakes and drinking water, habitat loss, and to top it off, we indemnify corn production with publicly supported crop insurance and a whole host of other economic trusses that keep the herniated system from blowing out. The patient keeps limping along, in obvious pain but nonetheless determined to maintain its stranglehold on the public and on 11,000 square miles of Iowa land, 20% of our state's area.

Ethanol is a thing because motor vehicles need liquid fuel, in this case organic compounds that ignite in the presence of oxygen to form CO_2 and water, producing usable energy in the process. But along come cars that use electrons that power not engines, but electric motors. And the electrons can come from photons intercepted not by corn, but by solar panels that don't need nitrogen fertilizer, tractors, pesticides, soil, or even farmers. And these solar panels stand ready to mothball the photosynthesis mine. An acre of them in Iowa produce *34 times*[1] the amount of usable energy as an acre of corn headed for the ethanol plant. Not twice as much, not three times as much, not 10 times as much. Thirty-four times as much.

This is causing Iowa politicians, many of whom identify as farmers, to soil not just our rivers but also their drawers, and start suggesting really, really stupid stuff. One is to force all filling stations in Iowa to provide E-15, gasoline blended with ethanol at an 85:15 ratio, above the typical 90:10 blend. Talking about a bill (HF 2128) currently being considered in the Iowa legislature, legislator-farmer Dan Zumbach (R-Ryan), he of the Bloody Run Creek/Supreme Beef fame, said that "This is about Iowa, this is about the people who live in Iowa, this is about supporting Iowans." Zumbach is chair of the Senate's agriculture committee. "This is about making Iowa a viable —economically viable—state where fuel is available everywhere."[2] Just a hunch, but I doubt there is an Iowan more than 10 miles from vehicle fuel.

The proposed law requires 50% of fuel pumps to deliver E-15, and fueling stations with just one pump would also have to sell E-15 exclusively if there's only one choice for fuel. Ever the do-gooder, Zumbach said that "We have a real opportunity to do well for Iowans. Good bills come hard. Good bills come with questions. Good bills come with controversy." Makes you wonder what bad bills come with. Performative politics, perhaps?

Iowa's governor Kim Reynolds also seems to be stalked by fears of corn ethanol's demise. She tweeted today (2/10/22): "Charging stations while ignoring a readily-available renewable energy source grown right here in IA. This is why we need increased access to E-15." This was in response to the Biden Administration announcing that the federal government would provide $51 million for electric car charging stations in our state.[3]

To say that the Ag establishment has the shakes because of ethanol is probably an understatement. I suppose it's possible that people like Zumbach and Reynolds think they can keep the corn-powered money machine chugging along so it can consume all the junk agri-business and big Ag corporations love to sell, a lot of which keeps Iowa in a polluted condition: seeds, fertilizer, chemicals, grain drying, grain storage, insurance, machinery. But it's always been inevitable that Isaac Newton was going to turn the Renewable Fuel Standard into the Renewable Fool Standard. And lest you think I'm being partisan here, there are many moronic democrats in the legislature only too eager to vote for this, and do their own performative skit when it comes to the environment.

The end of ethanol, whether it comes in 5 years or 50, is going to expose how selfish the industry and the state's politicians really are. There once was a day when politicians pontificated against government picking winners and losers. Those days are clearly gone. We're just going to go ahead and pick the losers here in Iowa, because we don't give a rat's behind about the common good.

Solar power does not have to displace Iowa agriculture. Solar can co-exist and commingle with all sorts of food production in ways that can and will make Iowa agriculture more prosperous once the statists get the hell out of the way. I'm just going to call it here. We have a generation or two of old and white and rich deadwood who are content to sit in their cozy room with the door closed reading cornography put out by their enablers that tell them they are victims of some grand conspiracy. These fetishists stand in the way of young and creative people who want to farm and who want to make Iowa a better and cleaner place.

BRAVE NEW IOWA

The perversities of Corn Belt agriculture could never endure without a deter-mined propaganda machine, mostly run by agribusiness and the Ag advocacy organizations. Propaganda is likely as old as civilization itself but has be-come increasingly difficult to separate from the truth with the emergence of social media. Some people saw this day coming—George Orwell, obviously, but also Aldous Huxley, the latter of whom inspired this piece.

At times it seems remarkable how Vladimir Putin brazenly messages what is rapidly becoming a genocide into a heroic existential strug-gle for the motherland.

Or is it that remarkable?

We see much the same thing here in this country, here in our state. Perhaps on issues of less moral importance and of less moral clarity than the Ukraine war, but it's here nonetheless. It's clear that the agricultural establishment views reality as less important than how that reality is communicated to its observers. During my brief four years working on the Ag side, someone used to frequently tell me "don't listen to the rhetoric, it's not important." Looking back, I can see now that this in itself was rhetoric, a tonic we swallowed to re-duce the nausea. It's so painfully obvious now that rhetoric matters that it's hardly even worth writing this sentence.

It would be wrong to say this contagion infects only agriculture. At various times throughout my career, I've heard people say, "If only we could make people understand that (the reality, whatever it might be) isn't all that bad, and that it's actually a good thing!" There are countless hardworking individuals in this country, but as a country, we're lazy. Rather than do the hard work of improving reality, we're content to pay "communicators" to throw some words and images onto it, thinking so much spray tan will fool people into thinking we're not old and fat and bald.

I was interviewed for a couple of recent media "products," I will call them, that featured Iowa's water quality within the backdrop of modern agriculture. These were targeted to national audiences. In the first couple of times through them, my feeling on both was, well done, nicely written, but basically, same-old in the story that they told, i.e., hogs, nutrient pollution, fertilizer, Des Moines Water Works, and so forth. Almost every Iowan has seen media products on these topics on a pretty regular basis. National audiences—I couldn't say.

I stewed on a couple of things while thinking about these pieces. Firstly, they were produced by communicators; how do I (or the public) reconcile contempt for agricultural artistry when it comes to the truth, with empathy for the communicators that are inclined to be industry critics? Obviously, it matters whether or not the content is objectively correct. Is that all that matters?

It isn't.

Aldous Huxley. Image from Wikimedia commons.

The great Aldous Huxley (*Brave New World*) said this: "Great is truth, but still greater, from a practical point of view, is silence about the truth. By simply not mentioning certain subjects, by lowering what [Winston] Churchill calls an 'iron curtain' between the masses and such facts or arguments as the local political bosses regard as undesirable, totalitarian propagandists have influenced opinion much more effectively than they could have done by the most eloquent denunciations, the most compelling of logical rebuttals. If persecution, liquidation and other symptoms of social friction are to be avoided, the positive sides of propaganda must be made as effective as the negative. The most important Manhattan Projects of the future will be vast government-sponsored enquiries into what the politicians and the participating scientists will call the 'problem of happiness'—in other words, the problem of making people love their servitude. Without economic security, the love of servitude cannot possibly come into existence; for the sake of brevity, I assume that the all-powerful executive and its managers will succeed in solving the problem of permanent security." Huxley wrote that in 1946. I thought about bolding "participating scientists," but didn't.

It hit me this morning that this is what Iowa's relationship with agriculture is about, and what isn't same-old about the two aforementioned media pieces. Whether intended or not, the pieces crystallized (for me anyway) Iowa's servitude to agriculture, even though the industry occupies a much smaller piece of our economy as many might believe, and some dishonest few would have you think. They want us to think that without them, our livings, and our lives, would become insecure. This is why we tolerate the pollution that is so maddeningly apparent to our senses, day in, day out, year in, year out.

It's apparent that the corn ethanol industry is entering a new era—one where its credible use as a motor vehicle fuel will be challenged almost daily. There's a lot of heated discussion on whether or not its use reduces greenhouse gas (GHG) emissions compared to gasoline. A recent paper[1] from the University of Wisconsin in the prestigious

Proceedings of the National Academy of Science says it does not. My feeling up to this point, based on some of my own work, was that it does, modestly. What I want to tell you today is, it hardly matters. The benefits of its use relative to the environmental consequences of its production have always been at best suspect, and at worst, scandalous.

Iowa is the best place on earth to harness photosynthesis for the benefit of our species. We should try to do that here. But doing what we're doing is an abomination. We grow only two plant species and use more than ½ of the calories produced to unnecessarily fuel engines. Because we can, and because it enriches a privileged few. And because we're lazy. The opportunity costs of using 11,000 square miles of Iowa land and 60,000 nationwide for corn ethanol are huge. Ethanol is a distraction and our continued devotion to it is dangerous.

In *Brave New World*, Soma is a drug that is handed out for free to all people for social control. A feeling of well-being is created by small doses; large doses send you on a pleasant trip and impart a sense of timelessness. People are encouraged to take it with pithy sayings like "a gram is better than a damn." Iowans, in the coming months and years, prepare yourself to be served up endless ethanol cocktails spiked with Soma roofies by the Ag establishment to make you feel warm and fuzzy and climate friendly when you fill your gas tank.

AGRIBUSINESS HATES CRP

People here in this country have tried to exploit Russia's invasion of Ukraine as an opportunity to make money. Agribusiness calls to release CRP land—land set aside for conservation—for crop and livestock production are one example. That's the theme of this essay.

I wrote the essay "Stop Saying We All Want Clean Water" on a snowy April weekend three years ago, and here I am again looking down at my keyboard and up at falling snow. Why does spring snow seem so aberrant to us when its appearance is a near certainty? I guess you could say that about other things too.

SSWAWCW was written as a manifesto of sorts, a stream-of-consciousness-volcano-of-frustration erupting because I'd had it with the brazen dishonesty that characterizes establishment agriculture and Iowa's water quality. Having been around a while, I had no expectation that the essay would change things, and the last time I checked, truth in agriculture is still about as common as an acre of Iowa farmland carpeted with a cover crop. Just like our bad water, this dishonesty isn't unique to Iowa; the entire Corn Belt is awash in both. I sometimes wonder if that old saying "a kernel of truth" wasn't conjured up in some Ag comm shop where the objective was to cornify literally everything, and gaslighting especially. But I digress. I want to focus today on how Russia's assault of Ukraine has provided yet one more excuse for the aggies to assault the truth and how this has been manifested in a call to release CRP land to production.

CRP—Conservation Reserve Program—sets aside agricultural production land whereby it is planted to native species such as perennial grasses, for example. Farmers are paid to do this—you can think of this as the government renting the land from the farmer for positive environmental outcomes such as wildlife habitat and improved water quality. Fields enrolled in CRP programs are usually a farmer's least productive and most environmentally sensitive land, and these fields remain uncultivated for ten years or more.

About a month ago, a noted Ag economist at the land grant university 150 miles east of here told his social media followers this: "I've been thinking about this all day and I came to the conclusion that it's time for the Biden Admin to consider opening up the CRP for cropping in 2022." This is indeed interesting. Something tells me it took him less than a day to come up with that idea. That's because this fellow happened to be featured in a 2013 *New York Times* article titled "Academics Who Defend Wall Street Reap Reward."[1] Here's a snippet: "[He] consults for a business that serves hedge funds, investment banks and other commodities speculators, according to information received by *The Times* under the Freedom of Information Act. The business school at the University has received more than a million dollars in donations from the Chicago Mercantile Exchange and several major commodities traders, to pay for scholarships and classes and to build a laboratory that resembles a trading floor at the commodities market."

And it keeps going: "Some of his recent research has been funded by major players in the commodities world. Last year, he was paid $50,000 as a consultant for Gresham Investment Management in Chicago, which manages $16 billion and runs its own commodities index fund. He also works for a business called Yieldcast that caters to agricultural producers, investments banks and other speculators, selling them predictions of corn and soybean yields."

U.S. politicians, who have been known to carry agribusiness' polluted water from time to time, have been only too happy to jump on this landwagon. This includes U.S. senators Marco Rubio, John Boozman, and Cynthia Lummis calling on USDA secretary Tom Vilsack to release CRP acres for planting.[2]

CRP has been blamed for a lot of things, including inflation of land values and the price to rent cropland. It has also been blamed for depopulating rural Iowa, and Iowa senator and weallwantcleanwaterer Joni Ernst has implied CRP is a driver of rural poverty. Increasing food prices and the risk of hunger and famine is the latest excuse by agribusiness and its patrons to frame CRP into an orange jumpsuit so they can exploit the current crisis at the expense of the environment, in this case, letting farmers opt out of CRP contracts and bring the land into production.

Now who among us wouldn't favor crop production on CRP to save starving people? But is that really the play here? Can they really think we're that dumb? We use an area the size of 20 Iowa counties to produce corn for ethanol—11,000 square miles—and this is just in Iowa alone. An area at least as large as the state of Mississippi is used to produce corn ethanol nationwide. And of course, Agribusiness soils their britches when people propose something that would actually lower commodity prices: waiving the Renewable Fuel Standard. And here's a nugget the Feedtheworldians don't want you to know: we could meet the caloric needs of hundreds of millions of people with just the land used for U.S. ethanol production.

What's the true objective here with these calls to release CRP? Obviously, it's so agribusiness can sell more junk—drain tile, seed, fertilizer, pesticide, machinery, and insurance, a lot of which is what pollutes your water. CRP, in case you haven't noticed, requires none of that stuff.

There is a natural constriction on growth in agribusiness: land. As they say, god ain't making any more of it, and these vultures would make you grow corn in your living room if they could. We All Want Clean Water, my ass.

So, I see our state government is still saying Iowa has made great strides on reducing phosphorus pollution.[3] Folks, there's just very little evidence of this in the water. Yes, there is evidence that farmers have adopted practices that can reduce phosphorus loss. These things are not the same thing. As I've said before, the real threat to Iowa's Nutrient Reduction Strategy is not criticism from its detractors, it's from people telling the public the water is getting better when there is empirical evidence that it is not. Iowa leaders can try to *1984* this all they want, but there's always going to be some crank like me around to take some measurements. And people aren't stupid—most know bad water when they see and smell it.

The core concept of the Nutrient Strategy—identifying practices that are known to work and then incentivizing farmers to adopt them—is old school and intuitive; it's not radical policy when it comes to Ag and the environment. The problem we have is that to solve a problem of this magnitude, we must collectively want and prioritize clean water, or this, or any policy for that matter, won't work. We don't prioritize clean water and we never have. Our priority is selling junk, and people who sell junk give a lot of money to our politicians. This is not complicated.

When we don't all want clean water, any policy is worse than nothing because it serves as a mirage of sorts that people can gaze at when they feel bad about the pollution. It provides the chimera that we're "doing something," when all we're really doing is entrenching the status quo. We are not addressing, nor does the Ag establishment want us to address, the core drivers of water pollution in Iowa. That might affect the junk sale, don't you know. The other component of this is that we still lack the courage to restrict bad practices. Cleaning the field by the highway with cover crops and the back forty with a bioreactor does not wash away the stain of more tile, more animals, and more fertilizer. This has nothing to do with whether or not "THE NUTRIENT STRATEGY IS WORKING!" People in Ag are about as concerned with that as they are with starving Ukrainian infants.

I have no expectation that Iowa's water will improve before the end of my life. That doesn't mean I'm hopeless on the subject, but I am a realist and what I see happening around me is not encouraging. We've tried appeals to conscience when it comes to land use for the better part of a century now in Iowa and other agricultural landscapes, and the truth is, these appeals have failed to hold back the agricultural horde. Iowans that want to enjoy nature have had to learn to cope with the debasement of post-European settlement Iowa or go somewhere else to find the nature they want.

If we want clean water, we need laws and we need people to have the courage to say that. A lot of people.

THE IOWA SINGULARITY

I've written several essays on the use of corn ethanol as a vehicle fuel, which I view as unnecessary and environmentally suspect. This practice has come to define our state and its politics, and our first-in-the-nation presidential caucus has entrenched corn and ethanol as the golden idols that wannabe presidents of both parties kneel to. There are so many other things we could do with the land we use to grow corn ethanol, an area the size of 20 Iowa counties and larger than nine other U.S. states. The current (2022) effort to use public money and eminent domain to construct pipelines that would transport carbon dioxide from Iowa corn ethanol plants to other states is yet the latest effort to keep the corn ethanol industry competitive and afloat.

A singularity is a mathematical term for a situation where all known laws break down, and nothing makes sense. Physicists often use this term to describe the first fractions of the first second of the universe's Big Bang origin, when even time didn't really exist.

It occurred to me recently that here in Iowa, we have our own singularity. It's called ethanol. A state of senselessness, where all laws break down and math and science and even logic cease to exist.

I've written about (some would say railed about) ethanol many times. Why? Because corn ethanol for fuel is stupid. The industry exists by virtue of one reason and one reason only: government policy. The environmental benefits of using corn to produce a liquid biofuel HAVE ALWAYS been more desperation-half-court-heave than slam dunk, its lower potential energy when compared to gasoline makes the 10% blend number an obvious head fake, and its dominance of American politics has kept higher energy players sitting at the end of the bench.

So why does ethanol get its ticket punched to the Big Dance year after year after year? Politics. Liberal politicians from Joe Biden to Amy Klobuchar to Dick Durban to Sherrod Brown to Cindy Axne to the Iowa City dogcatcher provide all the cover Republicans in general and Iowa Democratic state legislators in particular need to continue force feeding us this rancid cod liver oil until kingdom come.

How did this two-bit, two-carbon alcohol get enshrined as Iowa's golden calf? A generation ago, GMO seeds and a favorable climate continued to increase corn yields, and by god, nature truly does abhor a vacuum and something had to step in to gobble up all that junk organic carbon laying around, otherwise known as #2 Dent. Enter the Energy Policy Act of 2005, also known as the Renewable Fuel Standard (RFS) or if you're an Iowan, the 11th Commandment, that required blending of biofuels with gasoline. Grain-derived ethanol was to be a bridge fuel until cellulosic (ethanol made from leaves, stalks etc.) took over, but cellulosic flopped and is now riding the bench for the ANF's Sandhill Cranes D league team in Middleofnowhere, Nebraska.

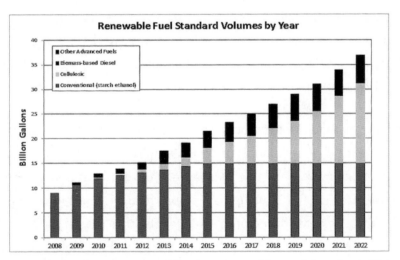

Liquid biofuel volumes required by the Renewable Fuel Standard. The cellulosic requirements have never been met and EPA has waived them every year. Source: Department of Energy.

So here we are, 2022, the RFS about to expire, EV cars coming, the world in dire need of wheat, and politicians are still tripping over each other to prop up corn ethanol so the panicked Ethanolians can build carbon pipelines that will pump more insanity from the ethanol plants out to the hinterlands, because......?

I have a theory.

In his book *Sapiens, A Brief History of Humankind*, Yuval Noah Harari explains that our species, *Homo sapiens*, once shared the earth with other *Homo* species: *Homo neanderthalensis, Homo erectus, Homo rudolfensis*, and *Homo denisova*. We coexisted with them all for thousands of years until we decided we wanted the neighborhood to ourselves and exterminated these other guys. What helped this along was the development of complex language in *Homo sapiens*. It seems that primate social structures start to break down at about 150 individuals. Language helps individuals of larger groups of our species bond and form alliances and complex social structures, and do stuff like wipe out competing species if we feel like it. We form these social structures by creating stories for members of the tribe to coalesce around—occasionally these are based on reality, but quite often they are not. Harari says that "the ability to create an imagined reality out of words enabled large numbers of strangers to cooperate effectively." And, as time goes by, the imagined reality becomes ever more powerful.

We see this everywhere in modern society, despite empirical evidence discrediting the story in plain sight. COVID is a bad cold. Trump won the election. Vaccines cause autism. School kids are relieving themselves in kitty litter. The culture of agriculture is no exception. Feeding the World. Regulation Can't Work. Ethanol— YEAH BABY (Barry White voice). One can imagine a few rich guys sitting around a bottle of Glenlivet about 20 years ago saying what in the X?!% are we going to do with all this corn? We gotta keep selling fertilizer and seed and machinery and we need someplace for this junk to go.

Voilà, the ethanol myth story is born.

Like all myth stories, the legend of corn ethanol has been as pliant and silly as silly putty, depending on the year and world affairs: reduces carbon monoxide emissions in cold weather, works on stains, relieves dependence on foreign oil, cures the heartbreak of psoriasis, reduces overall cost of fuel, solves toenail fungus, increases octane, regrows amputated limbs, and now—mitigates climate change.

Like many of the ancient myths, our corn ethanol myth sometimes makes use of phallic imagery. It's ironic that our legislature is now obsessing about groomers while all this time we've been towing corn penises through town on the 4th of July. Thanks to Dave Swenson for bringing this one to my attention.

It has given our state a reason to live and entrenched our caucus as the first. On cold winter nights, presidential candidates can be seen knocking back shots of corn whiskey at every Gus and Betty's Good Times Tavern from Lineville to Scarville and Centerville to Correctionville, all so they can bear homage to our myth story and declare themselves true believers and members of the tribe.

The 97% of us who don't farm are forced to pledge our allegiance to the 3 percenter's myth story, even though it has had dire environmental consequences here and downstream from us. Challenging this dogma means you're divisive, you hate Iowa, you hate farmers, and you hate agriculture, because you don't believe the myth. You're an infidel. The zealots become whatabouters and get in your face with whatabout the byproducts (dried digester grains, mainly), whatabout big oil, whatabout the jobs (probably 7,000 at best, 0.6 jobs per square mile of land investment, according ISU economist Swenson), and whatabout Uncle Harold and that new Airstream he was about to buy.

I'm proposing a new story, one built on empiricism: you can't achieve the state's environmental objectives until ethanol is killed and left for dead. And why not kill it? It parks its fat ass on an area equivalent to 20 Iowa counties, making millionaires out of a few while preventing food production on some of the best soil on earth.

What else could we do with that 11,000 square miles (7 million acres), you might ask? Let me think for a minute. (Opens up Excel spreadsheet.)

> 1.1 million acres: grow enough dried beans for every person in the United States

> 360,000 acres: grow enough potatoes for every person in the United States

> 220,000 acres: grow enough apples for every person in the United States

> 150,000 acres: grow enough canned sweet corn for every person in the United States

> 140,000 acres: grow enough onions for every person in the United States

> 37,000 acres: grow enough cherries for every person in the United States

> 26,000 acres: grow enough walnuts for every person in the United States

So right now I'm at a little over 2 million acres, and I think you probably get the picture. And there's still 5 million acres left.

So, for all the whatabouters reading, this is for you: Yes, I know the infrastructure doesn't currently exist to support these other production systems. Yes, I know there are some environmental consequences for growing some of these other crops, especially potatoes. Yes, I know farmers would have to buy different machinery. Yes, I know growing field corn is likely more profitable. But let's ask the question—why is it more profitable? Hmm. Could it be because THE RENEWABLE FUEL STANDARD GUARANTEES A MARKET AND A PRICE FOR A MONSTROUS CORN CROP?!? And it surely inflates the value of our land, preventing aspiring farmers from getting a start, at least some of which would like do something other than grow junk corn for a gutter fuel.

And I also want to say to the whatabouters, we spend MILLIONS of taxpayer dollars putting band-aids on the corn-soy system to try to get it to stop polluting, and to what benefit for the 97% of Iowans that don't farm? Could we not spend some of that to underwrite alternative crop production that would produce better environmental outcomes than the band aids, and provide us some actual food in the deal? Why do we mindlessly cling to a 17-year-old policy that's far beyond its use-by date?

Iowa has the good fortune to be the best place on earth to grow stuff, including annual crops. Growing corn for ethanol is lazy and betrays a complete lack of vision by Iowa's agricultural establishment. Why are we wasting this place on ethanol? It makes no sense, other than to fulfill the prophecy of the Ethanolians' myth story: ethanol today, ethanol tomorrow, ethanol forever! And don't forget to drop your envelope in the collection plate before you go.

LOOK AT THE PRICE THEY MAKE YOU PAY

One of the tragedies of our agricultural system is that we have on some level sacrificed the state's water quality to produce a transient vehicle fuel: corn ethanol. Corn ethanol was intended to be a bridge fuel that would soon be displaced by other forms of energy. Instead, it has become an entrenched part of the state's production system, and this at the expense of so many other things, both on our land and in our water. This essay shows how fuel ethanol ruined one of Iowa's constructed lakes.

Secchi depth is a water quality measurement of clarity. An 8□-diameter black and white disk is lowered into the water (flat side parallel to the water's surface) and the first depth at which it can't be seen is recorded. It's one of the oldest of all quantitative water quality measurements. Catholic priest Pietro Angelo Secchi demonstrated the technique to Pope Pius IX while onboard the pope's yacht in 1865.

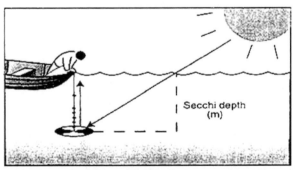

Measurement of Secchi depth. From: Carruthers, T.J., Longstaff, B.J., Dennison, W.C., Abal, E.G. and Aioi, K., 2001. Measurement of light penetration in relation to seagrass. Global seagrass research methods, pp. 370-392.

We still use this simple but elegant method today and Iowa DNR's ambient water monitoring program assesses lakes for clarity in this manner. Research shows that the public's perception of "good" water quality corresponds to a Secchi depth of about 3 feet; in other words, a depth where you can see your toes when standing in waist deep water.[1]

Iowa has a little over 100 lakes, and their degraded condition keeps DNR busy restoring them. You can easily make the case that lake restoration is the best thing Iowa DNR does. They know how to take a cloudy lake filled with sediment, phosphorus and carp and turn it into a clear one with bass and walleye in short order. The problem we have is that agriculture seems to prefer the former and so lake restoration in Iowa is more like a perpetual jobs program for earth movers to bulldoze sediment out of drained lakes on a regular and never-ending schedule.

There are several constructed lakes in southern Iowa where the topography is favorable for lake impoundment. Some of these serve as municipal drinking water source supply for nearby communities— Chariton, Corning, and Osceola are three, and some of these systems have struggled with atrazine impairment of the drinking water. Taylor County's Lake of Three Fires north of Bedford is the focal point for the state park of the same name, and, according to Iowa DNR,[2] "was dedicated in 1935 and is named after a group of Native Americans from the Potawatomi tribe who once inhabited the area known as the 'Fire Nation.'" There were a number of WPA and CCC projects in Iowa and elsewhere during the 1930s that focused on drinking water supply, lake construction, and natural resource enhancement in parks.

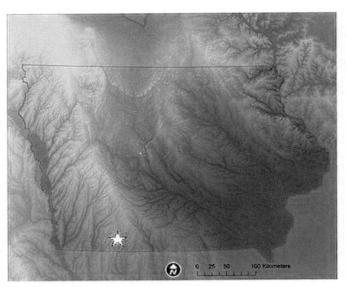

Location of Lake of Three Fires.

By the early 2000s, the volume of Lake of Three Fires had shrunk 40% and the maximum depth halved because of sedimentation. Iowa DNR and Iowa Department of Agriculture and Land Stewardship (IDALS) worked with watershed landowners to reduce sediment transport to the lake. The lake was drained in 2004 and about 400,000 cubic yards of sediment were removed. The lake was refilled and stocked with bluegill, catfish, and largemouth bass. Prior to this, the Secchi depth had never been greater than 18 inches. In the few years following restoration, lake clarity sometimes reached 6 feet, nearly unheard of for any Iowa lake this side of West Okoboji, which is kept clear by its enormous depth.

Then something happened. Ethanol happened.

Congress authorized under the Energy Policy Act of 2005 and this was expanded under the Energy Independence and Security Act of 2007.[3] The law began by requiring 4 billion gallons of renewable fuel in 2006 with an expectation that the amount would increase to

36 billion by 2022. This created a guaranteed market for corn and agriculture responded. Although Iowa has always had a lot of land planted to corn, this area of southern Iowa, discussed at length in Neil Hamilton's book, *The Land Remains,* has a lot of hilly ground that is considered marginal for corn production. Land value in Taylor County, where Lake of Three Fires is located, is ranked 93rd out of Iowa's 99 counties. The average value of Taylor County farmland tripled between 2000 and 2010, an increase slightly larger than state as a whole over the same period.

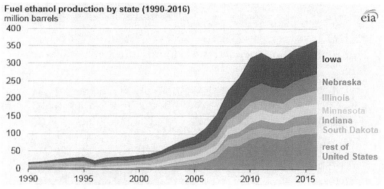

From: Energy Information Administration.

The guaranteed market for corn shepherded pasture and idle land into corn production in Southern Iowa. Corn area in Taylor County increased 34% between 2003 and 2013, and this wasn't just any ground—this was land vulnerable to erosion and other environmental degradation. The good stuff was already being farmed. This is apparent from aerial photos of Taylor County.[3] The images below show a hillslope in the lake's watershed just north of the park (the waterbody on the left is not Lake of Three Fires, but rather a pond). The 2004 image shows mostly pasture with a cropped field on the

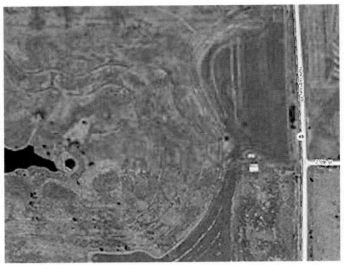
Hillslope in 2004 in watershed draining to Lake of Three Fires.

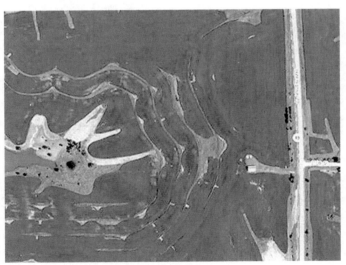
Same hill slope in 2010.

hilltop to the right. The 2010 image shows a sea of green corn planted to the entire hillslope.

The lake responded, predictably. By 2012, the lake had returned to its pre-restoration clarity, or lack of clarity, as the case may be.

The graph below shows a 3-year running average of Secchi depth, depicted with the solid line and corresponding to the y-axis on the left. I used negative numbers here to illustrate how you could see further down into the lake immediately after restoration. The graph also shows Taylor County corn acres in the dotted line, corresponding the y-axis on the right. Although Lake of Three Fires provides the best lake example of the degradation caused by fuel ethanol, you don't have to look far to find other examples, such as Lake Icaria in Hamilton's Adams County. The restoration project at Lake of Three Fires required $3.8 million, of which $2.3 million was spent on the lake itself and the balance spent on other park improvements.

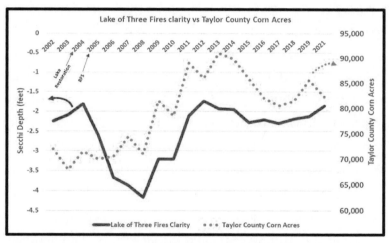

Three year running average of Secchi depth (top line right) in Lake of Three Fires and Taylor County Corn Acres (bottom line right).

I'm sure you know that using Iowa's natural environment to produce automobile fuel has wide bipartisan support, as demonstrated by the votes recorded on the recently passed E-15 law, which requires 15% ethanol blends be sold at all Iowa gas stations and provides taxpayer cost share for stations to purchase new pumps. Some quotes to that effect:

> Democratic State Senator and Johnson County farmer Kevin Kinney: "32 percent or more of our budget is directly related to the Ag industry" and E-15 is "a step in the right direction."[5]

> Senate minority (D) leader Zach Wahls, also from Johnson County: "This legislation is a win-win for the Iowa economy."[6]

> U.S. Congressperson (D) Cindy Axne: "I have been fighting tooth and nail to make sure biofuels is a part of the clean energy solution."[7]

> Governor Kim Reynolds (R), upon signing the E-15 bill: "I've never been prouder than I am today to be the Governor of the number one ethanol and biodiesel-producing state in the country."[8]

So, what are we to make of this and other similar situations? We've recently been told by our secretary of agriculture that farmers are not likely to adopt conservation unless it pencils out for them as profitable.[9] At the same time, we subsidize the activity that creates the pollution, indemnify the risk of that production, help the industry market their products, force the public to buy the products, and then, in the case of our lakes, ask our agency to travel the countryside to repair the damage that predictably results. The depravity of this is so perverse and so unexplainable and so illogical that this is what we're left with: we celebrate it.

Over the past few years, I've come to realize that Iowa's water quality will not recover in my lifetime to a condition that any reasonable society would consider adequate.

I think you should know why.

JUMPING THE SHARK

Des Moines Water Works is the municipal drinking water utility for the Des Moines metropolitan area, and a place I once worked. It's an institution in Des Moines, literally and figuratively, and has been led by some interesting people who were near celebrities in the community. The place had a reputation for leading the charge on water quality, advocating for its customers who were some of the most affected in Iowa from ongoing agricultural pollution. But since the death of former General Manager Bill Stowe, DMWW has taken a much less confrontational approach with agriculture, and now seems to have capitulated to the Ag giants on how the city and the state should approach water quality improvement.

I'm sometimes asked how the ideas keep coming for this blog. Believe me when I tell you this: writing this stuff is as easy as falling off a log backwards. As we say in the biz when we see some interesting data: this excrement just writes itself.

Last week Ag retailer Landus announced[1,2] that an area of land in Des Moines' Water Works Park will be used as a demonstration plot that will be planted with corn, soybeans, and cover crops. No word yet on whether the Agribusiness Association of Iowa will include this plot to pad the state total of cover cropped land. This comes on the heels of DMWW announcing they helped buy a cover crop seed planter that farmers can use.[3] Both projects purport to inspire more farmer adoption of conservation practices, in particular the use of cover crops, to reduce nutrient pollution. And if by some infinitesimally-remote chance you have been unable to see corn and soybean while living in or visiting Iowa, Landus states that "Members of the public will be able to see corn, soybean, and cover crops planted and grown in Des Moines Water Works Park, a 1,500-acre urban green space near downtown known for its wooded and open areas for bicycling, jogging, picnicking, fishing, hiking and participating in various group sports."[4] [I told you it writes itself!] So yeah, after you get bored with all that other outdoorsy stuff, you can go observe *Zea mays* and *Glycine max* in their (un)natural habitat. News is expected soon that grazing cattle will replace the DMWW grass mowing crew. Stay tuned. Some people are saying that negotiations with the Iowa Cattlemen's Association are imminent.

I suppose a little background here would be prudent if you are new to this:

> Iowa streams are polluted with nutrients (nitrogen and phosphorus) from two out of these three things: row crops, animal agriculture and golf courses.

> Cover crops are unharvested plants seeded in the fall that reduce loss of nutrients 32% on average from corn and soybean fields.

> DMWW uses the Raccoon and Des Moines Rivers as the drinking source supply for 1/5 of Iowa's population.

> DMWW operates perhaps the world's largest nitrate removal facility to keep the drinking water in compliance with Safe Drinking Water Act regulations.

Now I wish to say I don't object to the idea of demonstration plots. Or cover crops. Or even corn and soybeans on some level. But putting them in Water Works Park? Seriously? It's not like we have an abundance of parks or public land. In fact, Iowa is one of the worst in the U.S. when it comes to that. I've made jokes about Iowa agriculture forcing us to grow corn in cemeteries and school yards if they could, but this is no joke. This is a level of shark jumping not seen since Fonzie donned water skis on *Happy Days*.

Image credit: ABC.

It's beyond revealing that Landus couldn't find some of their own property, or some other Ag land somewhere, to locate these demonstration plots. They claim to have 7,000 farmer members all presumably with access to land, and their headquarters are centrally-located in Ames. And "Land" is part of their name, for crying out loud. But sure, let's put this in......A PARK. So convenient for farmers. In the middle of the city that tried to sue upstream polluters for nitrate pollution. On the grounds of the water utility. Talk about planting a flag, holy moly.

But I suppose to the victor go the spoils, and this is Harold the Red claiming the late king's young maiden daughter for his own. Landus was so giddy with their conquest that their agronomist Dan Bjorklund (a fine Viking name, by the way) offered up his own version[5] of Weallwantcleanwater: "EVERYBODY wants clean water," he bellowed from atop the dragon on the longship bow as it sailed down the Raccoon River, a phrase sure to please Harold.

But seriously. Never mind that Landus stands to benefit from the use of public property in this way by promotion of products and services featured in the plots, although there is plenty to object to there. The larger story here is this apparently is an unconditional surrender by the city and its drinking water utility and a nod to the Iowa power brokers that they're sorry about that little lawsuit thingy[6] of a few years ago. "Did you think I said lawsuit? Oh, I'm sure you misunderstood, what I really said was 'partnerships'! So come right into the people's park and demonstrate your good intentions." Because the road to polluted water is paved with them, I guess.

And after all, Cedar Rapids has gone all-in with the partnership approach, and look at the success they've had. The nitrate in the Cedar River is only 12 mg/L (!) as I write this, just 2 mg/L ABOVE the safe drinking water standard. (The Raccoon River is at 11.8 mg/L.) Those eastern Iowans shouldn't have all the fun. The pork loin, green bean casserole, and apple crisp served at those meetings in the Ag Co-op board rooms are tip top, let me tell you. Tip. Top.

Landus is predictably using the project to generate some top shelf cropaganda. From their website[7]: "Demonstrating the many sustainability practices Iowa farmers are implementing, Landus farmers seek to showcase modern, safe and stewardship-minded agricultural practices in the public setting." Well howdy-do. I guess there's so much conservation going on in the countryside, they need to bring some to the big city so those folks can see why their water is so doggone good.

Although there indeed may be a few farmers who will visit this plot, don't think for a second that farmers are the intended audience. Des Moinesians (or whatever you call yourselves), when you take a break from your run or bike ride to hydrate and find yourself alongside the demonstration plots, you'll know that high nitrate water cooling your innards was brought to you by those conservation-minded heroes at Landus Cooperative. Bottoms up!

Landus staff re-enacting Des Moines' "We surrender" moment in demonstration plot negotiations. Image from DMWW twitter account.

NO BUSHEL LEFT BEHIND

There's an idea floating around out there that we can meet our water quality objectives without simultaneously suffering a reduction in crop yields. This is fanciful thinking and most of the water quality insiders know it. Our institutions continue to approach our water quality problems, however, with this attitude. In effect, what agriculture is telling us is when comes down to bushels and water, the bushels are always going to win.

The Ag propagandists' lack of creativity is more than balanced by their relentlessness and the fact that they are unburdened by shame. Imagine if the Energizer bunny copulates (he is a rabbit, after all) with all the killer rabbits from the '72 horror movie *Night of the Lepus* (mutant rabbits terrorize Janet Leigh and DeForest Kelly) and their horde of offspring stampede the countryside devouring the truth. Or something like that.

Take phosphorus, for example. Iowa Secretary of Agriculture Mike Naig was recently quoted saying "We've come a long way on our phosphorus reduction goals in the state of Iowa due to a lot of management practices that have been put in place, cover crops, no-till, conservation tillage in the state of Iowa."[1] And not to be outdone, one-time Secretary of Agriculture hopeful and Iowa farmer Ray Gaesser was quoted saying in an EPA roundtable meeting that "Iowa has reduced phosphorus losses by 27%".[2] Reminds me of an old joke about Minnesota and Iowa and manure and the punch line is "Mr. RabBIT will soon be here with the shit."

These statements are detached from reality.

ChuckGrassley ✔
@ChuckGrassley
                                                    ...

Field cultivation a step to prepare field for corn
planting. Minimum tillage is a good conservation
practice. On Grassley farm abt 2wks behind last. Wet
cold spring #cornwatch

6:02 PM · May 15, 2022 · Twitter for iPhone

Here's an example of the hare-brained "conservation" the Ag spokespeople say has reduced Iowa
phosphorus levels 27%.

There is not a shred of water quality data that shows phosphorus
levels in our streams to be declining over the long haul, and in fact,
the opposite is probably occurring (graphs at the end). USGS long-
term phosphorus loading data in the basins draining to the Mississippi River at Clinton and the Missouri River at Hermann, Missouri, (which capture water from Iowa streamflow) show no such
decline. It is fair to wonder if Iowa is getting better while the states
upstream from us are getting worse, but this is not borne out by Io-
wa-centric stream data and in fact, Iowa could be driving increases or
non-improvement in the border rivers, as Iowa stream phosphorus
was found to be 43% higher in 2017 than 2004.[3, 4] The graveyard
whistlers make their claims based on the idea that we've put in some
terraces and that 75% of farmers have parked the moldboard plow
in a weed patch behind the shed where peaceful bunnies meet to
copulate.

Moldboard plow.

This narrative on phosphorus troubles me because I recall some big Ag jackrabbits saying at the onset of Iowa's Nutrient Strategy that the phosphorus objective (45% reduction, with 29% from agriculture) may have already been nearly or completely met. This was ten years ago now. And here we are, with Ag world celebrities saying exactly that. It's almost like....somebody knew something. The public should be hopping mad because these statements, which go unchallenged by the media and almost the entirety of the scientific community, do help mold policy, I can assure you. Federal agency staff and legislators, many of whom with little time and no ability to examine scientific data, hear such statements and take them at their face value.

We're also told by our government officials that "the state has to balance the concerns of clean water with crop production."[4] Are they not telling us that because we live in Iowa, we're less entitled to clean and safe water? Yes they are. Let's examine it.

We have 70,000 miles of streams and less than 20 stream stretches that meet all their designated uses, with 585 water bodies impaired.[5] We've had 6,600 private wells exceed the safe standard for nitrate since 2000.[6] The "balance" the industry has in mind is that none of this can get better if it means sacrificing bushels. They're entitled to their bushels, but we aren't entitled to clean water. There's no other way to read it.

Can we achieve meaningful water quality improvement with no sacrifice of bushels and no constraints on the livestock industry? In my view no, but if so, it will require virtual mountains of carrots (i.e. public money), just to give it a shot. And the Ag people aren't shy about telling you that. The mountains part, I mean. And if you're not happy with the current progress thus far, it's because the piles of money have only been of molehill proportions.[7]

In a new paper in the *Journal of the American Water Resources Association,*[8] researchers at Virginia Tech and elsewhere tell us that the problem is policy. They state that farmers and technical service providers at the agencies are rewarded for practice adoption, whether it improves the water or not (usually not and remember the claims on phosphorus improvements in Iowa have been made based on practice adoption). Here's another gem from the paper: "The use of conventional BMPs (best management practices), most of which do not address excessive nutrient mass imbalances, offers limited potential to reduce non-point source loads." Oh my. My poor heart goes all aflutter when somebody at a land grant Ag school (Virginia Tech and Penn State) is willing to say we we're applying more nutrients than what the crops need.

They go on to argue that the best solution would be to replace the current scheme, where farmers decide both whether and how they will control their pollution (we know how well that has worked), to one where a farmer or group of farmers is obligated to limit their pollution but has discretion and flexibility in deciding how that limit is met.

Now the statements of Mr. Gaesser[9] would seem to be consistent with this on some level: "How can somebody in Washington, D.C., tell us the best way to improve water quality without giving some deference to me and the 2 million other farmers who know their own land better than anyone else?" Ok, I'll take that statement on its face. But here's the rub: Iowa agriculture refuses to let us obligate farmers with limiting their pollution. Thus, there is no balance; the almighty bushel ALWAYS wins and your water suffers. You want clean water? PAY ME. And never mind if the only benefits your tax dollars produce are a good performance review for a USDA employee and a salve on the conscience of a guilty farmer.

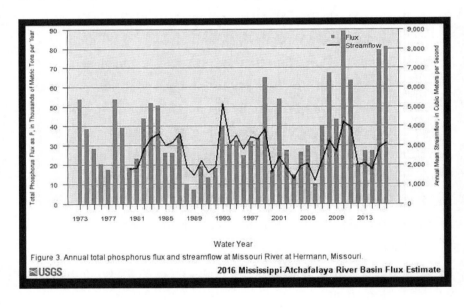

Figure 3. Annual total phosphorus flux and streamflow at Missouri River at Hermann, Missouri.

⚒USGS   2016 Mississippi-Atchafalaya River Basin Flux Estimate

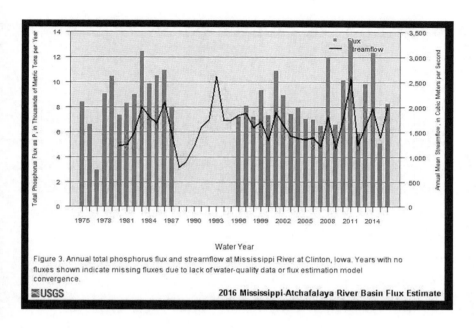

Figure 3. Annual total phosphorus flux and streamflow at Mississippi River at Clinton, Iowa. Years with no fluxes shown indicate missing fluxes due to lack of water-quality data or flux estimation model convergence.

≋USGS   2016 Mississippi-Atchafalaya River Basin Flux Estimate

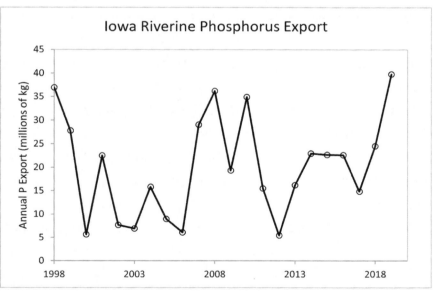

Iowa statewide phosphorus loading from PhD thesis work conducted by Elliott Anderson at the University of Iowa (2022).

BUSHELS OR BOBOLINKS

I love birds, but I am a lazy birder. I want them to come to me, whether I'm sitting in view of a feeder, waiting for a fish to bite, looking out my office window, or listening for night birds in bed at 3AM. I am definitely not the tweedy guy with binoculars in hand and guidebook in pocket, crawling from rock to rock to catch a glimpse of the northernspottedwhateverwarbler. I will, however, deliberately go to them from time to time, or try to, anyway. I once burned several gallons of gas chasing chat board postings of a snowy owl report in Central Iowa, and I will leave my cabin to peek at the spring and fall migratory waterfowl arriving at Pool 9 of the Upper Mississippi River. But long and short, I want my birds to entertain me on my terms.

The diversity of birds you can see in Iowa is impressive when you consider how profoundly disturbed our landscape is. The Audubon Society says that 390 species of birds have been recorded in the state, and I think I have seen close to half of those. This is slightly less than our bordering states, all of which report in the low- to mid-400s. But still, Iowa birders benefit from the Mississippi and Missouri river flyways as well as the convergence of prairie and eastern hardwood habitats. There's plenty to see here when it comes to birds.

Birds have provided me some of the most astonishing and memorable experiences of my life. Every Iowa kid remembers their first red-winged blackbird buzzing their buzz cut (or bob, as the case may be), and nobody who has heard a whippoorwill while enjoying a two-beer buzz on the back porch in the heat of a July night will ever forget it.

A great horned owl landing on the windowsill of an open college dorm window. The flying chihuahua—the red-bellied woodpecker—stealing a peanut before you finish filling the feeder. The blazing red of tanagers—summer or scarlet—setting your eyes afire on a May morning. A male catbird delivering a speech to early morning coffee drinkers sitting on their back deck.

A thousand or five thousand canvasbacks riding out a March snowstorm on the Mississippi River. A kingfisher landing on the branch that shelters the crappies you're trying to lure. The distinct voices of skyward trumpeter swans and sandhill cranes never failing to give you a half-second whatthehellwasthat before you can glance up.

Imagine what it must've been like, before we extirpated three eco-systems—the prairie, savannah, and wetland birds had to have been as numerous as stars. The Audubon Society says that North America has lost more than three billion birds just in the span of my life. Wetlands and their ducks were once so numerous in Iowa that hunters shot the latter on the wing from freight train box cars, leaving them lie like the buffalo hunters of the Great Plains left bison to rot in the prairie sun. Invasive birds that love us, starlings and house sparrows, have helped displace many of our native species. And some native bird species have evidently come to like us: Canada geese (turf grass), bald eagles (hog carcasses), and woodpeckers (emerald ash borers), and maybe a few others. I can't remember ever seeing a Canada goose during my childhood and now they're everywhere. We brought turkeys and trumpeters back, and would like to do the same with the prairie chicken, if we could.

But the grassland birds have suffered badly (down by 720 million since 1970) and will likely never regain even a sliver of their ancestral habitat. Fifty years ago, meadowlarks were almost as common as robins in town; it's tough to find one anymore, especially the eastern. The upside-down oddity—the bobolink—light on top, dark on the bottom—about gone. The grasshopper sparrow, Henslow's sparrow, common nighthawk, loggerhead shrike, bobwhite quail, all in decline. About three out of every four grassland species are declining, and many of them, like the shrike, declining steeply. The prairies are gone. The pothole wetlands that provided nesting and resting places for countless millions of waterfowl—99% gone. The floodplain bird habitat in Iowa's Missouri River corridor—levied and cropped. Do we care? I think we do. Do our politicians, and the agricultural industry they cater to, do they care? They don't seem to. If it comes to down to bushels or bobolinks, bet on the bushels; a safer bet has never been had.

A few years back, I got a tour of the farmland owned by the Eastern Iowa (Cedar Rapids) airport. Corn surrounds the runways, but that land was once planted to the giant grass miscanthus, which was ultimately baled and burned every year for heat and electricity generation. Miscanthus was abandoned because the wildlife (including birds) that colonized it became a hazard to the departing and landing planes, and so the airport returned to corn production. The lesson here is that anything, even a monoculture of a non-native grass, is superior to corn when it comes to habitat.

Sadly, I've resigned myself to the inevitable: Iowa land will be corn carpeted, come hell or high water, for the balance of my life. Birds will have to cope, find somewhere else to live, or perish. All three have happened and the process is still happening before our eyes.

Sometimes, however, nature will surprise you and nothing can give you hope like a bird. This spring (2022), a very large flock of American white pelicans set up shop in the Iowa River, right in downtown Iowa City. Now, I've seen a lot of pelicans in my life, especially while fishing in Canada. There, they can be seen sauntering around the boat like an old hound dog saunters around the porch, whiling the hours away. But to see a hungry hundred of them spiral down in the middle of town to feast on spent and dying shad, what a sight.

If a flock of pelicans can still make this place a little bit special every once in a while, then all is not lost.

FISH

My dad wasn't much of a fisherman, but his brother was, and I spent many a weekday evening and weekend morning in his boat with him and my cousin when I was a kid. The boat was a barely-seaworthy, 12' modified-v-hull aluminum tub with three bench seats, a mushroom anchor and a Sears Ted Williams 6 horsepower motor, back when the retired baseball titan was the outdoor gear spokesman for the now retired department store. The only time your butt left the bench seat was when your about-to-burst bladder couldn't take it anymore, because the fish were biting too good for my uncle to pull up the cast iron mushroom and motor you to shore.

Most of the time we fished for crappie at the newly-constructed Big Creek Lake north of Des Moines. One time we went to Clear Lake in northern Iowa and caught a big mess of bullheads, which my aunt fried upon our return. They were delicious. These days, most people won't mess with a hard-to-clean bullhead, but back then, my uncle (and my dad) had fond memories of fishing for bullheads with their dad at the Bullhead Capital of the World, Waterville, Minnesota. I remember my dad saying there were people in town who would dress bullheads with a paring knife for a penny apiece.

I fished with their dad, my grandad, a few times in Marion County, southeast of Des Moines. He liked fishing for bullheads from a bridge over Whitebreast Creek, and if you were lucky you might also catch a channel cat, which was cause for celebration. One time we had a stringer of bullies hanging from the bridge into the creek and the old man said you better grab the stringer, there's a turtle down there. I did—the turtle had already taken everything except the heads.

I still love fishing and go when I can. For my money, the Mississippi River from Red Wing, Minnesota, down to Dubuque, Iowa, is the best place to fish this side of Canada and the Rocky Mountains of Montana. I can't imagine a place on earth with a greater diversity of freshwater sport fish than the Upper Mississippi. And the scenery is just good enough to make you forget you're still in the Corn Belt. Here and there you can still see the King growing on top of a bluff, but not very often, thankfully.

To be a good place to fish, a lake or stream needs more than just the fish. For example, you can pay to catch tank-raised fish indoors in Japan, out of the elements. Plenty of fish, nothing else. Catching is not fishing. To me, fishing should be an opportunity to make observations and decisions within the same context that a walleye, or a heron, or a beaver, or a dragonfly, makes them. You're a part of their world—the heat and the cold, the wind and the rain, the sun and the dark. The water.

It's possible to catch good fish out of bad water, and some people do in Iowa. But to me, that feels more like catching than fishing. When the rivers are brown and the lakes are green—that's tough fishing for me. But that's the standard here for much of the year, brown in the spring, green in the summer. It doesn't have to be that way. We know the prairie streams were once clear.

I like to fish for what is biting, which is one reason I like the Mississippi. I don't like forcing the issue. So many folks, hook or crook, are going to fish for bass, or walleye, or trout, whatever their favorite is. There's no fish more beautiful than a redhorse sucker in its spawning colors, but rare is the fisherman who targets them—too bony for the knife and the plate. Or the mean-as-a-rattlesnake burbot, or dogfish, or bowfin, or whatever you want to call it. A fish from the Jurassic that somehow has managed to endure us. Only the bravest of fishers brings one into the boat; many would just as soon cut the line and bid their lure good-bye, as to try to extract it from a bowfin's mouth of knives. And it seems to me that even the humble but tasty channel cat is ignored by many these days—I guess familiarity breeds contempt, even when it comes to fishing.

The weekend warriors, with their $50,000 boats filled with $10,000-worth of electronics and tackle, want the glamour species of walleye and bass, the latter being either largemouth or smallmouth. Walleye mostly end up on the plate; bass are more of a living toy to these guys, released to be caught at the next play date.

I find it perverse that we'll spend our earnings on the expensive gear but not demand clean water. Almost one out of 10 Iowans buy a fishing license,[1] but participation in the sport here is below the national average (14%) and only about half the rate of the rest of the Midwest (17.5%). This is despite that fact that we have over 70,000 miles of perennial streams in Iowa. Unfortunately, many of them have been straightened and polluted with sediment, nutrients and organic matter from manure. Only a very few Iowa stream stretches meet the designated uses outlined by the Clean Water Act. The glamour species didn't evolve to live in the polluted ditches that were once clear and meandering prairie rivers. And our lakes...well, green and turbid water is the rule after Memorial Day, a result of nutrient-driven blue-green algae. Freakishly deep West Lake Okoboji entombs the nutrients in its great depth, and thus remains clear and mostly unplagued by algae. As a result, all of Iowa (and South

Dakota) seems to be there on summer weekends, leaving little space and solitude for the angler.

The natural fertility of our waters, and the diversity of species that could inhabit them, could make Iowa a destination state for fishing. The Dakotas, Minnesota, and Wisconsin, vacation destinations that Iowa fishermen and -women have dreamt about for generations, would have little on Iowa if we could clean up our water. It's always been sadly ironic to me that a casting Iowa farmer has forever been as common on a mid-summer Minnesota lake as the mosquitoes trying to bite him.

FIREWOOD

You don't truly realize it until you've tried to do it but heating your house with firewood and a wood-burning stove is no joke. No joke at all. Even the most hysterical climate change worrywart will cop to the upside of fossil fuels after spending a day cutting and splitting firewood. And they're ready to buy stock in Exxon when called on to leave the warmth of their bed to stoke the fire in the middle of a -20 degree night. It's also undeniable that producing one's own heat is something that scratches an Ice-Age-Cro-Magnon itch within our primordial unconscious. At least I think it is undeniable. And once you take the plunge from casual indoor fire user for ambiance, to full-on, fire-in-the stove or this house ain't livable, well, the nature of your existence will never be the same.

I bought a 1,000-square foot cabin a couple of years ago. Half the cabin is an old Amish abode with a small (8' x 15') front entry area on one end, a similarly sized kitchen on the other end, a 15' x 20' living space between the two, and two loft sleeping spaces at each end above the front entry and kitchen. The walls are rough-hewn boards and the peaked ceiling is tongue-in-groove pine that I put in. At my feet were plain floorboards when I bought it; I put in a hackberry hardwood floor atop those. A wood stove in the living space heats this half very nicely. The rest of the cabin is a modern addition with a bathroom, bedroom and a larger open room with the water heater and washer/dryer. The heat from the wood stove does not warm the addition.

There is also electric baseboard heat in both sections of the cabin. The cost to heat the cabin in this manner in the middle of winter is somewhere in the neighborhood of the mortgage payment. Maybe more if it is really cold, and so I'm highly motivated to use the wood stove.

About 20 acres of timber fan the hill behind the cabin, and soon after buying the place, I started looking about for the easy pickings of firewood, if it can be said that there is such thing. At my place, that's dead elm, about 6-8" in diameter. A lot of it is not only easy to get to but also disrobed of its bark, making it easy to spot. Its size doesn't require splitting, no bark means less mess and fewer bugs in the cabin, and it burns nicely—not the absolute best but pretty good. There are two problems with elm as I see it. One, in short order it transforms the cutting power of a sharp chainsaw into that of a rusty paring knife, and two, I always feel like removing a dead elm also takes one potential morel mushroom spot out of the pool of spots, and this always gives me some angst. Yes, I know the conventional wisdom is that an elm tree will be morel-less without bark, but it can also be said that the conventional of wisdom of morel hunting is there is no conventional wisdom when it comes to where they will be. The only conventional morel wisdom you can take to the bank in my neighborhood is that if you park your car within a quarter mile of Harold Anderson's timber in the month of May, you will return to find it with two flat tires.

My timber patch is loaded with invasive black locust. Mark Twain thought the existence of flies proved there was no god, and the same might be said about black locust. Evidently brought in to replace the logged-out oak and pine (there is an old log road up my hill, and every other hill around my neck of the woods), it grows fast and its horde lays claim to every patch of ground made bare for one reason or another. The new trees will grow 6" the first season and seem to leave the womb with thorns that would kill an armadillo. I once cleared a 50' by 50' patch of young black locusts and by the time I got them all dragged to the burn pile, my body looked like I had just climbed through the razor wire at Guantánamo. But the mature trees are straight and all trunk with little canopy to clean up, while the cut wood seasons quickly and burns hot. This combination of qualities makes me think Satan is burning black locust to keep Hell hot and the worst sinners are charged with clearing the young trees out of his back yard.

Ash is an underrated firewood in my estimation because it burns slow and hot and splits pretty easily. But you can't haul it anywhere because of the emerald ash borers, and I find it has a bit of an objectionable smell, both as a cut wood and while burning. An odd thing about ash is that the bark seems to retain moisture and is the last part of the log to burn in the stove. A stack of split white ash makes a beautiful wood pile, if that adjective can indeed be attached to a wood pile.

I don't have many softwood (conifer) trees on my property and thus don't burn it much. I did have a dead eastern red cedar tree that I eagerly cut up for firewood, thinking it would make the whole cabin smell like a sweater closet when burned, but it produced little heat and no cedar smell and disappointed. The red inner wood is beautiful to look at and I thought about making some discs for drink coasters, but then remembered I was more than 60 years old and didn't want to waste any remaining time doing crafts. By and large I don't like burning softwood like pine because the sparks popping out onto my hackberry floor have caused me four burned hands, two sprained ankles and one cut forehead as I lurched off the couch to prevent a burn mark. And let's just be honest, softwood is for sissies, unless you're in the far north and it's all you have. It cuts and splits just too easily for a job that was meant to take years off your joints. Look up any You Tube video on how to split wood by hand, and there's some personal trainer with a $100 haircut wearing crisp and spotless buffalo plaid from a Patagonia catalog acting like he's the terminator with an axe about to mince a pile of cut pine logs. Big deal.

Which brings me to the Babe Ruth of firewood, oak. Now let me say I would never, ever cut down one of the 500 or so oak trees on my property. Not even a dead one. They are important habitat and the acorns from one big oak tree feed countless deer, squirrels, blue-jays, turkeys and god knows what else, and pileated woodpeckers hammer out their rectangular doorways in the rotten ones. But I was offered a derecho-damaged, 50-year-old red oak tree by a friend in Iowa City, and with an immediate and unthinking YES I WANT IT, I entered the cult of serious firewoodism.

A private company felled and cut the tree into 18" lengths that were left to lie in my friend's front yard, which looked like the side lot of a sawmill when my 22-year-old daughter and I arrived to start removing the wood. An old firewood adage is that the tree always looks bigger once it is on the ground. Umm, yes, I can verify. The pieces were supposed to be of a weight that two people could lift. Well, the tree company must have thought those two people were going to be André the Giant and Arnold Schwarzenegger because the big pieces weighed about as much as a Toyota Corolla, while the smallest pieces were barely loadable into my pickup using a hand-cart pushed up ramps into the bed. The tree company was called back (at a cost of $180) to cut the big 18' tall cylinders into three tall pie pieces, which resulted in some being loadable using the hand cart and ramps. Most were still too heavy. And thus began my baptism by fire into hand splitting oak.

My strategy was to split wedges off the remaining big pieces with an 8-pound maul-axe until they were whittled down to a weight light enough to load. I thought about renting a hydraulic log splitter, but I knew these pieces were still too heavy and cumbersome for me to lift onto the splitter, and I didn't feel comfortable asking for help on a project that was bound to take days. Maul in hand, I began.

Patagonia boy might be able to halve a big piece of pine or spruce with one axe swing without mussing his haircut, but let me tell you, that's a fantasy with oak. You must carefully pick a spot a few inches from the edge, line up the point of impact so it's not crossing too many of the annual rings, and then let her rip and hope for the best. I like to have the maul head rest against my spine before starting the swing, such that it travels a near-360° arc before hitting the log, making the most use of gravity. Even then, hitting oak can be like hitting an anvil, with the recoil traveling back up through your arms and shoulders, and down through your spine to the bottom of your feet like a bolt of lightning. You're lucky if the first swing at a spot cleaves a wedge; a 2:1 or 3:1 swing:success ratio is more typical.

I could only take an hour or two of this at a time before succumbing to exhaustion. And this was a physical exhaustion unexperienced since running my last marathon 20 years ago. I really felt physically sick after each session. But little by little, I got the wood hauled away and stacked over a month's time. It helped that many of the days were very cold; I'm sure frozen wood splits best. The split oak is almost as white as ash on the day of splitting, but it starts to dry and yellow within days in the cold winter air, as oxygen and low humidity do their thing. And unlike ash, split oak smells good. It smells warm, and you can imagine the glowing coals warming your toes after a day of ice fishing, or serving as the backdrop for the fly tying vise on the days too cold or snowy to venture out with the ice auger.

Like rich guys and money, there's never enough firewood on the stack when you get serious about heating your living space with it. That little Ice Age Cro Magnon guy buried deep in your brain's back corner tells you that despite that huge stack of oak, you just might need that dead mulberry tree down there at the bend in the lane. Better see if the chainsaw is in working order. And there is no greater satisfaction than having your 29-year-old son-in-law ask in astonishment, "did you split all that by hand?"

(Gravelly Ice Age Cro Magnon voice): You're goddamn right I did, sonny.

DOWNSTREAM

When I speak to groups about the water pollution generated by Iowa agriculture, I'm often asked, "what can be done," or "what can I do," or, "how do we improve things" and various other similar questions. Often someone in the audience shouts out "Vote!" If only it were that easy. You don't get decades-long water quality degradation without the complicity of both political parties.

Some things have gotten better. The average clarity of our streams did improve in the years immediately following the 1985 Farm Bill, which included provisions for conservation compliance, i.e., farmers cropping on highly erodible land and wishing to participate in federal farm programs were required to adopt various soil conservation practices to prevent erosion. This had a noticeable and quantifiable effect on Iowa streams.[1,2] Along with that, the widespread use of glyphosate (Roundup) did reduce the use of many more toxic herbicides, and Bt corn genetically modified to resist corn borer larvae lessened the need for insecticides.

But nutrient pollution and the harmful algae blooms caused by it have continued to worsen and it's debatable whether or not soil erosion and stream clarity have improved much since 2000. Dense hog, cattle and poultry populations have made the presence of *E. coli* bacteria ubiquitous on our land and in our water, and the sand and gravel substrate of many of our smaller streams, needed by many clean water species for reproduction and other life processes, has been entombed beneath a layer of eroded soil and organic matter from manure. As a result, fewer than 20 stream stretches in Iowa's 70,000 miles of streams meet all their designated uses outlined under the Clean Water Act, and 585 Iowa water bodies are defined as impaired.[3] We've had 6,600 private wells exceed the safe standard for nitrate since 2000[4] and about 25% of Iowans drink water requiring nitrate removal at municipal treatment works.

Iowa's approach to agricultural water pollution has always been to let farmers decide whether and how to reduce the contaminants sourced to their own fields. This voluntary approach contrasts with a regulatory one which would obligate farmers to adopt various practices and demonstrate their efforts are being manifested in improved water quality. The industry rhetoric promoting voluntary approaches as good and regulation as bad has become accepted dogma such that it is even enshrined in Iowa code.[5]

While it is certainly possible to find fields and farms where voluntary adoption of stacked multiple practices have reduced contamination to streams receiving runoff from the treated fields, this approach almost always requires significant taxpayer investment in cost share funds to entice the farmer into adopting it.

These shared funds usually cover about half the cost of the practice, although much higher percentages can be the case, with 100% coverage with public funds sometimes available. The Iowa Flood Center has estimated that solving Iowa's water quality issues in this manner would cost on average $1 million for each HUC-12 scale watershed in Iowa, per year.[6]

Considering that there are 1,660 watersheds this size in Iowa, the total bill would come to $1.7 billion per year. This sort of public investment seems unlikely, and history shows that farmers and landowners (more than 50% of Iowa farmland is rented) will not make these sorts of commitments unless forced to do so.

The other critical factor that's rarely considered by policy makers is that our systems do not have stationarity; in other words, factors affecting the magnitude of agricultural pollution are dynamic. Thus, when we design improvement programs and conservation practices, we need to be cognizant of the reality that conditions external to these efforts are changing. These drivers are many, but the two biggest are climate and economics. Long-term climate and weather data for Iowa show that the state really has not warmed up much since the 1880s.[7] But the state has gotten *a lot* wetter, with some areas seeing precipitation increases exceeding 25% since then. And it's important to recognize that much of this increase has occurred during the early growing season when runoff and pollutant transport are more likely. Much of our pollution is what we call transport-limited, meaning the magnitude of the pollution is directly related to the volume of water available to transport it. For much of the year, there is a nearly inexhaustible supply of pollutants on the landscape: nitrogen especially, but also phosphorus and *E. coli* bacteria. More rain means more of these things enter our lakes and streams. And more rain means fewer days for field work. Farmers respond by installing more agricultural drainage tile,[8] which is the primary delivery mechanism for nitrate and dissolved phosphorus from farm fields to the stream network. The amount of new drainage tile across Iowa swamps the new and existing conservation practices installed to quench the resulting nitrate.

Likewise, the economics of Iowa agriculture are dynamic. Two huge factors have been the expansion of the hog industry over the past quarter century, and the entrenchment of corn ethanol as a motor fuel by federal policy. So much of our built and economic infrastructure in Iowa aligns with this system that changing it makes turning the *Titanic* look trivial. The trucking industry, the rail system, the lock and dam system on the Mississippi River, over a thousand Ag retailers, equipment manufacturers, skilled tradespeople, veterinarians, grain storage businesses, and ethanol producers, to name just a few, all are aligned with the existing production system, making change that will enhance environmental outcomes of the corn-soy-CAFO system difficult.

What approaches should we take to get cleaner water?

I see solutions to our water quality problems falling into one of three bins:

1. Regulate the existing corn-soybean-CAFO system. Agriculture often claims it is heavily regulated, but truth is there is very little environmental regulation, especially as it relates to crop production. The livestock industry can claim some regulations, but they helped write them and enforcement is kept tepid through weak funding by the legislature of Iowa's Department of Natural Resources. The mantra in agriculture is that every farm is different and thus one-size-fits-all regulations could never work. Look around at Iowa farms for yourself—they could hardly be more similar. They all grow the same two crops (corn and soy) with a small subset of those raising only a few species of animals (hogs, beef cattle, egg laying chickens), all within 2 degrees of latitude and 3 degrees of longitude. And the fact is that regulations can be tailored to specific situations.

There are certain practices in Corn Belt farming that are almost universally considered to range from sub-optimal to downright stupid but are still common. Why not ban or regulate these practices? Examples include fall tillage, application of nutrients beyond the crop needs, cropping up to the edge of streams, giving livestock (cattle especially) access to streams, and over-populating watersheds with livestock (hogs especially). Common-sense rules for farming would not inoculate our water from agricultural pollution, but they could go a long way toward improving things beyond the current status quo. Limits on new drainage tile and new CAFOs could arrest the decline in water quality in areas of the state where these drivers are major contributors to degraded water quality.

Regulation would also bring a level of fairness to ordinary Iowa taxpayers, who are asked year after year to provide funds to farmers if they desire clean water. How do we continue to give license to farmers to do whatever they want on their farms, and then ask taxpayers to pay for the environmental consequences? This is unjust and immoral policy in my view, especially because many of our farmers have very substantial accumulated wealth and farm operations are indemnified against natural and economic disasters by the federal government.

2. Diversify Iowa farms. I'm far from being the first person to suggest we need more biological diversity on Iowa farms if we wish to improve Iowa agriculture's environmental performance. No agro-ecological system based on only two species of annual plants is going to be resilient to bad weather. This is especially true in a place like Iowa that is situated in the middle of a continent and by virtue of that will have extreme and dynamic weather.

The evolution of agriculture in Iowa has decoupled the integrated crop-livestock production systems that relied on forage for animals and the result has been a confinement-style scheme where concentrated livestock are raised only on a small subset of farms and fed various formulations of grain.[9] Row crop production required to feed livestock and produce corn-derived fuel ethanol requires large inputs of fossil fuels for machinery operation, grain drying and chemicals, and especially for the ammonia produced from the natural gas that is used in various fertilizer formulations.[10] Fertilization of crops with both commercial formulations and confinement livestock manure has resulted in significant nutrient losses from agricultural watersheds, which degrades downstream aquatic ecosystems, including the Gulf of Mexico, which suffers from a seasonal Dead Zone (hypoxia) because of farm runoff from Iowa and other states.[11,12] Likewise, the emphasis on corn and soy production for livestock and ethanol has caused these two crops to displace others like oats and other small grains as well as forages like clovers and alfalfa. This has resulted in a loss of landscape diversity and an increase in nutrient inputs that degrade water quality at multiple spatial scales.[13]

As the Iowa population of hogs has nearly doubled over the past quarter century, the number of farmers raising hogs has plummeted; fewer than 1/10 of Iowa farms now have hogs. The average number of hogs raised by an individual farmer has increased from 200 in 1980 to 4,700 today.[14] And while the number of beef cattle declined 11% from 1997 to 2017, the number of farmers raising cattle shrunk by 41% and most notably, the number of cattle operations with more than 500 head increased 82%.[15] Thus, the concentration of animals onto a small subset of Iowa farms has made manure management a colossal challenge for the state, with consequences for both water and air quality.

Despite the concerns about the link between greenhouse gas emissions from cattle digestion (i.e. cow burps and farts), a return to cattle on pasture in Iowa is probably necessary if we are to diversify farms. And if farmers are to grow more environmentally friendly crops like oats, alfalfa, and clovers as forage, then they need something that can eat it, or they need a neighbor who has something that can eat it, and that means cattle. Federal cost share programs exist that help farmers set up fencing and watering systems that enable rotational grazing and restrict cattle from damaging stream banks and beds and defecating in streams.

3. Get rid of fuel ethanol. Although ethanol was first used to power an engine in 1826, the modern ethanol industry traces its origins to the 1970s when the Arab oil embargo increased gas prices and there was a need for higher octane fuels as the industry transitioned away from leaded gasoline.[16] I can recall filling my first car, a green 1969 Dodge Dart, with a 90:10 gasoline/ethanol blend (called gasohol in the old days) back when I was in high school in the 70s. It was at this time that corn became the dominant feedstock for fuel ethanol because the grain was so abundant even then, and the ease with which this two-carbon alcohol can be produced from the grain. The environmental rationale for use of corn in this way was that oxygenated compounds added to gasoline (ethanol contains one oxygen atom) reduced emissions of carbon monoxide, which accelerates the chemical reactions that produce photochemical smog.

The Federal Energy Policy Act of 2005 (also known as the Renewable Fuel Standard-RFS) codified the use of ethanol by mandating that gasoline sold in the U.S. contain a certain percentage of ethanol, with amounts increasing each year. This in effect created a guaranteed market for Iowa corn and the ethanol production industry responded by constructing about 40 plants with a production capacity of about 4.5 billion gallons per year, making Iowa the number one ethanol producing state.[17]

But the environmental costs of corn production are high and how we rationalize its use as a fuel has required not a small amount of creative thinking. The cleaner air argument is still around, evidenced by all the State of Iowa vehicles that sport *Cleaner Air for Iowa with Ethanol* bumper stickers. But as emission standards have reduced pollution from car exhaust, the Ag-ethanol complex has needed more than just cleaner air rhetoric to entrench corn as an energy source: reduces dependence on foreign oil, reduces costs at the pump, and home-grown energy and jobs (the number of which are usually wildly exaggerated) are but a few of the rhetorical nuggets we hear from the Ethanolians. Iowa's first in the nation presidential caucus has helped enshrine the state's corn and corn farmers as part of the country's energy portfolio, as candidates kneeling at the altar of corn ethanol are as much a part of the presidential campaign as eating breakfast pizza in the Casey's parking lot and a pork chop on a stick at the Iowa State Fair.

As the condition of our water continues to degrade, many keep wondering if the environmental benefits of corn fuel outweigh the degradation driven by corn farming. So now the industry, whose practitioners have long been ardent climate change deniers for the most part, want to hang their hat on the idea that corn ethanol helps mitigate climate change. Since the ethanol carbon burned in your engine was only in the atmosphere a few months prior, it's not a fossil fuel the way petroleum is, that is, carbon that was entombed in the earth's crust by decaying plants millions and even billions of years ago. Whether corn ethanol actually reduces carbon emissions relative to gasoline is still debated; a 2022 study from researchers at the Universities of Wisconsin and Minnesota published in the *Proceedings of the National Academy of Sciences* says no, and in fact corn ethanol may be worse than gasoline when the inputs and land use change needed to grow corn are considered.[18,19] Couple this with the emergence of electric vehicles (EVs) and the fact that demand for liquid fuels may have reached peak levels,[20] and a reasonable person can ask why we continue to double- and triple- and quadruple-down on corn ethanol.

The guaranteed market for corn has buckled a straitjacket onto Iowa land and our agricultural system. It has inflated land values and pigeonholed that land, some of the best on earth for growing food, into what at best is a superficial function and at worst is an abomination. More than half the calories produced by our land go to power motor vehicles, and an area of land the size of 20 Iowa counties is used to grow those calories.

Releasing those acres from their ethanol-enforced bondage will not be easy, but once free, that land could be used for something other than the corn production that drives so much of our water pollution. This needs to happen if we are to diversify Iowa agriculture and foster new crops and new farmers. It's true that many aspiring farmers, most of whom are young and would like to try something different than corn/soy, are limited by the availability of land. You can make the case that a young aspiring farmer has no right to expect a piece of Iowa farmland any more than a recent theatre arts graduate should expect to afford a Manhattan brownstone. But the truth is that ethanol and its guardian angel, the Renewable Fuel Standard, keep Iowa farmland prices inflated, adding wealth to those with a lucky birthright while bringing no real benefit to society.

Reducing corn acres by half (currently more than half our corn goes to ethanol production) could well benefit water quality specifically and the environment in general far more than regulating the corn-soy system. In fact, I'm pretty certain of that. We were sold the idea a quarter century ago that ethanol was a bridge fuel that would help us navigate the treacherous energy landscape until something better than petroleum came along. Something better is now here, and our state's leaders need to announce a last call for ethanol.

A lot of folks dream of an Iowa re-covered with prairies, wetlands, and oak savannahs. I agree we certainly deserve more of those things, and I am for more of those things. But I think it's unreasonable, impractical, and imprudent to have wholesale conversion of Iowa farmland to these other land uses. The world needs calories, and a place like Iowa, with abundant rainfall, fertile and thick (in most places anyway) topsoil, approximately level land, and a temperate climate, can produce a whole lot of calories. Because of those qualities, we could produce those calories here with a smaller overall environmental impact than almost anywhere else on Earth. If we wanted to. The problem is, we don't want to very badly. Iowa agriculture wants to produce junk carbohydrates, protein for mostly wealthy people and a liquid fuel we don't need, and they want to do it in a reckless manner without consideration for the 97% who don't farm.

I know some would read that comment as reckless and say wait a minute, we do everything very carefully, we apply our nutrients carefully, we practice soil conservation and so forth. Virtually all farmers lay claim to the title of Conservation Farmer. The problem we have is that it is not necessarily the individual actions that are driving degraded water quality; rather it's the fundamentals of the corn/soy/CAFO system that impel the practitioners to make decisions that are in their best self-interest, and not society's at large. Our dogmatic devotion to voluntary approaches necessarily relies on the individual actions of farmers and by extension, their willingness to make decisions that are *not* in their individual self-interest. It's delusional to think a problem of this magnitude can be solved against that backdrop.

Our problems arise from the fact that our production system has been designed to maximize and prioritize commerce over environmental and nutritional outcomes. I see no evidence that establishment Iowa has any intention of changing that dynamic. We have institutional, economic and built infrastructure constructed all over the state (and the entire Corn Belt) that aligns with the corn/soybean/CAFO scheme and almost no one willing to abandon even small parts of that infrastructure. Thus, we are left with a patchwork of taxpayer subsidized half-of-a-half-of-a-half measures that attempt to shore up the system at extremely small spatial scales (i.e., fields and small watersheds) without meaningful or measurable change at the system or landscape scales that people can recognize.

The idea that farmers are going to willingly transition to the diverse farming systems that we need and re-couple livestock and crop production on individual farms is a fantasy. The average age of the Iowa farmer is about 60, and many of the older farmers are financially comfortable, not exactly a demographic that lends itself to change. So, in the short term, we need to regulate agriculture in a way that we know will produce the water quality outcomes that we want. I think it's fine for farmers to have flexibility on conservation; yes, they do know what will work best on their individual farms. But instead of paying for them to implement practices, we should oblige them to produce objective outcomes and (perhaps) reward them when they do. The way things stand now, we're pouring public money down the drain for unmeasurable or non-existent outcomes—there's no accountability anywhere in this system.

We also need to take a very hard look at rented land. More than half of Iowa farmland is farmed by someone who doesn't own the land. This situation also does not lend itself to environmental improvement. Who's responsible for the pollution coming from that land is not an idle question. Land prices are kept artificially high by the demand for corn generated by the RFS and returns on that land are ensured by subsidized crop and price insurance and disaster payments. Young farmers can't break into this structure, essentially making Iowa a place where only the elite can farm and own land. We need land reform, and environmental regulations could force some. When you make landowners legally responsible for the pollution coming off their land, it stands to reason that you make ownership less profitable and you give a reason for the idle rich that own the land to divest, making it available to aspiring farmers that could lead change.

Meaningful and well-thought regulation could also help force more farmers into the alternative systems that will produce the environmental outcomes that we want. If farmers are made financially responsible for externalities generated by their farming system, we make it more favorable for them to explore different and lesser-polluting systems.

I write this at the end of a career where I observed and worked on these water quality issues from several perspectives: private industry, a municipal drinking water supply, an Ag advocacy organization, and finally, academia. If there is anything that distinguishes me from my colleagues, it's that I have been more willing to speak frankly and publicly about the problems than many. I got to that last place quite by chance on one consequential day, when I saw first-hand that a powerful Iowa institution was without question not operating in good faith. I decided that day that I couldn't go on doing what I was doing, taking the public's money as compensation for my work, unless I did it honestly and reported what I observed. The end result of that is this book.

As I write these words, I can tell you that among my close peer group of scientists and others who study these things, optimism is in short supply when it comes to cleaning up Iowa's water, at least within the span of their careers. That doesn't mean the situation is hopeless. But until the bulk of the folks earning their living in this sphere—probably less than 500 people in Iowa—start speaking up and creating space for decision makers (an idea I internalized from my colleague Silvia Secchi) and inspiring everyday Iowans to demand change, progress will be agonizingly slow.

Until then, I will take my inspiration from the words of Howard Zinn, a person whose ideas inspired many of the words in this book: To be hopeful in bad times is not just foolishly romantic. It is based on the fact that human history is a history not only of cruelty, but also of compassion, sacrifice, courage, kindness. What we choose to emphasize in this complex history will determine our lives. If we see only the worst, it destroys our capacity to do something. If we remember those times and places—and there are many—where people have behaved magnificently, this gives us the energy to act, and at least the possibility of sending this spinning top of a world in a different direction. And if we do act, in however small a way, we don't have to wait for some grand utopian future. The future is an infinite succession of presents, and to live now as we think human beings should live, in defiance of all that is bad around us, is itself a small victory.

Be defiant.

ACKNOWLEDGMENTS

I've always thought that writing was something that you can't know for certain that you do well, or not. Critics are at least as important as fans if you're going to get better at writing. I've had some of both and thank them all. I suppose I owe the most gratitude to Holly Carver, former director of the University of Iowa Press, who had faith that what I was writing would appeal to people. Ideas don't come out of nowhere, and there is no substitute for working with people that are smart and have active minds. I'm very lucky to have been around such people. Some of these folks include David Cwiertny, Silvia Secchi, Larry Weber, Dan Gilles and Kate Giannini, all at the University of Iowa; Iowa State Geologist, Keith Schilling; Iowa State University professor emeritus Matt Liebman; and *Cedar Rapids Gazette* columnist Orlan Love. I also want to thank my mother, Maxine Jones of Ankeny, Iowa, for keeping me abreast of water and political news from Des Moines, and for ramming my stuff down the throats of her Polk County pals.

NOTES

Upstream

1. Sayre, R.F., 2000. "The Landscape of Capitalism." *The Iowa Review*, pp.114-131.
2. Prior, J.C., 1991. *Landforms of Iowa*. University of Iowa Press.
3. Bishop, R.A., Joens, J. and Zohrer, J., 1998. "Iowa's wetlands, present and future with a focus on prairie potholes." *Journal of the Iowa Academy of Science*: JIAS, 105(3), pp.89-93.
4. Prior, *Land Forms of Iowa*
5. Kuck, G. and G. Schnitkey. "An Overview of Meat Consumption in the United States." *farmdoc daily*: 76, Department of Agricultural and Consumer Economics, University of Illinois at Urbana-Champaign, May 12, 2021.
6. USDA, National Agricultural Statistics Service (NASS).
7. Ibid.
8. Ibid.
9. Jones, C.S., Drake, C.W., Hruby, C.E., Schilling, K.E. and Wolter, C.F., 2019. "Livestock manure driving stream nitrate." *Ambio*, 48(10), pp.1143-1153. and Jackson, L.L., Keeney, D.R. and Gilbert, E.M., 2000. "Swine manure management plans in north-central Iowa: Nutrient loading and policy implications." *Journal of Soil and Water Conservation*, 55(2), pp.205-212.
10. Piekes, K. Lawmakers advance Gov. Reynolds' bill requiring E-15 at more fuel pumps. Iowa Public Radio, January 25, 2022.
11. Iowa Soybean Association. Biodiesel Blues on the Farm. 2019.
12. Lark, T.J., Hendricks, N.P., Smith, A., Pates, N., Spawn-Lee, S.A., Bougie, M., Booth, E.G., Kucharik, C.J. and Gibbs, H.K., 2022. "Environmental outcomes of the US Renewable Fuel Standard." *Proceedings of the National Academy of Sciences*, 119(9).
13. Stork, Gocke, and Martin, 2007. *The Golden Age of Pesticides*.
14. Ibid.
15. Munkvold, G.P. and Hellmich, R.L., 1999. "Genetically modified insect resistant corn: Implications for disease management." *APSnet Plant Pathology On-line* feature, 15.
16. Hladik, M.L., Kolpin, D.W. and Kuivila, K.M., 2014. "Widespread occurrence of neonicotinoid insecticides in streams in a high corn and soybean producing region, USA." *Environmental pollution*, 193, pp.189-196. And Klarich, K.L., Pflug, N.C., DeWald, E.M., Hladik, M.L., Kolpin, D.W., Cwiertny, D.M. and LeFevre, G.H., 2017. "Occurrence of neonicotinoid insecticides in finished drinking water and fate during drinking water treatment." *Environmental Science & Technology Letters*, 4(5), pp.168-173.
17. Uri, N.D., 2001. "A note on soil erosion and its environmental consequences in the United States. Water, Air, and Soil Pollution," 129(1), pp.181-197. And Jones, C.S. and Schilling, K.E., 2011. "From agricultural intensification to conservation: sediment transport in the Raccoon River, Iowa, 1916–2009." *Journal of environmental quality*, 40(6), pp.1911-1923.
18. Force, H.T., 2008. Mississippi River/Gulf of Mexico Watershed Nutrient Task Force, Gulf Hypoxia Action Plan 2008 for Reducing, Mitigating, and Controlling Hypoxia in the Northern Gulf of Mexico and Improving, Water Quality in the Mississippi River Basin.

Iowa's Real Population

1. Jones, C.S., Drake, C.W., Hruby, C.E., Schilling, K.E. and Wolter, C.F., 2018. "Livestock manure driving stream nitrate." *Ambio*, pp.1-11.

Ransom

1. "Toledoans to Vote on Lake Erie Bill of Rights." January 29, 2019. Cleveland.com.https://www.cleveland.com/news/2019/01/toledoans-to-vote-on-lake-erie-bill-of-rights.html.
2. Eller, D. "Is Iowa's new $3B fertilizer plant worth $110M in state subsidies?" April 19, 2017. *Des Moines Register*.

Ransom the Sequel
1. "The Productivity-Pay Gap. Economic Policy Institute." Updated August 2021. https://www.epi.org/productivity-pay-gap/
2. USDA Economic Research Service: Food Dollar Series. https://www.ers.usda.gov/data-products/food-dollar-series/documentation.aspx.

INPL
1. Public land data from US Bureau of the Census, Statistical Abstract of the United States.
2. Schilling, K.E. and Libra, R.D., 2000. "The relationship of nitrate concentrations in streams to row crop land use in Iowa." *Journal of Environmental Quality*, 29(6), pp.1846-1851.
3. Iowa Department of Natural Resources. 1988 Iowa Open Spaces Plan.

Drunk Dad
1. Eller, D. "Iowa farmers say Army Corps puts endangered species above people." *Des Moines Register*, March 27, 2019.
2. McPhee, J., 2011. *The Control of Nature*. Farrar, Straus and Giroux.

Hello Darling
1. "How Wet is Your State?" U.S. Geological Survey, Water Science School, June 8, 2018.
2. Allen, J. "Expedition Through Iowa Territory in 1844, to follow the Des Moines River to its source and to explore the general area to the east, west and south."
3. Brown, E., 2008. *Nutrient Criteria for Iowa Lakes Recommended Criteria for Class "A" Recreational Uses Report of the Nutrient Science Advisors* February 14, 2008 (Doctoral dissertation, Iowa State University).
4. Love, O. "New life for Iowa's downtrodden Lake Darling State Park." *Cedar Rapids Gazette*, February 13, 2014.
5. Animal Feeding Operations Databases. Iowa Department of Natural Resources.
6. Khanal, S., R.P. Anex, B.K. Gelder, and C.F. Wolter. 2014. "Nitrogen balance in Iowa and the implications of corn-stover harvesting." *Agriculture, Ecosystems & Environment* 183: 21-30.
7. Jackson, L.L., D.R. Keeney and E.M. Gilbert. 2000. "Swine manure management plans in north-central Iowa: Nutrient loading and policy implications." *Journal of Soil and Water Conservation*, 55: 205-212.
8. Jones, C.S., Drake, C.W., Hruby, C.E., Schilling, K.E. and Wolter, C.F., 2018. "Livestock manure driving stream nitrate." *Ambio*, pp.1-11.

Stop Saying We All Want Clean Water
1.*Des Moines Register*, Iowa Poll, February 26, 2015.
2. Muller, M. "Nitrates in drinking water causing friction in Iowa." McKnight Foundation, April, 2015.
3. Anderson, D. "Winter Manure Application Tips." Iowa State University.https://www.extension.iastate.edu/dairyteam/files/page/files/Winter%20Manure%20Application%20Tips.pdf.

From Golf to Gulf?
1. Iowa Department of Natural Resources, Environmental Protection. Watershed Basics.
2. Steimel, D. "Vilsack touts voluntary conservation efforts." Iowa Farm Bureau, January 19, 2015.
3. Iowa Nutrient Reduction Strategy, public comment #1089.
4. Iowa Nutrient Reduction Strategy, public comment #109.
5. Rogers, C. "Fertilizer rule debate intensifies." *Winona Post*, April 25, 2018.
6. Schilling, K. "How much do golf courses contribute to Gulf of Mexico hypoxia?" *Golf Course Management*. June, 2017.

This is Why We Can't Have Nice Things
1. Zhang, W. 2021 "Farmland Value Survey." Iowa State University. https://www.extension.iastate.edu/agdm/wholefarm/html/c2-70.html.
2. USDA Farm Service Agency. Conservation Reserve Program Statistics.
3. Des Moines Water Works, 2019 Budget and Water Rates. http://www.dmww.com/about-us/announcements/2019-budget-and-water-rates.aspx

4. Swoboda, R. "Fishing for a Solution to Iowa Water Quality Lawsuit." *Farm Progress*, September 10, 2015.
5. Iowa Natural Resources and Outdoor Recreation Trust Fund, Amendment 1 (2010).
6. Duffy, M. Voter approve Linn County conservation bond. *Cedar Rapids Gazette*, November 9, 2016.
7. Ellis, S. "Administration tips its hand when it comes to prospect of trade agreement." *Herald & Review*, May 28, 2019.

Fifty Shades of Brown
1. U.S. Department of Agriculture, National Agriculture Statistics Service, https://www.nass.usda.gov/Quick_Stats/.
2. Khanal, S., R.P. Anex, B.K. Gelder, and C.F. Wolter. 2014. "Nitrogen balance in Iowa and the implications of corn-stover harvesting." *Agriculture, Ecosystems & Environment*, 183: 21-30.
3. Jackson, L.L., D.R. Keeney and E.M. Gilbert. 2000. "Swine manure management plans in north-central Iowa: Nutrient loading and policy implications." *Journal of Soil and Water Conservation*, 55: 205-212.
4. Jones, C.S., Drake, C.W., Hruby, C.E., Schilling, K.E. and Wolter, C.F., 2018. "Livestock manure driving stream nitrate." *Ambio*, pp.1-11.
5. Cullen, A., 2018. *Storm Lake: A Chronicle of Change, Resilience, and Hope from a Heartland Newspaper*. Viking.
6. Kolbert, E. "Louisiana's Disappearing Coast." *The New Yorker*, April 1, 2019.

The Swine Republic
1. Johns, L. "Iowans should not be so perturbed about poop." *Des Moines Register*, June 25, 2019.

Middle of Nowhere is Downstream from Somewhere
1. Eby, C. "Iowa River Lands on Endangered List." *Waterloo Cedar Falls Courier*, April 17, 2007.
2. Jordan, E. "Wastewater plant upgrades stress small Iowa towns." *Cedar Rapids Gazette*, August 16, 2019.
3. Iowa DNR, Animal Feeding Operation database.
4. Armstrong, M. "Swine manure can protect water quality." *Farm Progress*, January 30, 2018.

Demand Clean Water Now
1. Villarini, G., Schilling, K.E. and Jones, C.S., 2016. "Assessing the relation of USDA conservation expenditures to suspended sediment reductions in an Iowa watershed." *Journal of Environmental Management*, 180, pp.375-383.
2. Jones, C.S., Nielsen, J.K., Schilling, K.E. and Weber, L.J., 2018. "Iowa stream nitrate and the Gulf of Mexico." *PloS one*, 13(4), p.e0195930

It's Their Way or the Highway
1. Payne, K. "Conservationists Call for Mandatory Stream Buffers." Iowa Public Radio, September 13, 2019.
2. Hill, C. "Iowa farmers make true progress on water quality." *Iowa Farm Bureau Federation*, August 1, 2019.
3. Schilling, K.E., Streeter, M.T., Seeman, A., Jones, C.S. and Wolter, C.F., 2020. "Total phosphorus export from Iowa agricultural watersheds: Quantifying the scope and scale of a regional condition." *Journal of Hydrology*, 581, p.124397.
4. Stein, J. "As billions flow to farmers, Trump administration faces internal concerns over unprecedented bailout." *Washington Post*, September 9, 2019.

Fishing in the Rain
1. Van Meter, K.J., Van Cappellen, P. and Basu, N.B., 2018. "Legacy nitrogen may prevent achievement of water quality goals in the Gulf of Mexico." *Science*, 360(6387), pp.427-430.
2. Johns, L. "Iowans should not be so perturbed about poop." *Des Moines Register*, June 25, 2019.

MMPs are CRAP
1. Jones, A. "What they put on the fields contaminates our water: Iowa's pollution problem." *The Guardian*, September 26, 2019.
2. Libra, R.D., Wolter, C.F. and Langel, R.J., 2004. "Nitrogen and phosphorus budgets for Iowa and Iowa watersheds." Iowa City, Iowa: Iowa Department of Natural Resources, Geological Survey.
3. "Corn Nitrogen Rate Calculator, Finding the Maximum Return to N and Most Profitable N Rate. A Regional (Corn Belt) Approach to Nitrogen Rate Guidelines." Iowa State University.
4. Stanford, G., 1966. "Nitrogen requirements of crops for maximum yield. Agricultural anhydrous ammonia technology and use." *Agricultural Anh*, pp.237-257.
5. Fox, R.H. and Piekielek, W.P., 1987. "Yield response to N fertilizer and N fertilizer use efficiency in no-tillage and plow-tillage corn." *Communications in soil science and plant analysis*, 18(5), pp.495-513.
6. Camberato, J., 2012. "A historical perspective on nitrogen fertilizer rate recommendations for corn in Indiana" (1953-2011). Purdue Extension.
7. Johns, L. "Iowans should not be so perturbed about poop." *Des Moines Register*, June 25, 2019.

Iowa is Hemorrhaging Nitrogen
1. Jones, C.S., Nielsen, J.K., Schilling, K.E. and Weber, L.J., 2018. "Iowa stream nitrate and the Gulf of Mexico." *PloS one*, 13(4), p.e0195930.
2. Jones, C.S. and Schilling, K.E., 2019. "Iowa Statewide Stream Nitrate Loading: 2017-2018 Update." *The Journal of the Iowa Academy of Science*, 126(1-4), pp.6-12.
3. Corn Nitrogen Rate Calculator, Finding the Maximum Return to N and Most Profitable N Rate. A Regional (Corn Belt) Approach to Nitrogen Rate Guidelines. Iowa State University.
4. Iowa Water Quality Information System (IWQIS). University of Iowa.
5. United States Geological Survey, National Water Information System: Web Interface. Current Conditions for Iowa.
6. Schilling, K.E., Jones, C.S., Wolter, C.F., Liang, X., Zhang, Y.K., Seeman, A., Isenhart, T., Schnoebelen, D. and Skopec, M., 2017. "Variability of nitrate-nitrogen load estimation results will make quantifying load reduction strategies difficult in Iowa." *Journal of Soil and Water Conservation*, 72(4), pp.317-325.
7. United States Department of Agriculture, National Agricultural Statistics Service.

Cry Me a Raccoon River
1. Houser, M., Gunderson, R. and Stuart, D., 2019. "Farmers' Perceptions of Climate Change in Context: Toward a Political Economy of Relevance." *Sociologia Ruralis*, 59(4), pp.789-809.

Don't P Down My Leg and Tell Me It's Raining
1. Executive Summary—Iowa Science Assessment of Nonpoint Source Practices to Reduce Nitrogen and Phosphorus Transport in the Mississippi River Basin. Iowa State University, 2013.
2. Schilling, K.E., Streeter, M.T., Seeman, A., Jones, C.S. and Wolter, C.F., 2020. "Total phosphorus export from Iowa agricultural watersheds: Quantifying the scope and scale of a regional condition." *Journal of Hydrology*, 581, p.124397.
3. Jones, C.S., Nielsen, J.K., Schilling, K.E. and Weber, L.J., 2018. I"owa stream nitrate and the Gulf of Mexico." *PloS one*, 13(4), p.e0195930.

Free Iowa Now
1. Mee, L., 2006. "Reviving dead zones." *Scientific American*, 295(5), pp.78-85.
2. Procopio, S. and Mitro, R. "Reviving the Gulf of Mexico's Dead Zone." *KTBS3*. January 16, 2020.
3. Bakhsh, A., Kanwar, R.S. and Karlen, D.L., 2005. "Effects of liquid swine manure applications on NO3–N leaching losses to subsurface drainage water from loamy soils in Iowa." *Agriculture, Ecosystems & Environment,* 109(1-2), pp.118-128.
4. Iowa State University, Iowa Nutrient Reduction Strategy, 2022.
5. Iowa Pork Producers, Updated Iowa Nutrient Reduction Strategy released. May 30, 2013.

Fool Me Once...

1. https://twitter.com/IowaAgWater/status/1227600127260532736?s=20
2. Naig, M. "Farmers are working to reduce nitrate levels." *Des Moines Register*, June 28, 2018.
3. Procopio, S. and Mipro, R. "Reviving the Gulf of Mexico's Dead Zone." *KTBS3*, LSU Manship School News Service, January 16, 2020.
4. Baker, J.L. and Johnson, H.P., 1981. "Nitrate-nitrogen in tile drainage as affected by fertilization." *Journal of Environmental Quality*, 10(4), pp.519-522.
5. Iowa State University Digital Repository. Agena, U., Bryant, B. and Oswald, T., 1990. "Agriculture: environmental problems and directions." https://lib.dr.iastate.edu/icm/1990/proceedings/34/.
6. White, V., 1996. "Agriculture and drinking water supplies: Removing nitrates from drinking water in Des Moines, Iowa." *Journal of Soil and Water Conservation*, 51(6), pp.454-455.
7. Hooper, B. "World's oldest Twinkie marks 40 years on display at Maine school." UPI, June 27, 2016.

They Break It, You Buy It

1. REDUCING NITROGEN APPLICATIONS COULD SAVE FARMERS MILLIONS, STUDY SHOWS. Iowa Soybean Association, February 20, 2020.
2. Meeting of the Water Resources Coordinating Council, June, 2019, Altoona, Iowa.
3. Jones, C.S., Seeman, A., Kyveryga, P.M., Schilling, K.E., Kiel, A., Chan, K.S. and Wolter, C.F., 2016. "Crop rotation and Raccoon River Nitrate." *Journal of Soil and Water Conservation*, 71(3), pp.206-219.
4. Continuum Ag, LLC. October 30, 2019. 60-INCH CORN TRIAL 2019.

The Ethics of a Pig

1. https://en.wikipedia.org/wiki/O._Henry.
2. Herriges, J.A., Secchi, S. and Babcock, B.A., 2005. "Living with hogs in Iowa: the impact of livestock facilities on rural residential property values." *Land Economics*, 81(4), pp.530-545.
3. Iowa Pork Facts. 2019. https://www.iowapork.org/news-from-the-iowa-pork-producers-association/iowa-pork-facts/.
4. "U.S. Hog Giant Transforms Eastern Europe." *New York Times*, May 5, 2009. https://www.nytimes.com/2009/05/06/business/global/06smithfield.html.
5. M. Perret. "JBS sees growth in revenue and profits." April 1, 2019. https://www.globalmeatnews.com/Article/2019/04/01/JBS-sees-growth-in-revenue-and-profits.
6. https://www.gourmetsleuth.com/articles/detail/pork-cut-yield-per-hog.
7. K. Blankfeld. JBS: "The story behind the world's biggest meat producer." April 21, 2011. https://www.forbes.com/sites/kerenblankfeld/2011/04/21/jbs-the-story-behind-the-worlds-biggest-meat-producer/#77013a587e82.
8. https://www.reuters.com/companies/0288.HK.
9. T. Polansek. "At Smithfield Foods' slaughterhouse, China brings home U.S. bacon." November 5, 2019. https://www.reuters.com/article/us-china-swinefever-smithfield-foods-foc/at-smithfield-foods-slaughterhouse-china-brings-home-u-s-bacon-idUSKBN1XF0XC
10. H. Devlin. "Thousands of pollution deaths worldwide linked to western consumers—study." March 29, 2017. https://www.theguardian.com/environment/2017/mar/29/western-consumers-fuelling-tens-of-thousands-of-air-pollution-related-deaths
11. United States Census. https://www.census.gov/prod/www/decennial.html
12. "Post-Farmgate Employment in the U.S.," book chapter. Davidova, Sophia; Mishra, Ashok; and Thomson, Kenneth eds. "Rural Policies and Employment: Transatlantic Experiences." *World Scientific*. 2019.http://www2.econ.iastate.edu/prosci/swenson/Publications/17_Swenson_PostFarmgate_KJT22Corrected.pdf

I'm Not a Scientist

1. Membership of the 115th Congress, A profile. Congressional Research Service, December 20th, 2018.
2. Chotiner, I. "The Contrarian Coronavirus Theory that Informed the Trump Administration." *The New Yorker*, March 29, 2020.

3. Drake, S., 1957. *Discoveries and Opinions of Galileo*. New York: Doubleday.
4. Anderson, T.R., Hawkins, E. and Jones, P.D., 2016. "CO2, the greenhouse effect and global warming: from the pioneering work of Arrhenius and Callendar to today's Earth System Models." *Endeavour*, 40(3), pp.178-187.
5. Boyd, I.L., 2019. "Scientists and politics?" https://science.sciencemag.org/content/366/6463/281.full.

Ripe as a Roadkill Raccoon
1. Stowe, W. "What will it take to get meaningful water quality legislation in Iowa? Iowa View," *Des Moines Register*, April 24, 2018.
2. Watershed Management Authorities in Iowa. Iowa Department of Natural Resources, Environmental Protection Division.
3. "Iowa Watershed Approach, A Vision of Iowa's Future." Iowa Flood Center, University of Iowa, 2016.
4. Cullen, T. "Raccoon watershed authority can barely give it away." *Storm Lake Times*, May 8, 2020.
5. Cullen, T. "Raccoon watershed board ponders its future as few landowners are interested." *Storm Lake Times*, May 15, 2020.

When The Ship Comes In
1. Dickinson County Board of Supervisors, Letter to Iowa DNR, January 12, 2015. https://iagreatlakes.com/wp-content/uploads/2015/01/Guge-Farm-Letter-Signed.pdf
2. Iowa Counties by Per Capita Income. Census of the United States. https://en.wikipedia.org/wiki/List_of_Iowa_locations_by_per_capita_income
3. Johns, L. "The scoop on poop: how Iowa farmers manage manure responsibly." June 19, 2019. Iowa Farm Bureau Federation. https://www.iowafarmbureau.com/Article/Between-the-Lines-The-scoop-on-poophow-Iowa-farmers-manage-manure-responsibly
4. Procopio, S. and Mipro, R. "Reviving the Gulf of Mexico's Dead Zone." LSU Manship School News Service, January 16, 2020.
5. Jordan, E. "New Violations for Walz Energy feedlot and biogas site." December 14, 2018. *Cedar Rapids Gazette*.
6. Scheinblum, "J. Cedar Rapids fish kill may cost city around $20,000." KCRG TV-9. August 7, 2017.

Everyone is Responsible so No One is Responsible
1. Livingston et al. "The Economics of Glyphosate Resistance Management in Corn and Soybean Production." https://www.ers.usda.gov/webdocs/publications/45354/52761_err184.pdf?v=42207.
2. https://crops.extension.iastate.edu/blog/bob-hartzler/historical-perspective-dicamba
3. "Dicamba 2020: What went wrong in Iowa?" https://crops.extension.iastate.edu/blog/bob-hartzler-prashant-jha/dicamba-2020-what-went-wrong-iowa.
4. "PERFECT STORM' LINKS TO DICAMBA INJURY." https://www.iasoybeans.com/news/articles/perfect-storm-links-to-dicamba-injury/.

Land of Milk and Money
1. Ostrom, E., Burger, J., Field, C.B., Norgaard, R.B. and Policansky, D., 1999. "Revisiting the commons: local lessons, global challenges." *Science*, 284(5412), pp.278-282.

On Brothels and Cathedrals
1. https://www.iowadnr.gov/idnr/Fishing/Where-to-Fish/Trout-Streams/Stream-Details/lakeCode/TBR22.
2. https://www.kcrg.com/content/news/I9-Cedar-Rapids-fish-kill-may-cost-City-thousands-of-dollars—439077123.html
3. Khanal, S.K., 2011. *Anaerobic biotechnology for bioenergy production: principles and applications*. John Wiley & Sons.
4. https://www.thegazette.com/subject/news/monona-iowa-biogas-facility-law-

suit-walz-energy-feeder-creek-energy-20191030

5. https://www.thegazette.com/subject/news/monona-iowa-biogas-facility-law-suit-walz-energy-feeder-creek-energy-20191030

6. http://cnrc.agron.iastate.edu/.

7. Klatt, J.G., Mallarino, A.P., Downing, J.A., Kopaska, J.A. and Wittry, D.J., 2003. "Soil phosphorus, management practices, and their relationship to phosphorus delivery in the Iowa Clear Lake agricultural watershed." *Journal of Environmental Quality,* 32(6), pp. 2140-2149.

8. Schilling, K.E., Jones, C.S., Clark, R.J., Libra, R.D., Liang, X., Zhang, Y-K. 2019. "Contrasting NO3-N Concentration Patterns at Two Iowa Karst Springs: Insights on Aquifer N Storage and Delivery." *Hydrogeology Journal.* https://doi.org/10.1007/s10040-019-01935-y.

9. Jones C.S., Drake, C.W., Hruby, C.E., Schilling, K.E., Wolter, C.F. 2018. "Livestock Manure Driving Stream Nitrate." *Ambio. doi*: https://doi.org/10.1007/s13280-018-1137-5.

10. Porter, S.A. and James, D.E., 2020. "Using a Spatially Explicit Approach to Assess the Contribution of Livestock Manure to Minnesota's Agricultural Nitrogen Budget." *Agronomy,* 10(4), p.480.

No Country For Old Men

1. Calvin Wolter, Iowa DNR, personal communication.

2. USDA, Economic Research Service, Farm Income and Wealth Statistics, 2022.

3. Sweeney, C. Oklahoma, "Arkansas agree to create cleanup plan for Illinois River." *The Journal Record*, November 15, 2018.

Defending Paris

1. Stormwater Discharges from Municipal Sources. U.S. EPA. National Pollution Discharge Elimination System.

2. Environmental Working Group. Farm Subsidy Database.

3. Iowa Farm and Rural Life Poll. Highlights from the 2021 Poll. Iowa State University Sociological Extension.

4. Payne, K. "State Report Finds the Rate of Impaired Iowa Rivers, Lakes, Streams Continues to Increase." Iowa Public Radio, December 1, 2020.

This Might Hurt Some Feelings

1. National Agricultural Statistics Service, 2017.

2. Iowa Nutrient Reduction Strategy 2018-19 Annual Progress Report, Iowa State University.

3. Personal Communication, Calvin Wolter, Iowa DNR, December 8, 2020.

4. Zinn, H., 1995. *A People's History of the United States*. 1980. Nord Amerikakunnskap. Noram, 2321(4321), pp.31-54.

Big Pollution

1. Take action now to promote soil health. Wayne Fredricks in letter to the *Des Moines Register*, March 3, 2021.

Environmental Injustice

1. National Agricultural Statistics Service, Selected Producer Characteristics, 2017 and 2012. https://www.nass.usda.gov/Publications/AgCensus/2017/Full_Report/Volume_1,_Chapter_1_State_Level/Iowa/st19_1_0052_0052.pdf.

2. State Library of Iowa. Median Household Income, 2019. https://www.iowadatacenter.org/data/saipe/saipe-income

3. Perret, M. "JBS sees growth in revenue and profits." *Food Navigator-USA.com*, April 1, 2019.

4. Oster, J. Radio Iowa. "Iowa Ag secretary asks Biden administration to back effort to curb 'dead zone' in gulf." March 5, 2021.

iIfyoucantbeatemjointemitis

1. Eller, D. "Could Polk County's Water Quality Initiative Work for All of Iowa?" *Des Moines Register*, June 3, 2021.

2. "Hundreds Flood Capital for Bills," *Des Moines Register*, March 4, 2019.

Take This Stream and Shove It
1. Gerlock, G. "Raccoon River Water Quality Lawsuit Dries Up In Iowa Supreme Court." Iowa Public Radio, June 18, 2021.
2. Agren, Inc. "Raccoon River Watershed Water Quality Master Plan." Iowa DNR Portals, November, 2011. https://www.iowadnr.gov/Portals/idnr/uploads/water/watershed/files/raccoonmasterwmp13.PDF.

The Swine and the Swill
1. Franta, B. "On its 100th birthday in 1959, Edward Teller warned the oil industry about global warming." *The Guardian*, Jan 1, 2018.
2. Maulsby, D. "Farmers are the original environmentalists." *Thrive* newsletter. Syngenta Corp. Winter 2021.
3. Harris, T. "How do we meet Iowa's goals for cover crops?" *Wallaces Farmer*, Jun 24, 2021.
4. U.S. Department of Agriculture. USDA Invests $21.7M in Research Innovations to Improve Soil Health and Climate Smart Agriculture and Forestry. Apr 21, 2021.
5. Murphy, E. "Ag Secretary Tom Vilsack wants conservation efforts to focus on incentives, not regulations." *Cedar Rapids Gazette*. May 24, 2021.
6. U.S. Department of Agriculture. National Agricultural Statistics Service, Quick Stats. https://www.nass.usda.gov/Quick_Stats/.

Mamas, Don't Let Your Babies Grow Up To Be Farmers
1. Elliot, E. "Students Learn That 'Three Times A Day You Need A Farmer'". Harlan (IA) online.com, October 7, 2022.
2. North American Grasslands & Birds Report. Audubon Society. https://www.audubon.org/conservation/working-lands/grasslands-report.
3. Villarini, G., Schilling, K.E. and Jones, C.S., 2016. "Assessing the relation of USDA conservation expenditures to suspended sediment reductions in an Iowa watershed." *Journal of environmental management*, 180, pp.375-383.
4. Eller, D. "Erosion estimated to cost Iowa $1 billion in yield." *Des Moines Register*, May 3, 2014.

Breaking Wind
1. Burnett, H.S. "Iowa crop yields are setting records, not failing, amid modest warming." *Des Moines Register*, July 6, 2021.

Cropaganda
1. https://www.youtube.com/watch?v=bBQ52LLccYw.
2. USDA Census of Agriculture. https://www.nass.usda.gov/Publications/AgCensus/2017/Full_Report/Volume_1,_Chapter_1_State_Level/Iowa/st19_1_0047_0047.pdf.
3. USDA Economic Research Service. https://data.ers.usda.gov/reports.aspx?ID=17883.
4. Schilling, K.E., Tomer, M.D., Gassman, P.W., Kling, C.L., Isenhart, T.M., Moorman, T.B., Simpkins, W.W. and Wolter, C.F., 2007. "A tale of three watersheds: Nonpoint source pollution and conservation practices across Iowa." *Choices*, 22(2), pp.87-95.
5. Gassman, P.W., Tisl, J.A., Palas, E.A., Fields, C.L., Isenhart, T.M., Schilling, K.E., Wolter, C.F., Seigley, L.S. and Helmers, M.J., 2010. "Conservation practice establishment in two northeast Iowa watersheds: Strategies, water quality implications, and lessons learned." *Journal of Soil and Water Conservation*, 65(6), pp.381-392.
6. Leopold, A., 2014. "The land Ethic," *The ecological design and planning reader* (pp. 108-121). Island Press, Washington, DC.
7. Schilling, K.E., Streeter, M.T., Seeman, A., Jones, C.S. and Wolter, C.F., 2020. "Total phosphorus export from Iowa agricultural watersheds: Quantifying the scope and scale of a regional condition." *Journal of Hydrology*, 581, p.124397.
8. https://media.giphy.com/media/FmlOfgAxVx1eM/giphy.gif?cid=ecf05e473kpyyxucns6vn2oklsmccpfyh9t1b31tparnj09m&rid=giphy.gif&ct=g.
9. Jones, C.S., Nielsen, J.K., Schilling, K.E. and Weber, L.J., 2018. "Iowa stream nitrate and the Gulf of Mexico." *PloS one*, 13(4), p.e0195930.

God Made Me Do It
1. Payne, K. "Des Moines Water Works Advances Plans to Build New Wells in Light of River Pollutants." Iowa Public Radio, April 22, 2021.
2. Zinn, H., 1990. *Declarations of Independence Cross-Examining American Ideology.*
3. Leopold, A., 2014. "The Land Ethic," *The ecological design and planning reader* (pp. 108-121). Island Press, Washington, DC.

Rancid Turkey
1. Strong, J. "Farm co-op fined $6,000 for ammonia discharge." *Iowa Capital Dispatch*, October 19, 2021.
2. Iowa Department of Natural Resources, DNR News Releases, July 22, 2020.
3. Jordan, E. "Iowa State University's fertilizer recommendations 'flawed,' Farm Bureau says." *Cedar Rapids Gazette*, September 17, 2021.
4. Iowa Nutrient Research & Education Council. https://www.iowanrec.org/

On Popcorn Farts and Porcupine Piss
1. Strong, J. "Farm co-op fined $6,000 for ammonia discharge." *Iowa Capital Dispatch*, October 19, 2021.

Call Me Crazy
1. Ag Decision Maker File C1-10, 2021 Iowa Farm Costs and Returns. Iowa State University.
2. Clayton, C. Sen. "Grassely Explains Why Farmers Need a Safety Net." *Progressive Farmer DTN*, December 18, 2018.
3. Jordan, E. "TREADING WATER: Iowa Ag groups wield clout to stymie conservation land buys." *Cedar Rapids Gazette*, April 26, 2019.
4. U.S. Bureau of the Census, Statistical Abstract of the United States.
5. U.S. Bureau of Labor Statistics. Occupational Employment and Wage Statistics.
6. Zhang, W. "Who owns and rents Iowa's farmland?" *Ag Decision Maker*, Iowa State University, File C2-78.

C is for Carbonalism
1. Jenny, 1941, 1961; Jenny & Raychaudhary, 1961
2. Payne, K. "Proposed carbon dioxide pipeline draws opposition from Iowa farmers and environmentalists alike." Iowa Public Radio, October 13, 2021.
3. Jordan, E. "Researchers say carbon dioxide could be stored underground in Iowa." *Cedar Rapids Gazette*, December 13, 2021.

The Maginot Line
1. "The Hagstrom Report." *Farming and Ranching*, September 20, 2021. https://www.thefencepost.com/news/farming-ranching/vilsack-counters-eu-farm-to-fork-strategy-eu-groups-raise-productivity-concerns/.
2. Senatus, R. "The Nature Conservancy is building a portfolio of agtech ventures to improve soil health." *Agrifood Tech*, March 24, 2021. https://impactalpha.com/the-nature-conservancy-is-building-a-portfolio-of-agtech-ventures-to-improve-soil-health/.

Catch-2022
"Iowa Water Needs What Legislators Have: Money." *Des Moines Register*, January 9, 2022.

Malice in Wonderland
1. *Corridor Business Journal,* January 28, 2022.
2. Strong, "J. Polk County buys newfangled cover crop tractor for upstream farmers." *Iowa Capital Dispatch*, January 27, 2020.
3. https://www.legis.iowa.gov/legislation/BillBook?ga=89&ba=HSB536.

Iowa is Addicted to Cornography
1. How I calculated solar/ethanol comparison. The West Dubuque solar farm covers 21 acres and produces

200,000 kw hours of energy per acre per year. There are 3412 BTU in a kw hour. So an acre of solar panels in Dubuque County produces the equivalent of 682 million BTUs. An acre of corn producing 175 bushels will generate about 500 gallons of ethanol. That ethanol has 37.5 million BTU of energy but required 17.5 million BTU to produce, for a grand total of 20 million BTU of net energy. 682 divided by 20 is 34.

2. Strong, J. "Committee clears path for final E-15 vote." *Iowa Capital Dispatch*, February 8, 2022.
3. KCCI. Iowa to receive $51M for new electric vehicle charging stations. February 10, 2022.

Brave New Iowa

1. Lark, T.J., Hendricks, N.P., Smith, A., Pates, N., Spawn-Lee, S.A., Bougie, M., Booth, E.G., Kucharik, C.J. and Gibbs, H.K., 2022. "Environmental outcomes of the US Renewable Fuel Standard." *Proceedings of the National Academy of Sciences*, 119(9), p.e2101084119.

Agribusiness Hates CRP

1. Hart, B. "Academics who defend Wall Street Reap Reward." *New York Times*, December 28, 2013.
2. Douglas, L. "U.S. senators call for planting on conserved land in response to Ukraine crisis." *Reuters*. April 1, 2022.
3. Iowa Press. Iowa Public Television, April 1, 2022.

Look at the Price They Make You Pay

1. Brown, E., 2008. "Nutrient Criteria for Iowa Lakes Recommended Criteria for Class "A" Recreational Uses," Report of the Nutrient Science Advisors. February 14, 2008
2. Lake of Three Fires State Park. Iowa Department of Natural Resources.
3. "The Renewable Fuel Standard (RFS): An overview." Congressional Research Service, January 31, 2022.
4. Iowa Geographic Map Server, Iowa State University Geographic Information Systems Support and Research Facility. https://ortho.gis.iastate.edu/client.cgi?zoom=1&0=358597&y0=4511058&layer=naip_2005_nc&action=layernaip_2010_nc&pwidth=800&pheight=625
5. Belin, L. :Iowa Democrats won't speak truth to ethanol power." *Bleeding Heartland*, April 28, 2022.
6. Office of the Governor, May 17, 2022. "Gov. Reynolds signs bipartisan Biofuels Bill into law at farm in Prairie City."
7. Hoffman, D. "IDALS working to better water quality in Iowa. IDALS working to better water quality in Iowa." Iowa Agribusiness Radio Network, May 25, 2022.

Jumping the Shark

1. Terrell, L. "Des Moines Water Works teams up with cooperative to clean drinking water." KCCI News. May 31, 2022.
2. Crumb, M. Landus, "Des Moines Water Works collaborate on agricultural, clean water project." *Business Record*, May 20, 2022.
3. Strong, J. "Polk County buys newfangled cover crop tractor for upstream farmers." *Iowa Capital Dispatch*, January 27, 2022.
4. Eller, D. "With Water Works' lawsuit dismissed, water quality is the legislature's problem." *Des Moines Register*, March 17, 2017.
5. AN UNLIKELY COLLABORATION: LANDUS AND DES MOINES WATER WORKS BUILD UPSTREAM-DOWNSTREAM PARTNERSHIP. https://www.landuscooperative.com/news-events/blog/an-unlikely-collaboration-landus-and-des-moines-water-works-build-upstream-downstream-partnership. May 17, 2022.

No Bushel Left Behind

1. "A focus on nitrate reduction: Naig says federal grant will help Iowa with water quality." KCCI News, June 10, 2022.
2. "Neeley, T. Farmers to EPA: Need Partners, Not Regs." *DTN Progressive Farmer*, May 24, 2022.
3. Schilling, K.E., Streeter, M.T., Seeman, A., Jones, C.S. and Wolter, C.F., 2020. "Total phosphorus export from Iowa agricultural watersheds: Quantifying the scope and scale of a regional condition." *Journal of Hydrology*, 581, p.124397.

4. Elliot Anderson, PhD thesis, University of Iowa, 2022.
5. Jordan, E. "Iowa impaired waters list grown in 2022." *Cedar Rapids Gazette*, February 21, 2022.
6. Iowa Environmental Council. "Iowa's Private Wells Contaminated by Nitrate and Bacteria." April, 2019.
7. DeGood, K. 2020. "A Call to Action on Combating Nonpoint Source and Stormwater Pollution." Center for American Progress. https://www.americanprogress.org/issues/economy/reports/2020/10/27/492149/call-action-combating-nonpoint-source-stormwater-pollution/.
8. Stephenson, K., Shabman, L., Shortle, J. and Easton, Z., 2022. "Confronting our Agricultural Nonpoint Source Control Policy Problem." *JAWRA Journal of the American Water Resources Association*.

Fish
1. U.S. Fish and Wildlife Service. National Survey of Fishing, Hunting, and Wildlife-Associated Recreation. Revised 2018.

Downstream
1. Jones, C.S. and Schilling, K.E., 2011. "From agricultural intensification to conservation: sediment transport in the Raccoon River, Iowa, 1916–2009." *Journal of Environmental Quality*, 40(6), pp.1911-1923.
2. Uri, N.D. and Lewis, J.A., 1998. "The dynamics of soil erosion in US agriculture." *Science of the Total Environment*, 218(1), pp.45-58.
3. Jordan, E. "Iowa impaired waters list grown in 2022." *Cedar Rapids Gazette*, February 21, 2022.
4. Iowa Environmental Council. "Iowa's Private Wells Contaminated by Nitrate and Bacteria." April, 2019.
5. Hamilton, N. *The Land Remains*, Ice Cube Press, 2022.
6. Weber, L. Personal communication, 2022.
7. *Iowa Environmental Mesonet*, Iowa State University, 2022.
8. Singh, R., Helmers, M.J., Kaleita, A.L. and Takle, E.S., 2009. "Potential impact of climate change on subsurface drainage in Iowa's subsurface drained landscapes." *Journal of Irrigation and Drainage Engineering*, 135(4), pp.459-466.
9. Liu, Q., Wang, J., Bai, Z., Ma, L. and Oenema, O., 2017. "Global animal production and nitrogen and phosphorus flows." *Soil Research*, 55(6), pp.451-462.
10. Leigh, G.J., 2004. "Haber-Bosch and other industrial processes." *Catalysts for nitrogen fixation* (pp. 33-54). Springer, Dordrecht.
11. Jones, C.S., Drake, C.W., Hruby, C.E., Schilling, K.E. and Wolter, C.F., 2019. "Livestock manure driving stream nitrate." *Ambio*, 48(10), pp.1143-1153.
12. Turner, R.E., Rabalais, N.N., Alexander, R.B., McIsaac, G. and Howarth, R.W., 2007. "Characterization of nutrient, organic carbon, and sediment loads and concentrations from the Mississippi River into the northern Gulf of Mexico." *Estuaries and Coasts*, 30(5), pp.773-790.
13. Hatfield, J.L., McMullen, L.D. and Jones, C.S., 2009. "Nitrate-nitrogen patterns in the Raccoon River Basin related to agricultural practices." *Journal of Soil and Water Conservation*, 64(3), pp.190-199.
14. Legislative Services Agency, Iowa Legislature. Livestock inventory historical trends. November 4, 2019.
15. Gustafson, C. "History of Ethanol Production and Policy." *Energy Briefs*, North Dakota State University.
16. Iowa Renewable Fuels Association. Ethanol Biorefineries, 2002-2022.
17. Lark, T.J., Hendricks, N.P., Smith, A., Pates, N., Spawn-Lee, S.A., Bougie, M., Booth, E.G., Kucharik, C.J. and Gibbs, H.K., 2022. "Environmental outcomes of the US renewable fuel standard." *Proceedings of the National Academy of Sciences*, 119(9), p.e2101084119.
18. Hill, J., 2022. "The sobering truth about corn ethanol." *Proceedings of the National Academy of Sciences*, 119(11), p.e2200997119.
19. Randall, T. and Warren, H. "Peak Oil is Suddenly Upon Us." *Bloomberg*, December 1, 2020.

Chris Jones is a Research Engineer with IIHR-Hydroscience & Engineering at the University of Iowa. He holds a PhD in Analytical Chemistry from Montana State University in Bozeman and a BA in chemistry and biology from Simpson College in Indianola, Iowa. Previous career stops included the Des Moines Water Works and the Iowa Soybean Association. As an avid outdoorsman, he enjoys fishing, bird watching, gardening, and mushroom hunting in both Iowa and Wisconsin. While he spends most of his time in Iowa City, he is especially fond of the Upper Mississippi River and the Driftless Area of Iowa, Minnesota, and Wisconsin.

The Ice Cube Press began publishing in 1991 to focus on how to live with the natural world and to better understand how people can best live together in the communities they share and inhabit. Using the literary arts to explore life and experiences in the heartland of the United States we have been recognized by a number of well-known writers including: Bill Bradley, Gary Snyder, Gene Logsdon, Wes Jackson, Patricia Hampl, Greg Brown, Jim Harrison, Annie Dillard, Ken Burns, Roz Chast, Jane Hamilton, Daniel Menaker, Kathleen Norris, Janisse Ray, Craig Lesley, Alison Deming, Harriet Lerner, Richard Lynn Stegner, Richard Rhodes, Michael Pollan, David Abram, David Orr, and Barry Lopez. We've published a number of well-known authors including: Mary Swander, Jim Heynen, Mary Pipher, Bill Holm, Connie Mutel, John T. Price, Carol Bly, Marvin Bell, Debra Marquart, Ted Kooser, Stephanie Mills, Bill McKibben, Craig Lesley, Elizabeth McCracken, Derrick Jensen, Dean Bakopoulos, Rick Bass, Linda Hogan, Pam Houston, Paul Gruchow, and Bill Moyers. Check out Ice Cube Press books on our web site, join our email list, Facebook group, or follow us on Twitter. Visit booksellers, museum shops, or any place you can find good books and support our truly honest to goodness independent publishing projects in order to discover why we continue striving to "hear the other side". 2023 Iowa Governor's Art Award Winner

Ice Cube Press, LLC (Est. 1991)
North Liberty, Iowa, Midwest, USA

Resting above the Silurian and Jordan aquifers
steve@icecubepress.com
Check us out on Twitter and Facebook.
www.icecubepress.com

Celebrating Thirty-Two Years of Independent Publishing.

To Fenna Marie, MSW!!!
for all the reasons,
for all of time, you
are always the ultimate GK!